WHERE YOU END AND I BEGIN

WHERE YOU END
and
I BEGIN

A Memoir

Leah McLaren

HARPER

An Imprint of HarperCollins*Publishers*

WHERE YOU END AND I BEGIN. Copyright © 2022 by Leah McLaren.
All rights reserved. Printed in the United States of America. No part
of this book may be used or reproduced in any manner whatsoever
without written permission except in the case of brief quotations
embodied in critical articles and reviews. For information, address
HarperCollins Publishers, 195 Broadway, New York, NY 10007.

HarperCollins books may be purchased for educational, business,
or sales promotional use. For information, please email the Special
Markets Department at SPsales@harpercollins.com.

FIRST EDITION

Designed by Emily Snyder

Library of Congress Cataloging-in-Publication Data has been applied for.
ISBN 978-0-06-303718-2

22 23 24 25 26   LSC   10 9 8 7 6 5 4 3 2 1

For Joanna

Author's Note

THIS book is a factual account of my life, drawn from memory and the diaries I kept from the time of my parents' divorce, when I was about eight, through to university, as well as many conversations with family and friends.

It is not intended as a work of investigative journalism, nor should it be read as one. Entire years have been compressed into sentences and fleeting moments are teased out over pages, making them longer to read than they were to live. Memories diverge and others will undoubtedly recall things differently or not at all. As in most memoirs, dialogue has been reconstructed from recollections and notes, and should not be read as verbatim quotes, with the exception of certain conversations that were transcribed from audio recordings or correspondence.

I have tried my best to stay true to the facts, conferring with many of the real people involved and making alterations where appropriate and necessary. Having said that, there will undoubtedly be disagreements and lapses, for which I apologize in advance. The memoir form, like memory itself, is inherently subjective and impressionistic, which is to say fallible. I do not pretend the book you are about to read is an empirical rendering of events but rather an honest representation of my life and experience as I recall it.

The overwhelming sense of dread I felt while parenting my daughters was no passing affliction. For years motherhood felt like a prison. Because I love them, the realization that I have let them down again and again is too much to bear. If I had known then what I know now I would not have chosen motherhood and its unbearable love.

—CECILY ROSS, *CHATELAINE*, APRIL 2007

Demeter held her dear child in her arms
When, suddenly, her heart suspected treachery
And she trembled terribly.
She stopped hugging her and at once asked her:

"My child, tell me, you did not,
did you, eat any food while you were below? . . ."

Then the very beautiful Persephone faced her and said:
"Mother, I shall tell you the whole truth . . ."

—"SONG OF DEMETER," *THE HOMERIC HYMNS*

WHERE YOU END AND I BEGIN

1

WHEN I was thirteen I left Cobourg, the town where I'd grown up, and moved to Toronto to live with my mother. To celebrate my arrival, she unrolled a foam mattress on the mudroom floor of her one-bedroom rental flat and taped a sign on the leaky mustard-yellow fridge. It was a letter-sized computer printout in block capitals with a single declarative sentence:

COMMITMENT SUCKS THE LIFE RIGHT OUT OF YOU.

"This will be our family motto," she said.

Then Mum laughed; we both did. A few days later I asked her what it meant. She was curled up in the deep-white sofa she'd liberated years before from the living room of the gray house on Hamilton Avenue. Her head was tilted back against the cushioned armrest, its creamy upholstery tattered and soiled by all the moves. Dragging an upside-down spoonful of peanut butter over her tongue she smiled at me quizzically, closed her lips, and swallowed with effort. In a voice that was both gentle and cutting, she said two words she has said to me many times since.

"You'll see."

✦ ✦ ✦

In the spring of that year, my first year at drama school, a heat wave envelops the city. The temperature rises twenty degrees in a single day. My friends and I tear off our coats and scarves and fall into each other's arms sighing, as if reunited after a long absence. The humidity settles in and after a few days everyone is bewildered, listless from lack of air-conditioning and sleep. All we can talk about is summer, but the holiday is still weeks away. On Friday afternoon in the half-empty cafeteria, Scott stands up on a table and announces his camp friend Jeff is hosting a pool party that night. Everyone is invited, he says, meaning just our group. The table cheers and Scott punches the air. Holding his fist aloft, he bows his head and does a little victory dance, shaking his mane of dark curls. The beads his ex-girlfriend braided into it swish and click. A couple of the rugby guys grab Scott around the waist and lift him up. He howls like a wolf.

"There is a god," Hannah whispers.

Joni wriggles in her seat beside me, spreads her fingers wide and claps her palms together, beaming like a baby. I lay my face down sideways on the glitter-specked Formica of the cafeteria table, dreaming of swimming at night.

Joni and I arrive late to the party, awkwardly adjusting our tankinis under the antique slips we're trying out as cover-ups, our bare feet swollen in combat boots, eyeliner half sweated off our faces from the bus ride. All our group is here and some other kids we don't know: Skater Dan and Scott's camp friends, the Deadheads from Eglinton Park in caftans and greasy bandanas playing Hacky Sack. I spot Teddy, the pacifist drug dealer, with his endless supply of cheap magic mushrooms, acid, and pills, which he sells to pretty girls on interest-free layaway. Hannah produces a bottle of schnapps she paid the busker outside the liquor store five bucks to buy. The three of us sit beside the pool, taking sips from the green glass spout and passing it along, wincing as the sweetness burns a path down our throats. We help each other up, clambering, arm over arm, laughing at nothing, falling back then rising again. Furtively we strip off, heads bowed hoping no one will look, then jump in holding hands, legs bicycling the humid evening air. The water takes us fast and soft, like an opioid plunged from a drip. Our fingers slip apart and we glide and turn in opposite directions somersaulting like selkies, tossing our heads back and forth to feel the pull and push of our hair. When the sun sets, the pool light comes on, illuminating the water with a cerulean haze. We play sharks and penguins, sea lions and otters. Hannah hosts an underwater tea party, daintily tonging sugar cubes into our invisible china cups. Joni and I sip with our pinkies up, wearing closed-lipped smiles as the bubbles stream out our noses, rising up and vanishing until we follow them to the surface, gasping for breath.

Joni and I stay in the pool. We linger on after everyone else has got out, pushing our bellies against the warmth of the jets, locked in conversation. People try to join us but then give up and slide away, alienated by the intensity of our closed loop. We talk quickly, overlapping each other, a rush of words devoid of polite pauses. Our friendship is a work of performance art. We're building a cathedral out of conversation.

Hannah towels off and changes into dry clothes, then goes around the pool deck collecting empty beer bottles in case one breaks and someone cuts their foot. Watching her, Scott hollers over the reggae, "Marry me, Hannah!" She rolls her eyes and continues scooping up bottle tops and damp cigarette butts. Scott turns to his camp friends, who silently nod matching Habs caps. "Seriously, dudes, you gotta marry a Hannah."

Just before midnight, the party thins out. Hannah is one of the first to leave. She has to get up early to open the shop where every Saturday she spends six hours refolding sweaters and telling rich ladies how nice their bums look in $200 designer jeans. Kids beg off one by one, citing curfews, early morning rugby and band practice. There's talk of night buses and shared cab fares. A jar of Skippy is passed round and spooned into mouths to mask the smell of booze.

Joni and I linger in the water. The temperature has dropped slightly and now the air is cooler than in the water. Our lips are grayish-blue, fingertips like wizened grapes. Unlike the others, we have no curfew.

Our mothers are restless, busy with work or at parties of their own which makes them distracted. Each mother assumes we're at the other's home. A standing crisscross alibi. Every weekend is a perfect crime.

On his way out, Teddy crouches down beside the pool and says he has a little present for us. He holds out his fist, which is soiled with oil and paint because he's an art major. When he opens his hand there are two tiny squares of paper printed with yin yang symbols sitting on his palm. He tells us to close our eyes and open our mouths.

"Let me know how it goes," he says, then smiles at our squeals of *thank you, thank you, thank you!*

Joni and I look at each other and giggle through closed lips, letting the paper flecks dissolve before washing them down with a warm can of vodka-spiked Sprite. Hardly anyone is left now. One of Scott's camp friends sits with his head drooped over a guitar, fumbling the chords for "Smoke on the Water." On one of the sun loungers a girl and a boy are writhing under a towel like a Chinese dragon puppet. Joni finds an abandoned scrunchy by the side of the pool and slips her ankles inside it. We take turns swimming like mermaids, undulating our bellies, legs bound. When we resurface, minutes or hours later, the party is over. Jeff has gone to bed and now it's just me, Scott, and Joni in the pool. We take turns staring at each other's faces. Joni's eyes glitter like sapphires, then begin to rotate clockwise until they are spinning like pinwheels, crackling with violet light.

"Can you see that?" I say to Scott, who is also super wasted but on something that unfortunately for him is not acid.

"See what?" he says, then licks my shoulder.

The pool is like a glass elevator filled with water. It hoists itself up, up, up, then falls, catching itself softly, only to begin climbing slowly again. I hold onto the ledge, trying to catch my breath. Scott says he wants me to kiss Joni so he can watch.

"Come on," he says. "Just once?"

We obey his dumb command, nibbling each other's lips and chins, then turn to Scott, snorting into the hollows above his collarbone. He scoops us up and for a moment cradles a girl in each arm, like Atlas the human scale, comparing and contrasting our weights. "In the pool you're way heavier," he says to me. I spurt water in his face then sink down to the bottom with Joni, interlacing our fingers around Scott's knees, laughing a stream of scornful bubbles. It's all going to plan.

Here's what you need to know about Scott: he's a music major. The most talented classical guitarist in his year. A perversely funny boy with a monstrous ego. In his wallet he keeps an enormous yellowing scab, peeled from his elbow last summer, which he throws at girls for sport. One of his favorite games is to walk around the halls pinching the flesh above our bra straps, testing for back fat.

Scott and his friends have a list of the hottest girls in the city, ranked by a complex, ever-changing set of criteria based on body parts: face, ass, legs, arms, feet. They take their troglodyte rating system so seriously it's like they're hoping to one day turn it into a trillion-dollar business. Joni and I have a rating system of our own. A secret one. We call it the Hit List. On it are the names of the boys at school we'd like to murder, and how. Scott is number five. Castration by steak knife then death by drowning. On the bus ride from the subway station we'd conspired to seduce him into a late-night threesome in the pool. Then, at a crucial, unspecified moment, slip away laughing, leaving Scott humiliated and alone, doubled over with the agony of thwarted desire, clutching his throbbing testicles, which, contrary to sexist urban legend, do not turn blue.

But something's gone wrong. What started as a practical joke has evolved into an improvised performance. Joni and I are kissing. I'm surprised to find how gentle it feels. Not sexy but comforting, as familiar as laying my head in my mother's lap. We make out for a while, maintaining the pretense it's for Scott's benefit, then draw apart and swim around a bit as Scott splashes after us, roaring and growling. On the count of three we all close our eyes and take off our bathing suits, then watch them sink listlessly to the bottom of the pool. Time seems to stretch open then snap back into place. At one point I am arcing backward off the diving board. Then I am in the shallow end with Joni doing something with Scott's penis. Later I am crawling along the turquoise floor of the deep end collecting the pennies that wink at me like copper eyes. Finally I am back in the shallow end and Joni is flung back over the edge, and Scott is trying to have actual sex with Joni, without much success. The plan has changed; what's not clear is why or how.

Scott strains forward once, twice, three more times, then exhales, deflated, and falls back into the water, turning and diving down bare-assed for his trunks. I fall back into the water, away from the ledge, and sink down to my chin in the shallow end. Joni slips into the pool and wraps her weightless limbs around me in a full body hug. Scott says he's going for a piss. We swim to the edge of the pool and hang there for a moment, holding hands.

"You okay?" I say to Joni.

"I think so." She grins through her tears, then reaches forward and with two fingers wipes something from my lip, flicking it onto the concrete.

"Snot rocket," I say, and she laughs.

We get out and huddle together by the side of the pool, warming our gooseflesh under a damp towel. Because I am cool and experienced, I smoke a cigarette. Behind us Scott clears his throat. We turn. He stares back at us, waiting for something. Back in the safety of our friend fortress, we gaze back at him blankly.

"I'm turning in," he says. "Jeff says you're welcome to stay over. Or not. Your call."

Hours later, I wake up alone and shivering in a vast white bed. No memory of how I got here. The room smells like the inside of a fridge. Disinfectant masking vegetal rot. My skin itches and my mouth seems coated in hot sand. Scott turns over on the bed beside me and props his head on his hand. *How long has he been here?* He opens his mouth to say something but then seems to think better of it. Instead, he reaches over and squeezes my breast through the bedsheet like a cautious shopper weighing up an orange. I pull the sheet higher. *Where's Joni? Where are my clothes?* I ask Scott these questions, or I think I do, but if he hears them, he just shrugs, then swings his square face over my round one and pushes his tongue into my mouth. The wool of Scott's hair falls over my face like a shroud. The smell of his damp scalp and patchouli oil. He pushes a finger inside me and smiles.

"I can't believe you're still horny," he says.

I intend to say something sarcastic and withering, the kind of thing my mother would say, but first I need to turn over, prop myself up, get out from under him, and in trying to do this I somehow miss the moment. My arms and legs seem disconnected from my brain, which must be the acid, or maybe the schnapps or the vodka or the three bottle tokes I did before. After a while Scott stops what he's doing and sighs, not with pleasure but in thought.

"That thing in the pool with Joni," he says. "It was super weird."

"Whatever. You were into it."

"I dunno. I mean, Joni's my little friend."

"So?" I try to shrug but it's hard lying down with a large dopey boy half on top of me. I wish I had a cigarette.

Scott tips his head to the side so his face is parallel to mine. I close my eyes. Again he squeezes my breast, this time under the sheet. I shudder. His hand is like ice.

"Seriously, Scott, don't," I say in a voice that is neither playful nor mean.

"You owe me," he says.

"Whatever, dude."

"C'mon, Lucy, I've got a condom," he pleads in a dumb-guy voice, a reference to the cringiest episode of *Degrassi Junior High*.

I laugh then say, "Seriously, Scott, fuck off. I'm so tired."

We go back and forth like this for a while—him pushing, persuading, cajoling, me resisting, twisting, mumbling. A half-hearted not-quite-joking low-grade tussle in which neither one of us is brave or sober enough to force the moment to its crisis. Our voices never rise above stage whispers, half muted by the hum of the whirring ceiling fan. Scott probes my ass, my mouth and breasts, prying me apart. He is plodding, determined, and I am flagging. I'm relinquishing my hold on the moment; one by one my fingers slip from the edge of the cliff.

"No," I say. "Don't." I whisper these incantations once, twice, three times, softly but with purpose, the way I was taught in sex ed, but nothing happens. Of course it doesn't. The magic, if there is magic, is on Scott's side. The Force is with him, not me. What he wants to happen is alchemizing into what will happen. The problem is that he wants it more than I don't.

"Fine," I say at last. "Do what you want. I'm going to sleep."

Scott says nothing. He slides over me like the lid of a cast iron pot. He pushes my legs apart gently and proceeds to settle the debt. It only takes a few minutes.

As it's happening I think, You know what? Maybe he's right. I do owe him. Because that stuff in the pool earlier, whatever that was, it was super weird. He probably feels bad. Also the hit list. That was so cunty. Scott can be a massive douche but he doesn't deserve to be castrated with a steak knife or drowned. Tomorrow I'll suggest to Joni we amend it to overdose and suffocation by pillow. No seriously. Why are girls such bitches? Literally what is wrong with us?

As I drift into sleep I think of my mother. Not her face or her voice, just that if she were here she would hold my hand the way I held Joni's. She's the only person I know who would do that.

WITHIN days, rumors of the "druggy threesome" sweep through the school. Joni breaks up with me, saying she can't breathe. I am adrift. For weeks my mind hovers just outside my body, following it to class, then home. I begin to experiment with not eating, teaching myself to survive on cigarettes and Diet Coke. I allow myself three dry rice cakes a day. I consume them slowly, ritualistically, breaking them up into smaller and smaller pieces until they are just piles of papery kernels, then I let them dissolve slowly, one by one, on the tip of my tongue.

"You're getting thin," my mother says, not disapprovingly. "Are you on a diet?"

"Not officially."

"Well, it's working."

For the last month of school I skip all my classes except English and read novels in the library. I do fine on my exams, but I will have to repeat math. During a choir rehearsal of Pergolesi's *Stabat Mater*, I stand in the back row of the first sopranos trying to relax my diaphragm as we've been taught to do. When I get to the *Quando corpus morietur* part, two black bars appear in the periphery of my vision. I continue to sing, observing as they advance slowly toward each other like the walls of a compactor closing in. The thing I think is *So this is what it's like to faint.*

In the infirmary, the nurse says she's going to call my mother to come pick me up, but I tell her that won't be necessary. Mum has a car, but she hates driving, especially if it involves retrieving me from somewhere. It's a Friday, so she'll be in production at the weekly magazine where she works, frantically editing copy. I pull a book of cab chits from my backpack, rip off the top one, and ask the nurse to get the school office to call me a Diamond taxi. The nurse looks at me with pity before going to make the call. I'd taken the chits from my mother's purse, which I feel guilty about, but I'm pretty sure she knows. This is how a lot of things are between us: we talk about everything except the things we don't.

Later that night, at the kitchen table, I break down and tell my mother everything that's happened—not just at the pool party but afterward with me and Joni. The fact that I have lost my best friend. "I miss her so much," I say. "I hate myself for missing her. It's stupid."

We are sitting at the kitchen table. My mother listens calmly, and for a golden moment I have her full attention. When I finish the story, she gets up and makes me a cup of Raspberry Zinger. She puts the china mug in front of me, then pours in some Scotch from her tumbler.

"Just a nip," she says. "It'll help you sleep."

I plug my nose internally and take a sip. I hate Scotch.

Mum smiles and covers my hand with hers. She is in her late thirties, slim and blond, with a face that strangers often compare to Joni Mitchell's. Her brow is creased and her hands are mottled with premature age spots, which she blames on racing sailboats with my father when they were still married.

"Listen, Pumpkin," she says finally. "It's a long life."

"I know," I say, though I don't.

"You get plenty of chances."

Inwardly I roll my eyes, not knowing this truism will reverberate in my brain for decades to come, like all her kitchen wisdom. *If you're hungry, drink a glass of water first. Don't leave a wooden spoon to simmer*

in the pot. Beware ambitious people and men who hate their mothers. Wait
ten minutes before having seconds; hunger is mostly in the mind.

Mum looks at me for a while, making a calculation.

"What?"

"Never mind," she says, shaking her head.

"Tell me."

"Are you sure?"

"Yes, of course," I say, because it's true. Whatever she has to tell, I want to know.

She hesitates, swirls the ice in the bottom of her drink, and watches it until the tinkling stops.

"When I was your age, something happened to me," she says. "I fell in love with an older man. Much older. It was terrible and wrong, but I was also young and desperately in love, or I thought I was. I thought I'd never get over it, but I did."

"How old?"

"Your age," she says, then corrects herself. "No, a bit younger. I was twelve."

"And him?"

"Oh, gosh, older. He was married with four kids. Two of them were older than me, actually."

"*What?*"

"He was my riding instructor. At the riding club. Your grandad hired him. He liked him, at first."

I look at my mother in a fog. My grandad had liked my father too. In the context of our family, this counted for a lot. My parents split up when I was eight, after twenty years together, twelve of them married. They'd met on the first day of high school in Erin, Ontario, in the farm country northwest of Toronto, where they'd both grown up. Because they were so young, I'd always assumed they'd lost their virginity to each other.

I stare at my cooling tea, mind swimming.

Mum strokes my wrist, summoning me back to the kitchen table.

"I'm telling you this for a reason," she says. "Bad things happen. You might think you won't survive them, but you will."

That was the first time I heard my mother's story about her self-described first love. Later I would learn the details of what the Horseman did to her young body, all of which were banal and unsurprising in their evil. The Horseman's legacy was the shameful secret he left her with. In the years to come, the story would haunt us both. For her it would serve as a touchstone, the key to the map of her life. I, on the other hand, would be consumed by a growing desire to hunt down the Horseman and demystify him. If there was one belief I cleaved to, it was that I could help my mother, even heal her. The Horseman was the problem, but in order to fix it, first I had to bend him into a mystery—one that only I could solve.

Even at fourteen, I sensed our talk was not just a female bonding moment, like something ripped from a *Gilmore Girls* script. A transaction had taken place. I felt it move through me, shivering up from the roiling unstable center of everything. The past grinding into the present. From that moment on my mother and I were engaged in volcanic experiment. A chain reaction building toward a force majeure that would flatten us both. But that night at the kitchen table, I understand none of these things. Instead, I am overcome by an overwhelming sensation of relief. It is the realization that my own story, the one about what happened at the pool party, is not as important or interesting as I'd believed.

My mother and I sit in silence after that, sipping our whisky-spiked tea. Cigarette smoke quavers in the air between us; it swirls and disperses then slips away entirely like a forgotten dream.

It doesn't matter, I think. And maybe I am right.

Mum rises to open a window.

2

"Hello caller?"

Rob answers the phone like an AM radio host, his bemused way of indicating he can't talk long or ideally at all. I'm calling him from the airport tarmac the way I always do. When I left early this morning he was still in bed with the boys—under the duvet, a pancake stack of early edition broadsheets piled on his chest, the kids on my side, hunched over an iPad devising a smoothie for a finicky Swedish monster. I'd found it hard to leave. Three hours later on the phone I can hear Solly and Frankie bickering in the background over the sound of robots and laser fire.

"Leah? Hulloo?"

"I'm not sure about this trip. I think it might be a bad idea."

Rob pauses. "Are you on the plane?"

"Of course. We're about to take off."

"Good."

Silence.

My husband is a newspaper man. A ruffian poet of hard deadlines. For him the phone is like a transom—a crude device for the immediate transfer of pressing information. His listening face is a handsome ticking clock.

"Don't start this," he says in a low, smooth voice.

"Start what?"

"Tarmac catastrophizing."

The only time I seriously consider the unlikely scenario of my children coming to serious physical harm is when I'm buckled into an economy window seat, watching a safety demonstration performed by a bored-looking air steward in a neckerchief. Hard as I try to scroll through the new releases or decide on the least worst in-flight entrée, my mind will not cooperate. It's normal, even instinctive, to be regularly seized by the fear that one or all of your children will die. There are entire industries built on the exploitation of this anxiety. Fear of flying is similarly commonplace, especially alone, hurtling across time zones, continents, and oceans. These irrational panics are so common they have a weird quotidian logic, like the impulse to pray to a god you don't believe in—just to be on the safe side.

But you know what is neither logical nor instinctive? The all-consuming belief that your children are going to die *because* you are about to embark on a long-haul flight alone, specifically without them or their father. *Rather selfishly*, my superego adds. Because this particular trip isn't even officially for work.

It's in these moments the awful visions come; the tiny bodies that arc through the air, then slam down, rubber-limbs starfished on windscreens that crackle, then pop. They remind me of the time we watched Frankie trip and then pinwheel down the stairs. The steep and slippery black-painted stair of our early Victorian baby-death-trap of a house. The visions are similar but this time Frankie doesn't cry. He does not get up. Fear is the wrong word for it. If you've ever had a visceral, throat-clutching premonition, you will know that whether or not you believe in the show unfurling on the screen of your mind's eye is utterly irrelevant. You are there, an engaged participant, however unwilling. You can see it. *The future is nigh.*

I've learned to live with it. What are my options? The National Health Service won't prescribe tranquilizers unless you're about to be involuntarily committed to a psychiatric hospital. Hard liquor on day flights makes me nauseous. Prayer would be hypocritical. So instead what I do is call Rob and pour a steady stream of persistent, delusional thoughts in his ear. I'm not doing this in the hope of being comforted. My husband hates catastrophizing. I get why it's irritating, even a bit insulting. I am, after all, implying the boys are going to die on his watch. If he called me up to whinge and borrow trouble before flying off to a hotel in a foreign city, leaving me alone with the kids, I'd be rightly annoyed. So I quickly skip over my irrational premonitions and move on to the marginally firmer ground of geopolitical doomsday scenarios instead.

"What if they close the borders and I get stuck over there?"

"Won't happen."

"Okay, but what if it's like that novel where half the population dies and there's a woman who gets stuck on the other side of the world?"

"The clue is in the word *novel*."

"And what if there's a second American civil war and I have to walk to Canada with a band of minstrels, sleeping in ditches and selling my body for scraps?"

My husband is silent.

"I know it's an unlikely scenario, but it's not impossible. Rob, I should not be on this plane, it's—"

"Leah, *stop*."

I press on, ignoring the blade glinting in his tone. "Or—or what if I can't get home? And I end up trapped in New York, in a tiny hotel room, for days? With *her*?" Meaning my mother.

Rob snorts.

In the background, Frankie begins to whine for an ice lolly. I can almost feel him, my baby boy, tugging on the loose bit of trouser above Rob's knee. His curls, which we still call blond even though they've faded to light brown, creeping over the edges of the purple Elton John glasses I let him pick out for himself. Smudged lenses, frames chipped within a week—like both his front teeth. Milk teeth. We should really get his hair cut.

Rob starts to laugh. Is he mocking me? Then suddenly I get it. He's amused by the mental picture I've painted. Not the dystopian second civil war, which I'd only half meant as a joke, but the other thing, the one I'm really frightened of. The scenario where I end up trapped in a small room with my mother. My own private existentialist vision of hell: Cecily and me, sardined on narrow beige beds, reading paperbacks under matching polyblend bedspreads. The air crackling with silent mutual resentment. Closed-lipped smiles concealing the poison pooling in our mouths.

Now that we're laughing, I remember how much I like the feeling. We're good at it too. Rob and I fill each other's ears with mirth until I am intercepted by a hard-faced stewardess who orders me to put away my phone "immediately, please," and as if by command the line goes dead. The cabin crew is preparing for takeoff. I want to call Rob back, but I can't.

I'm going to New York City to meet my mother. A long-anticipated girls' weekend in February 2020. Fun is the ostensible reason. Three lovely days of theater and galleries and eating in restaurants. A rare treat.

But I have a deeper aim. I'm trying to get to the bottom of us—to unpick the tangled knots of our attachment. I'm not doing this out of masochism or duty or even curiosity, although these are all a part of it. I'm flying to New York because I am writing a book about our strange and complicated relationship. Not a book about her—a book about us. I want it to be a story about the ties that bind and chafe, steadying and suffocating us both with their relentless twist and pull. And I need to tell my mother this, officially, and in person. In a place where we can talk and not turn away from each other.

MUM had suggested we book a room at the Chelsea, a seedy mid-price hotel immortalized by the Leonard Cohen song in which he describes getting a blow job from Janis Joplin. Soon after the song was written, Joplin died of a heroin overdose. "It's where Basil and I always stay," Mum explained wistfully over the phone. Because their romantic loyalty to the Chelsea is something I'd rather not consider in detail, I overrule my mother and book us a double room at a boutique hotel in the Flatiron District. The rate is cheap, because tourism is down because of the Chinese flu. I'd been informed of this by the guy at the front desk when I called to request a spacious room on account of my mother's mobility issues (not a *total* lie: she'd had a second hip replacement a year earlier, though if anything it made her more mobile, not less). When I asked the concierge where we should eat, he advised me to go anywhere but Chinatown.

"I'm not saying it's not safe," he added. "It's just boring. Empty. Zero buzz."

When I get to the hotel, I discover it's "locally art themed," whatever that means, the building converted from an old cinema. The door girl grins at me like an eager-to-please Cardi B. Her hair is scraped back and she's wearing enormous gold hoop earrings and a quilted satin bomber jacket. Walking around the hotel is like a disconcerting form of time travel. No space is in any way connected to the next. There are two bars: one Colonial, wood-paneled, with estate sale oil paintings, like something out of Edith Wharton, the other a rooftop Hawaiian-themed tiki bar. The main restaurant is low-lit, sleek, mid-century modern, like an Edward Hopper painting. Breakfast is available in a cafeteria-style fifties diner. Everything about the hotel is so self-consciously curated to look authentic, I decide it must be secretly owned by the Marriott.

Mum hasn't arrived yet, so I wander into the gift shop looking for toothpaste and a phone charger. I find neither. Instead the shelves are stocked with sage smudging kits, essential oils, and a wide array of energy-channeling crystals. I pick out a large strawberry obsidian the size and shape of a half-used bar of soap and surreptitiously slip it into my jacket pocket, where it stays for the rest of the trip.

That's when I see my mother across the lobby, talking to the young man with the pointed beard at the front desk. I find myself curling my fingers around the smooth, cool weight of the stone. From this angle I can almost see her clearly. A midsize sedan of a woman in a quilted olive-green coat, one hand on the counter, the other on the handle of her silver plastic wheelie suitcase. The familiar soft shoulders, a crop cut the color of burnished nickel. I wave at the pointy-bearded boy-man, who looks relieved, then points, which causes my mother to turn.

She swivels, mindful of her new hips, and in doing so is momentarily returned to her natural state: a slim, freckle-tanned flyaway-blonde with devouring blue eyes that alight upon me with interest, then slide away.

"Mumsy."

"My little Leah."

We hug awkwardly, pat-pat, no kisses, minimal contact. Perfunctory, but for us this is a lot. My mother draws back and examines me visually from bottom to top without comment. Then she poufs up the front of her hair, forgetting she no longer has bangs.

Our hotel room is on the second floor, a bright but cramped corner suite with bunk beds and a view of Lexington and East Twenty-Third Street. I joke that it looks like a prison cell for hipsters. Mum is impressed. "Very cool," she keeps saying. "So chic."

We wander around the block to buy toothpaste at a drugstore, and then get pedicures and head massages in an Asian nail bar. Apart from us, the place is empty. The staff are all in masks and surgical gloves. My mother and I share a conspiratorial Canadian eye roll at the antiseptic hyper-vigilance of American health and safety measures. Once we are reclining in our massaging chairs, I wonder if now is the moment to bring up the subject of the book.

I look over and see that my mother's head is tilted back, eyes closed, while the spa attendant presses her fingertips to her temples. She sighs. I haven't seen her this relaxed since the last time we were alone together, almost two years ago at Easter.

THE last time Mum came to London, I bought us a pair of theater tickets for the night of her arrival. The play was *Downstate*, a critically acclaimed US production having a second run at the National. I'd booked hastily, on a whim, not knowing much about the play.

Just before she was due to arrive, I googled the play, and as the reviews bloomed on the page, I felt my stomach flip. *Downstate*, it turned out, is about a group of convicted pedophiles living in a halfway house in Florida. The program synopsis on the National Theatre's website was covered in trigger warnings about graphic descriptions of child abuse and rape and links to victim support charities.

When Mum turned up on my doorstep, she was cheerful in spite of her fatigue, fresh off the red-eye from Toronto with her carry-on, having refused a lift from Paddington Station. I made her a cup of coffee and carried her case upstairs to the trundle bed in the baby's room. Once she was sitting down at my kitchen table with coffee in hand, I brought up the play.

"You know what it's about, right?"

"Oh, sure," she said. "Pedophiles—a sympathetic view. Uplifting stuff. Were all the musicals sold out?"

"Do you really want to see it? We could just go to dinner instead."

"Why wouldn't I?" she said, looking genuinely confused. "It's supposed to be brilliant."

Silence descended and before I could toss off the moment, she flinched in understanding. Almost immediately, she collected herself with a sniff and an involuntary fluff of her hair.

"Don't be ridiculous," she said. "You know me—I love dark and depressing stuff. It's optimism I can't stand."

We shared an uneasy laugh.

After the theater that night, Mum and I went out for a late supper on the South Bank. She was in unusually high spirits. Over mescal margaritas and guacamole, we talked about my younger sister Meg's second pregnancy, marveling at the statistically unlikely yet somehow inevitable news that the baby—like every other child born to the women of our extended family in the past decade—was a boy. So far there are eight and counting—a solidly male generation of Ross offspring.

Tacos arrived and we moved on to the well-worn subject of my mother's four siblings. She likes to discuss them one by one, updating me on the news in their lives, the health issues, real estate developments, recent holidays, work news, and relationship gossip, all of it relayed in a tone of empathetic sisterly concern.

Though I'd heard most of the stories before, I didn't mind hearing them again. Her reflections on her siblings, the childhood they had shared, and the lives they'd chosen since soothed me with the varied constancy of a sea view. It wasn't until we'd shared the last plate of carnitas that Mum brought up the play. It was very good, we both agree. Good and unsettling.

Downstate is set in a Florida halfway house for recently released sexual offenders. The plot centers on a visit with a social worker as part of a survivor's therapy program. Over the course of the first act it emerges that one of the residents, a doddery, sweet-natured old chap in a mobility scooter who practices Chopin on an electric keyboard, was in fact a serial abuser who fondled and raped his young piano students. He's paralyzed from the waist down after a vicious prison attack, though he's remarkably devoid of bitterness about it. One of his victims, now a father with children of his own, aggressively confronts the old man, delivering a speech he's rehearsed with his therapist while his wife shakes and weeps. The piano teacher offers a bland but sympathetic apology. Then he asks if the man and his wife want a biscuit, which they refuse.

Later in the play, the former student comes back to see the piano teacher alone, without his wife. He collapses in the old man's arms. "You were the only one who ever made me feel special," he sobs as his kindly abuser pats his back and says, "There, there. You poor boy." His voice is full of an odd kind of sympathy—one that is both genuine and utterly devoid of guilt. Again the piano teacher offers his former student a biscuit, and this time the man, now reduced to the needy, damaged boy he once was, accepts.

The scene is excruciating, my mother and I agreed, almost unbearable in its honesty: a testament to the lasting emotional dependency that pedophiles often foster in their victims—a bond that is so deep and richly complicated, it can easily pass for love. We understood in this moment that the love the man felt as a boy—the love he *still feels* toward his elderly teacher—is the problem he cannot unpick. The love is what haunts him. Whatever the piano teacher did to his body—the crimes he committed—is almost incidental by comparison.

The topic of the play flowed naturally into the inevitable subject of my mother's childhood, to what happened to her at the Caledon

Riding Club in the summer of 1964. The facts of what transpired are an open family secret. My mother has told the story of the Horseman in countless iterations and contexts, to therapists and husbands, friends, lovers, family, including me. She'd written a thinly veiled novel based on the story, which she despaired of getting published. Later, years after our dinner on the South Bank, she will publish the story in a magazine. By then, the spring of 2019, my mother's story was not a secret but a story. But it was already a problem.

While no one in the family questioned the facts of my mother's narrative, her insistence on airing it publicly, introducing it into the official family canon, engendered a certain degree of discomfort—resentment born of a collective cognitive dissonance. The Horseman conflicted with another cherished narrative, one agreed upon by her siblings: the story of an idyllic rural childhood—a halcyon dreamscape of ponies and grass tennis courts, bifurcated by the roaring Credit River. A Narnia ruled by the five blond Ross children, where, to their consternation and my mother's insistence, the Horseman now lurked in the woods.

My mother's habit of telling the truth—*her* truth, a lawyer might say—meant that all of us are, to some degree, haunted by what happened to her that summer at the riding club. Unlike my aunts and uncle, who are fiercely protective of their shared childhood nostalgia, I'm less bothered by the specter of the Horseman. The pall he casts over their childhood fascinates me. My whole life I've been treated by my aunts and uncle as an honorary sibling—the elder daughter of the eldest daughter, another writer in a family of writers. People say I look more like them than I do my mother. When I lived in Canada, I'd occasionally be stopped on the street, at the airports, or in the office by people who'd say, "Nicola?" mistaking me for my aunt. Or "Are you by any chance related to the journalist Oakland Ross?"

But strictly speaking I am not a Ross. I did not grow up playing tennis or riding my pony to a one-room schoolhouse. I did not help my sisters kidnap our only brother and hide him in the woods as a willing hostage until Dad agreed not to send him back to boarding school. Their Narnia, for me, is a box of black-and-white photographs. Their Aslan (my grandfather) was hobbled by the time I was born, his weak heart powered by a pacemaker, mind ravaged by early-onset dementia. I never went foxhunting or galloped bareback into a quarry. There were no midwinter holidays at luxury resorts in Jamaica or Montreal weekends at the Ritz. Their nirvana was my bedtime story.

Like the wheelchair-bound pianist in *Downstate*, the Horseman was my mother's teacher before he became her lover. Like the boy in the play, she mistook his attentions for devotion. Then later—much later, after a painful divorce and years of emotional chaos and therapy—she understood her mistake and revised her view. Today, sitting on the South Bank, we both know the Horseman was a predator and what occurred between them was a violation. A transaction designed to benefit him alone. We do not need to state the obvious. What the Horseman did to my mother's body was a crime, an abomination, but it was not nearly as complicated or lasting as what he did to her mind, which was, perhaps, to create a kind of confusion, a set of limitations, when it came to her ability to love or be loved—especially by me, her elder daughter.

My mother loves me. I know this because she has assured me of it my entire life. I have spent my whole life trying to love her back, with mixed results. It's hard to love a mother whose bottomless desire for connection is delineated by an abject fear of being needed. It's hard for a daughter not to depend upon her own mother, especially when her mother has, at times, depended heavily upon her. This fear of my mother's—of being truly needed and wanted by a child—is the Horseman's legacy. It's a trauma my mother and I have shared and suffered over the years, in ways that are entirely separate and indelibly linked. I despise the Horseman for many reasons, but if there is one trick I'll never forgive him for, it's the way he rendered the story of everything that happened after him pale and meaningless by comparison. He is, my mother has often said, the "central defining event" of her life. He has been offered to me as the explanation and excuse for all the circumstances of my childhood. He's not my father, but he is the reason I was born. If there is a problem with us, it's all down to him. This is the story my mother told me and that for a long time I accepted as truth. So long as we both believed it, everything was fine. But lately, since having children of my own, I've started to question the story of the Horseman—not the facts of what occurred but their import, as an explanation for what later happened. Every time my mother and I are together, I find myself picking at the Horseman like a loose thread on a sweater. My mother is unnerved by this but also flattered, curious. Like me, she likes to talk about herself. Like me, she is not afraid of darkness. Neither of us, it seems, was born with that instinct so many other women have: the trick of knowing when to leave well enough alone.

Looking back at that night on the South Bank, I think we both sensed the danger of the undertaking. Disassembling the Horseman down to his moving parts and holding them up to the light would force us to confront a number of bitter truths that ran counter to the ones we held dear. Foundational truths we'd long ago accepted and built our lives upon would be rendered fragile, in danger of buckling and collapse. We both sensed this and yet we kept talking about him, peering into the void wondering what was down there and debating whether to jump. We did not do this because we are clever or wise or brave or even because we are writers. It's just how we are.

"Don't you want to find out what happened to him?" I said, picking a fragment of avocado off the platter.

Mum shrugged. "Not really. If anything, I've spent half my life trying to forget him."

"But aren't you even curious?"

She considered this, tapped a sun spot on the back of her wrist. Twisted the familiar gold-and-garnet ring she's worn all my life and most of hers too.

"Not really," she said after a while. "Maybe a bit? But anyway, he's probably dead. He was a chain-smoker."

"That's irrelevant, isn't it? Unless you wanted to confront him."

She makes a face. "Er, no, thank you."

"But don't you want to find out if he ever got caught?"

As my mother considered this, her frown lifted. She was, after all, a retired journalist.

"Didn't you say there were other victims? Don't you want to know what became of them?"

"There were at least two girls in my year at school; probably more."

A pause as we both let my mother's words hang in the air. I knew there were other victims, but for some reason I still found the fact jarring. I wondered, not for the first time, if those girls had grown up and had children of their own and, if so, whether their children had been told the story. A while back my mother found one of them on Facebook, a girl she'd gone to high school with. She showed me the picture on her phone—a plump, sweet-faced grandmother type. Her bio said she was a retired teacher in Florida. The woman looked perfectly normal, we both agreed. My mother did not add her as a friend.

"You should find him," I said with sudden urgency.

Mum scoffed. "Where would I look? It would be like a needle in a haystack."

In my experience, it's not that hard to find things if you just keep looking. My uncle, also a journalist, once told me that any story is interesting if you focus on it long enough. I've found this to be true, especially of long stories. Complicated ones. Investigations. You just have to be persistent, relentless. Scratch at a brick wall long enough and it will give way.

"Death records. Employment records. Police records. Reach out to other victims. Find his living family. They might know something. People don't just disappear without a trace. They leave marks on the world, especially men like him."

My mother took off her glasses and rubbed the tiny pink indentations under her eyes. I could see she was flagging. She had been such a good sport, flying over to London, staying out past ten despite her jet lag, letting me drag her to see the play. *She's getting old,* I thought with a stab of affection mixed with alarm because it meant she would die, then Rob would die, then I would, then the boys and everyone else. An incomprehensible and inevitable chain of events that for some irrational reason always began—for me—with my mother. Mum once told me she saved up the opioids from both her hip replacements and is planning to swallow them in one gulp if she gets dementia like her father. Assisted suicide is legal in Canada, but only if you're mentally sound. Half-jokingly, she worried Basil is too sentimental and won't let her stick to the plan.

"Leave it with me," I'd offered. We both laughed.

That night on the South Bank, I changed the subject back to writing. The investigation. The seed that was sprouting in my mind. "You should write about it," I said again.

She shook her head. Snorted. "I can see how it's interesting, but really, Leah, I have no desire." Then she looked at me. "Why don't you do it?"

"Do what?"

"Find him and write about it."

We sat in silence for a few moments. A foghorn bleated across the Thames. The waitress brought the bill. I drained the last of my margarita.

"Okay," I said. "Maybe I will."

Ten days later my mother flew home, and for a few months after that we looked for the Horseman together. We treated it as a collaboration and told ourselves it would bring us closer together. For a while it seemed to work. Over the spring and early summer of 2019 we talked more often than normal, emailed, texted, and spoke on the phone almost every day. There was something galvanizing about the project, a sense of danger that made us feel at first that we were onto something. But ultimately the center would not hold. The end of our collaboration began as most disastrous, life-altering quarrels do, with a silly argument, in this case a dispute on a familiar theme: my mother's deep dislike of having to drive me places. A hangover from the past. There was a mix-up over who would pick up me and my son at the airport when we came to visit that summer, then another over whether I should rent my own car. Our visit that summer was short, fraught, unbearably tense. We did not speak of the "project."

After I got back to London, Mum called out of the blue. The moment I saw her face on the screen that day, her owlish spectacles hovering over the graduated pearls she had given to me, then taken back when her better string was stolen. I understood somehow that this was the fight we'd been working up to for months, even years, possibly since the day I was born. It was terrible, of course, but also strangely inevitable, almost familiar, as if an unseen writer had scripted the call in advance. My mother began by apologizing crisply, then declaring she wanted nothing to do with the project.

"I want you to drop it," she said.

"What? Why?"

"Because it's my story."

"But it's my story, too, Mum."

"No, it's not. You didn't live it."

"But I lived *with* it," I said. "Which is different, I know, but it affected everything. And thinking about how it did has led me to think about other stuff, like my own childhood. All of it."

"You've got to be kidding," my mother scoffed. Then she hissed, "*I'm telling you to drop it.*" It was less a command than a warning.

"Why?"

"Because I don't trust you, Leah. I feel violated."

"Violated! You can't be serious, Mum."

"I'm allowed to feel this way."

I told my mother she was allowed to feel however she wanted. She was the victim, after all. The Horseman was her story. Then I added, "But, Mum, it's too late—"

She hung up. My mother and I often hang up on each other. Usually one of us calls back, but this time no one did, so I didn't get to explain. But what I said was true. It *was* too late.

I meant to write about the Horseman, but the more I tried, the less I wanted to. The harder I tried to find him—combing the birth records, death records, archived microfiche from local papers scanned and posted online—the further he seemed to recede. The harder I focused on him, the less interesting he became. Eventually, slowly, I began to understand that who he actually was, what became of him, didn't matter.

What I failed to tell my mother on the phone that day, the thing I had just begun to grasp myself, was that, for me, the story of the Horseman had become something else—a story that was my mother's but also indisputably mine. In that story, my story, there were no obvious victims or predators, just a mother and a daughter trying and failing to love each other.

3

I AM six, maybe seven. It is late May, maybe June. I'm pedaling my red Raleigh ten-speed toward the big gray house on Hamilton Avenue in Cobourg. Skidding to a stop on the dirt shoulder, I toss my bike on the lawn, then push open the heavy front door and run down the long hall to the open-plan kitchen and family room, where I know I'll find my mother. I am bursting with school news and starving for a snack, but more than anything I want to get out and play. My friends and I have recently discovered a vacant lot full of abandoned concrete sewer pipes that we've repurposed as make-believe animal dens. I'm a raccoon nesting for winter; Tracey's a beaver; Melanie and Meg are twin rabbits. It's frantically busy in our absorbing parallel world. We are gathering a nest of supplies, acorns, twigs, and pebbles we pretend are nuts and berries, preparing to grow fat for the long winter's nap.

I throw open the kitchen door and find my mother sitting on a chair directly in front of me. Her face is pink and swollen. In her hand is a wadded Kleenex. On the kitchen table behind her, an ashtray overflows with half-smoked menthols. It's not her distress that unnerves me so much as where she's sitting. When my mother isn't sleeping or cooking, she is normally in one of two positions: standing at the sink or curled up with a book on the sofa my father calls a sectional and my mother calls the chesterfield.

What her position announces is that my mother has been waiting for me. Meg is already out playing. The scene has been stage-managed for my arrival. Mum has something to tell me.

I ask what's wrong and Mum's face trembles until tears spill over her cheeks.

"Your father is leaving us," she says.

I think she must be confused and I attempt to comfort her by petting her shoulder. "No, no," I say. Mum shudders and buries her face in a handful of tissues. Standing beside her, I feel the pretend world receding like a mirage. The safety and warmth of my groundhog burrow in the concrete sewer pipe is replaced by the shifting emotional sands of reality. Eventually I start to cry, too, less out of feeling than sheer confusion. If my mother knows the reason, she doesn't tell me. We cling to each other for a while, sobbing, keening, moaning. Every so often I beg her to explain. I keep thinking there must be a way to make sense of it. Why would my kind, even-keeled father just . . . leave?

"He'll be home soon," my mother sniffles. Then her face brightens. "Why don't you ask him?"

A bit later, Dad's black Toyota Celica pulls in the drive. Just as my mother had done, I position myself where he can't miss me, on the front steps of the house. Our black Lab, Duffy, who'd been sitting at my feet, runs to meet him with such slobbering enthusiasm, I wish I'd left him locked up in the backyard.

"Hey there, honey!" Dad hollers, dropping his briefcase on the ground and pulling off his already loose tie as Duffy races circles around him. I watch sullenly as they wrestle on the front lawn. When Dad finally strolls up to where I sit, he is sweating slightly in the heat. He sits down beside me and reaches into his pocket and withdraws a packet of cherry Chiclets, shakes them once, then drops a hard white candy rectangle into my open palm. If Dad senses my sulking, he isn't showing it.

"Why don't you want to live with us anymore?" I demand in what I hope is an imperious tone, soon undermined by a gush of tears that sweeps all the anger from my voice.

Dad's chin twists. I watch him weigh the situation, assessing how much I know or need to know. He keeps petting Duffy, who thumps his tail on the ground, tongue licking Dad's hand.

"Let's go down to the lake," he says.

It isn't a solution so much as an effort to buy time, but he knows I'll be up for it. I'm the only kid I know who enjoys going for walks with grown-ups. The girl who says yes to everything. The one who always throws up her hand, eager to be picked in class.

Dad ropes me up in his strong arms and perches me on his shoulders for a ride. I haven't had one in ages. Neither of us knows it yet, but this will be my last.

He strides out fast and hard, around the house and across our big backyard, then down Fitzhugh Lane, a dirt road long abandoned, named after a rich American family who'd owned a grand mansion there that burned down on Christmas Day years ago. As Duffy rambles through the brush, sniffing, pissing, scattering dead leaves, I take in the view. On top of Dad's shoulders, I am exhilarated. My mother's anguish is instantly forgotten. I don't wonder how Dad is feeling. My father is impenetrable, reliable, an ironclad military vehicle that will run forever. But even his strength has limits. When he lifts me down, I notice he's sweated through his dress shirt.

"You're tall for your age, honey," he says, catching his breath by lighting a cigarette. "Just like I was."

We walk on in silence through the overgrown ruins of the Fitzhugh mansion, through the field behind it and all the way to the cliff that overlooks the lake. We scramble down the path to the beach and sit on our favorite log, staring out at the thick green skin of the water, inhaling the lake's familiar murk. It's a calm evening, clear, the sun still high at suppertime. In the distance, a couple of sailboats bob along the horizon. Dad licks his finger and holds it up beside his ear and nods at me to do the same, which I do. After a few seconds I point south, toward Rochester, New York, a place I've never been in a country called America, which I've only seen on TV.

"Prevailing winds from the northeast. How many knots you think?" he asks.

I shrug. "One? Maybe two? Not much."

Dad nods, eyes on the white triangles riding the horizon. My parents have recently bought a sailboat and joined the yacht club. My father, a suburban furniture salesman, has been spiritually reborn as a seaman. He listens to Stan Rogers on high rotation. I've learned all the words and harmonies to "Northwest Passage," an East Coast folk song about the Franklin Expedition. Sometimes we sing it together in the car.

"Still, a beautiful night for it."

Dad stands up and paces the pebble beach. Lights a new cigarette off the old one, then picks up a pale gray stone, thin and flat as a biscuit. He flings the stone with a practiced flick and watches it skip across the water before it skitters and sinks without a splash. Dad's arms are unnaturally long, disproportionate even to his lanky frame. I wouldn't have noticed except it's something my mother has always remarked on. It's not a criticism—not exactly. My mother doesn't believe in short men. She notices everything about other people's bodies. Dad flicks his cigarette into the lake, then sits back down on the log and ruffles my hair.

"Sorry about all this," he says. His eyes are fixed on the boats. Or maybe he's looking at the spot where the stone vanished. He doesn't look at me, which is good. "Your mum shouldn't have told you like that."

"Don't you love us?"

"Of course," he says. "More than anything."

"*All* of us?"

Dad sighs. Our eyes meet, just for a second. A painful spark. He looks at the lake again, nods. Affirmative.

"Then you're just being stupid."

"Hey, now, honey—"

"You told me yourself grown-ups do stupid stuff sometimes."

"When did I say that?"

"The time Mr. Billing got drunk and fell off the dock."

Dad laughs. "Yeah. Well, that *was* stupid. But drunk is a different kind of stupid. This is more complicated. It's a grown-up problem between me and your mother."

"But it affects all of us."

Dad laughs. Not a real laugh; a wordless admission.

I pick up a bit of shale and cast it forward. It doesn't make it off the beach.

Dad rises and, cigarette clamped in his teeth, skips a few more stones. His technique is perfect. He could be a professional stone skipper. I wonder if that's where the sailing word *skipper* comes from. The wind picks up, shifting the gulls who shriek and flap above us, catching the new breeze and hovering just offshore in hopes we'll toss out something other than rocks. Sky rats. Shit hawks. That's what Dad calls them while we're scrubbing the decks.

"So what am I going to do?" He poses the question like an answer.

"You're not stupid. Sorry I said that."

Dad thinks awhile, then nods. "Well, I guess it's settled, then."

Wʜᴇɴ we get back to the house, my sister, Meg, is at the kitchen table. She dips a lime Popsicle into a bowl of Kraft dinner, then pops it into her mouth. Beside her, Mum is drinking a can of Tab, her face puffy and dry. *Doctor Who* is on the family room TV even though we're not allowed to watch it at dinner.

I run straight up to Mum, bury my face in the shallow, vanilla-scented nest of her hair. I cup my hands over her ear so my sister can't hear and whisper into the tunnel that leads to her brain that she mustn't worry. "Everything is going to be fine," I say. "He's staying."

"Oh Pumpkin," she says quietly. "What would I do without you?"

4

On Good Friday the year I turned seven, my grandfather died of a stroke and my mother quit ironing. At the time, these two events seemed unrelated, but in retrospect they were a two-step catalyst that would culminate in the end of my parents' marriage. The news of my grandfather's death came the old-fashioned way: a phone call after midnight. I suppose my parents were devastated—they both revered him for his gentleness and wisdom—but as a child I was barely aware of their grief.

To me, Grandad was a benignly worrisome presence, a slow-moving lantern jaw in a silk paisley ascot. He smoked a pipe and took daily "walks" round and round the main floor of my grandparents' house, whistling tunelessly on a contented stroll to nowhere, a grown-up man who was not allowed outdoors for fear he might get lost. He smelled of leather, cherry tobacco, and woodsmoke. The single clear memory I have of him is of crawling into the warmth of his sunken corduroy lap with a Time Life book—it had a purple jellyfish on the cover—and asking him to read it. He looked at me with what I took to be tenderness, though it may have been confusion, and began patting down his pockets for spectacles. My grandmother appeared and shooed me away gently, whispering about aluminum pots and the holes they had put in his brain.

The day of my mother's ironing strike is more vivid. A bright spring morning, sunlight streaming in. My father and I were sitting at the kitchen table, eating Cheerios from white porcelain bowls. There was a bulging bag of milk in the brown plastic pitcher on the round table between us. Dad was reading a story about the Blue Jays in the sports pages. Mum entered the room carrying a plastic laundry basket full of my father's tumble-dried dress shirts and set it down on top of the newspaper with emphasis.

"From now on, Jim, I'd appreciate if you could do your own shirts." Her tone was crisp, expectant.

Dad nodded, then silently lifted the basket off the table and went back to reading the box scores.

Mum went to the sink and rattled a load of plates into the dishwasher, then turned it on and swept from the room. It was as if nothing had happened, but then Dad raised his head and met my gaze. I brushed my finger across my upper lip to indicate there were crumbs in his mustache. He swiped them away and gave a cockeyed grin, revealing the magic teeth that cleaned themselves each night in a tumbler of Polident. When I was little I'd spent ages trying to pull mine out while he and Mum laughed.

"She only had to ask," he said.

"Are you mad?"

Dad shook his head. Salt was already creeping into the pepper of his sideburns, though he was just past thirty.

"Can I let you in on a little secret?"

I leaned in, thinking he was going to whisper, but he didn't.

"I like ironing. I'm actually pretty good at it."

At the time, my mother thought the end of her marriage to my father was the start of her third act, but she was young then, so much younger than she knew. Later she would offer a different assessment of the timeline, one in which her "journey toward selfhood" had begun two decades earlier, on a warm spring evening at the Caledon Riding Club when she was just a few weeks shy of her thirteenth birthday. After her riding lesson, the club's stable manager, her instructor, the man we are calling the Horseman, led my mother into the empty clubhouse and calmly eased off her britches, then raped her on the yellow vinyl sofa. He was forty-five, married, with four children of his own, two of whom were older than she was. Utterly unknown and perfectly familiar, a man hired by her father.

What to say about this man who stole my mother's girlhood? He was quiet and gruff, a man whose hands were calloused from years of literally shoveling shit for money, who smoked in the stables, near straw bales, patting down the horseflesh of the rich. A man saddled with a duty of care for animals and children he did not own and perhaps for that reason resented. An undistinguished rider but a charismatic teacher, one who engendered the devotion of his mostly young female students with a combination of grim self-seriousness and dearth of praise. He was a man who broke horses and girls, taking his pleasure where he could.

After she was raped, my mother fell hopelessly in love. It's the oldest story in the book. A classic. Years later this love would be reinterpreted by therapists, by me, by my mother herself, as a child's attempt to survive, a romantic conflation of violation and desire. But love is what she called it at the time.

They carried on all through that summer until being discovered by my grandfather in an empty cottage on the grounds of the family farm on a clear, hot night in late August 1964. My grandfather wept openly; my mother burned with shame. For two weeks she was grounded. The Horseman and his family vanished overnight. They never spoke of it again.

For my grandfather the story was over but for my mother it had just begun. The Horseman moved to the next county over, a few miles down the road. He picked her up in his truck after school, then drove her out to the woods. They corresponded through a post office box. She broke it off two years later, when she was fifteen, indignant and jealous, having learned she was not the only one.

After that, she focused on her studies, began dating a boy from high school, a gangly, affable hockey star who lived with his parents and two older sisters in a cramped flat above the family shop, the Silver

Dollar in Hillsburgh. Grandad approved of Jim. Everyone did. He was reliable, hardworking, handsome, and unerringly kind. He didn't ride or ski or play tennis, but horses and dogs calmed under his hand. He had an easy laugh, big competent hands that could mend a fence and change a flat. He never smoked in the barn.

My parents were engaged by eighteen and married at twenty-one the summer after my mother graduated with an English degree at her father's insistence. They moved to Winnipeg, where my father managed a mattress factory and Mum worked as a bank teller, a job she loathed and escaped by quietly going off the pill. By the time I was born, they were safely ensconced on a farm in Grafton, the down payment a wedding gift from my grandfather. Meg arrived a couple of years later. Dad became a traveling furniture salesman. Mum stayed home. She was lonely in the country so they moved into Cobourg, to the big gray house on Hamilton Avenue.

Then my grandfather died and my mother stopped ironing. It was, she would later write, "as if his death opened a gap in the thicket of my inertia, a gap that became a portal to change, to another kind of life." Another happy ending that was in fact the beginning of a very different story, the one that became mine.

AFTER the ironing strike, Mum went back to university. She wanted to complete her honors degree in English, writing the optional thesis she had skipped in her rush to marry my father.

She chose Trent, a small liberal arts college in Peterborough, a forty-five-minute drive north of Cobourg, attending classes on the Bloomsbury group and poetry of the First World War. The experience transformed her. She threw out all the Harlequin romances she and I used to pass back and forth and instead filled her hours with Virginia Woolf, James Joyce, Siegfried Sassoon, and Rupert Brooke. Penguin paperbacks piled up on the family room coffee table. The radio in her Honda Civic was now permanently tuned to Classical FM. When I complained, begging her to let me change the dial to the Casey Kasem countdown on CHUM, she explained that I was too young to understand Mozart. "One day, when you're older," she assured me, "you'll learn to appreciate the sublime."

The Penguins, with their tissue-thin pages and tight, constricted type, looked menacing to me; I regarded them as tedious interlopers, mean substitutes for a beloved, chronically ill teacher. Like Mozart they were designed to bore me to death.

Mum became entranced by one of her professors, a weedy little man with receding tufts of hair who was an expert on polyphony and storytelling. Years later, in one of life's strange coincidences, I would fall deeply in love with his cousin, with whom I would live happily for six years. My mother and the polyphony prof embarked on a short-lived affair during which she invited him sailing with my father on their boat, *Eilween*. It was a bright, gusty day on the lake, clouds scudding across the sky. I still remember my mother's high excitement, the anticipation with which she approached her professor's arrival, the way she kept repeating his full name at moments when a pronoun would do.

I still have a photograph of the three of them on the boat: my father, my mother, and her professor. I may have taken the picture myself. My parents both look happy, ruddy, at home on the water. Between them sits the professor, older, smaller, balding, drowning in a borrowed yellow mackintosh as panic scrambles across his face. How do I know my mother had an affair with this man? She told me so. Not while it was going on, but just after the divorce, when she started telling me everything. "Your father also had affairs," she added. "Or at least the one he told me about." (Later, when we are living on our own in Toronto, my mother would tell me about a recurring dream she had in which we are all still together as an intact family, living happily in the big gray house on Hamilton Avenue. She and my father have managed to broker a deal: she will stay so long as she doesn't have to sleep with him anymore. In the dream, he happily accepts.)

My mother's honors thesis was on the subject of water imagery in the novels of Virginia Woolf. I remember her typing it furiously for hours on an electric typewriter, having taken over the small, dark study we still called Daddy's office, though my father was mostly on the road, his desk a neglected heap of fabric swatches. We continued to call it this long after my mother took over, no matter how long or hard she worked.

Daddy's office was just off the front hall. It was the sort of room that's dark even on bright days; a veil of smoke tinted the air blue regardless of whether anyone was smoking. (Mostly someone was, though soon my mother would quit, a moral accomplishment she would hold over my father for thirty-five years, until he was able to wean himself off by vaping.) As a child, it seemed to me that Daddy's office was the most unpleasant place in our house. It was a house of secret balconies, laundry chutes, trompe l'oeil rugs, and high, slanted ceilings. There was light and loveliness all around, but it was also full of secret passages. The garden went on forever, into the birch forest, then the real forest, the cornfields, the cliffs, at the bottom of which was the lake. We were living surrounded by magic, but Mummy couldn't see it because she had fallen in love with a boring machine. The electric Epson had sat on my father's desk, gray and heavy, for years, collecting dust, out of ink, under a plastic cover. Now suddenly it was alive, purring, my mother's fingers flying across the keyboard. It sounded like tap shoes on a flagstone floor. The Epson didn't compete with me for my mother's attention the way books or the radio did; it completely consumed her. The hated thing whirred and hummed and *pa-ding*ed! It returned automatically, slamming itself back each time she reached the end of a line.

"Mummy's working," she said when I tried to interrupt her. "Mummy *needs* to work."

The page, I see now, was the secret place she'd been trying and failing to find as she wandered around the house, pretending to be a housewife, thumbing through Laura Ashley patterns, pitting plums for jam, polishing wedding silver, cutting lilies from the garden and placing them in a vase. Did she really do any of these things? Am I inventing them? I'm not. But what she did at night with the Epson was something different.

In retrospect, the signs of her desperation were obvious and everywhere. The times I came home from school and found my sister, then just a toddler, beet-faced and howling, fists raw from battering the door to the master bathroom, behind which my mother was often locked.

"I'm fine, sweetheart," she'd call out to me, her more-reasonable eldest daughter. "I just don't want to hit her."

My mother was vehemently anti-spanking, which I understand now was part of her liberalism, a principle that required true restraint at a time when most kids got smacked, many of them ritualistically, bent over a father's knee with lashings counted out, painfully administered with a belt or a spoon. "Never hit a child in anger" was the accepted wisdom of the time. Emphasis on the last two words.

Mum was emphatic: she did not have tastes or opinions, but *principles* and *beliefs*. There were many things she "did not believe in" that seemed confusingly normal to everyone else. She didn't believe in calling people we weren't related to Auntie or Uncle. She didn't believe in having godparents on the grounds we didn't believe in God. She didn't believe in taking off her shoes indoors or wall-to-wall carpeting or plastic on furniture or keeping things for best. She didn't believe in driving children to school—or anywhere, in fact, under any circumstances, ever, if she could help it. She didn't believe in stripping old houses of character. She liked things that were old—wavy glass and crown moldings—and was suspicious of things that were new. She didn't believe in overheating houses or in refrigerating certain foods—tomatoes, bread, butter, except during a heat wave—or in eating salad before dinner. In a time and place where there was no such thing as a vanguard, she found ways to set herself apart. It was a long time before I parsed the difference between progressive politics and petty snobbishness. In her mind I don't think there was a distinction; aesthetics and values were one and the same.

W E lived at 60 Hamilton Avenue for five years; my parents split when I was eight. It was the longest time I ever lived anywhere until I became a mother myself. In my mind's eye those years have gelled into a montage of snow fort building and games of pretend in the forest. Much of my contentment, I suppose, was material—financial security really does buy a modicum of happiness—but I also suspect it stemmed from something deeper. It wasn't just having my own bedroom or a big garden and corn fields to play in, or being able to come home for lunch on school days to buttery grilled cheeses Mum served with steaming bowls of tinned tomato soup cooled with milk. I was a happy child then, not just for what my mother gave me but for what she managed to conceal and withhold.

It's said narcissists treat people as resources, but so do children. And happy children are the worst.

THE day she moves out is sweltering, a Saturday in July. Mum splits the cost of a full-sized U-Haul with her best friend, Maureen, who also happens to be leaving her husband, Ron, an appliance salesman.

Once the van is packed, Mum climbs up into the cab. She looks like a Virginia Slims ad, I think, in her sweaty white singlet and frizzed-out blond perm. Dad stands beside me, silent as a sentry. I sink down on the front step, scratching at the scabs on my knees, sweating from the humidity, though it is only midmorning. Dad, who'd been up since dawn helping to load the boxes into the van, raises a bottle of Labatt Blue to his mustache. Its brown glass surface is beaded with condensation. Maureen backs the truck across the front yard in a clumsy three-point turn. Up in the cab, the women burst into laughter, hiding their faces and shaking their heads at their own mechanical incompetence. My father shakes his head and chuckles. I am startled. It is so unlike him not to help with anything, especially two women trying to drive a truck. Later, I will marvel at his restraint.

Dad reaches down and ruffles my hair in the damp place at the nape of my neck. I know I'll get to see Mum next weekend, but this fact does nothing to soften the impact of the moment. Maureen gets the van into gear and it swings out onto the road. Mum gives one quick backward wave, then turns forward, chin jutting out, eyes on the road.

After she leaves, Mum's restlessness lingers on in the house, unseen but insistent, the constant maddening hum of a magnetic field. After my grandfather, it was my father who had lived with her secret—the story of the Horseman—the longest. Years later he told me he rarely thought of it, he tried his best. My father is competent and practical, but also innately squeamish. The sort of man who can hold down a whimpering dog and extract porcupine quills from its muzzle with pliers but cannot bear to change a dirty diaper. A sailor who could helm the boat through any gale but gagged at the smell of other people's sick. If he had to, Dad would apply first aid but it would never, ever occur to him to pause to probe a wound. Tell him a secret and he will not just keep it; he will lock it in a box and swallow the key. In the years after the divorce he did not tell anyone else my mother's story, not even my stepmother, after thirty years of marriage. When I asked him why, he shrugged and said he didn't see it as having anything to do with him. This stood in stark contrast to how I felt. In my mother's narrative of our lives, the one I accepted and understood, the Horseman was both the clue and the final reveal. He was the keystone in the arch, the signature at the bottom of every page. As Homer Simpson once observed of beer, the Horseman was the cause of and solution to all of life's problems. I mean my mother's problems, which after the divorce became impossible to distinguish from my own.

My parents were both unfaithful but it wasn't adultery that did them in. According to my mother, it was her own shame and self-loathing. Shame, she has always maintained, was the reason she married my father in the first place. When my grandfather died, she was released from us. The family she'd created was not what she wanted after all. The fact that it involved actual people who loved her desperately did not make up for the fact that she'd been dreadfully miscast in a play she accidentally wrote for an audience of one: her father. The point of the pantomime was to prove that the Horseman hadn't soiled her completely, that she was, if not good, at least capable of acting the part. Now that her father was dead, the show was over. My mother stepped offstage and embarked on her "journey toward selfhood"—an exploration into the darkest recesses of her own suffering and desire for self-abnegation at the hands of men. Even if she'd known what was coming, I wonder if she might have welcomed it. Torture was what she thought she was made for. She was the daughter of a gentle, loving man and she'd married a gentle, loving man, but because of the Horseman what she wanted was to be punished. This was her story, the one she later explained to me at the kitchen table. My grandfather died and within the year she was gone.

After she leaves, the big gray house on Hamilton Avenue seems structurally compromised, as if it has shifted on its foundations. Cracks appear in the drywall. My father goes on mowing the grass, changing the storm windows, applying spackling paste to the fissures, but nothing seems to help. The cracks in the walls lead to blurry in-between places I fear but find I am drawn to. The half-furnished rooms where I once played with my sister, choreographing dances to records, building forts out of sofa cushions, I now walk through guardedly. Eventually I learn the spots to avoid. In the gap where the sideboard meets the curtain just behind where her reading lamp used to sit, there's a wormhole; if I stand at a safe distance and tilt my ear to the left, I can hear a low sucking sound. There's a portal to a netherworld in the cupboard beside the oven, right at the very spot where the Cuisinart used to sit. The objects my mother took with her in the moving van still exist, of course—I've seen them with my own eyes in her apartment across town—but the unfaded square on the wall where the oil painting of the rowboat used to hang is more real to me now than the painting itself. "A presence of an absence," my mother would have said.

HER new apartment is a second-floor walk-up. She'd chosen it for its location, right across from the *Cobourg Daily Star*, where she'd found a job as a general reporter. We stay with Mum only on weekends at first, because it's far from our school. Meg and I share a room with pink metal Ikea bunk beds. I let my younger sister have the top bunk. After we go to bed, even on the weekends, Mum sometimes goes back to the newsroom to work.

One night when Mum is out, Meg wakes up crying with an earache. I remember fetching the drops from the bathroom and squeezing them into my sister's ear. I open the childproof bottle and feed her two sugary orange dots of baby aspirin, swallowing a couple myself as a treat. I rub my sister's back but she will not stop crying, her sobs turned to wails. I become worried about Mr. Garish, the crotchety landlord who lives downstairs. He bangs on his ceiling with a broomstick when my sister and I play records and complains when we run in the flat with our shoes on. Mum says he's trying to kick us out because she didn't bother to mention she had children when she signed the lease. She says it's none of his business, that he doesn't have a legal leg to stand on, and besides it's only two weekends a month. But it still worries me because I can see it worries her. I wonder what he might say if he hears my sister wailing. What will I say if he knocks on the door and demands to speak to my mother? I know he will judge her for leaving us alone and that somehow this will add to his case, that he will use it somehow in his plan to evict us. Because I know all of this I talk Meg down the way I do when she has tantrums and I'm afraid we'll both get punished.

"Hey, Meggles, it's not so bad. Do you want me to read you a story?"

She holds her ear moaning, her voice rising. "It's hurting. Get Mummy. I DON'T WANT YOU I WANT HER."

"She'll be home soon," I promise. "Do you want me to kiss it better?"

My offer plunges my sister back into a howling spiral. Desperate action is called for. I fumble around the hall for the light switch. We've moved in so recently, I have to look for a while before I find it. The kitchen phone is fixed high on the wall, my fingers covered in my sister's tears and snot. They slip on the rotary dial. I'd promised Mum I'd memorize the number and I had, I swore I had, but somehow the raw animal panic deleted it from my brain. Meg's wailing lifts to a dreadful crescendo.

I return to my sister and look at her seriously in the half-light of the bedroom as I contemplate what to do.

"Stay right here and try to be quiet," I say finally.

"Where are you going?" she whispers.

"Shhhhhh, I won't be long."

I run down the stairs barefoot, mindful not to wake Mr. Garish, then sprint across the street toward the *Cobourg Daily Star*, a low-slung, windowless office building that smells of ink, a printing press churning in its basement. Through the gaps in the frosted glass of the front doors I note the flickering of fluorescent lights but there is no one behind the front desk. I bang and bang and bang, I may have even shouted. Finally, from behind a glass partition I see a figure stirring. I must have looked comical to the security guard who eventually ambled his way toward me—a skinny buck-toothed child with stringy bobbed hair, clutching the sleeves of her Snoopy night shirt and hopping from foot to foot. He looks at me with befuddled curiosity and something else I can't quite place but will later understand as wariness. The suspicion adults reserve for unkept children who roam the streets in the night. Perhaps he thought I was going to sell him Girl Guide cookies I had no intention of delivering or beg him for food. I try to compose myself as he fumbles with the locks then opens the door. He opens his mouth to say something, but I cut him off.

"Have you seen my mother?"

5

By the time I join her at the hotel bar on our first night in New York, Mum is halfway through what I'm certain is not her first martini and am hoping isn't her third. She leans back when she sees me and raises her arms in a silent *whoop!* I smile and give a tight little wave, elbows pressed primly against my waist. As I weave my way through the tables, I can feel her conducting a full height-weight-hair-clothes assessment. I instinctively brace for the inevitable appraising remark then remember: *Oh wait, she doesn't say those kinds of things anymore.*

Since turning sixty, my mother has put an enormous amount of energy into letting herself go. She had her hair defiantly clipped, Judi Dench–style. Not long after, she gave up on belts and heels. She bought dresses that floated, blouses that skimmed, trousers with elasticized waistbands, cardigans in which she could wrap herself from shoulder to hip. She posted photos of her unscaled feet in silver Birkenstocks on Instagram with the hashtags #gettingold #dontcare.

"Why shouldn't I eat crème fraîche?" she began saying. "I could get hit by a truck tomorrow, and besides, my husband is madly in love with me."

Mum pats the empty stool beside her. I clamber up and she reaches over to administer an awkwardly familiar sideways hug. We've booked a table for dinner, but I already know this is where we'll stay. Without appetite, I shovel a handful of salted cashews into my mouth.

"Oh, Pumpkin, I'm so glad we did this."

"Me too."

"Can you believe it? Just the two of us together in New York. I'm excited about the play on the last night."

"Thanks for booking it."

"Well, you found the hotel, and it's fabulous. *So hip.* So much better than the Chelsea, which is obviously *wonderfully historied* but in truth a bit grotty. Basil and I just have this romantic tradition . . ."

"It's where you always stay."

"Yes! It's silly, isn't it? But I always say, the thing about Manhattan is that you barely spend any time in the room anyway. The only time we ever go to the theater now is here or London. Toronto is *hopeless.* So mediocre. We go to the opera once a month at the movie theater in Collingwood. Fifteen minutes away and just the price of a movie ticket. I really don't know why anyone would pay for a full ticket and subject themselves to a three-hour drive through a blizzard when it's practically as good as the real thing."

I'm not sure if my mother has actually been to a live opera. No, that's wrong: she's been at least once, though it was years ago. With Richard—the man with whom she had a tortured, on-off, decade-long affair after leaving my father. It must have been a last-minute invitation. I remember it because we were still living in Cobourg and my mother picked us up from school and drove us straight to my grandmother's house in the city. We got to miss school the next day.

"Basil *adores* the opera," my mother is saying. "He's getting to be a true aficionado. I get a bit fidgety, though. I mean, four hours. Apart from sleep, I can't think of anything I'd choose to do nonstop for four hours."

"Drink?"

"*Ha ha ha.* The last time we went, I looked over and there he was, sobbing like a baby," she says. "The full waterworks. Luckily, I had Kleenex in my purse. He's so sensitive, my Bodo is. Anyway, it's good for men to cry. Don't you think?"

I say that I encourage the boys to cry, especially when they're frustrated. It's better than lashing out.

"So tell me," she says. Her gaze rises over my head and circles round the room, then drifts back in my direction. "How often does Rob cry?"

I stiffen, remembering how she does this now. Contrasts our marriages, our husbands, in the way she once compared our bodies and faces and hair.

"Rob cry? Not a lot."

"Never?"

I think of the last time I saw Rob cry. It was just a few weeks ago after a fight about I forget what. He was sitting on the red sofa in my writing shed.

"Only when Liverpool beats Everton. Why?"

I wave to the bartender, but he doesn't see me. I keep waving.

"Just curious," my mother says with a shrug.

Finally, the bartender strolls over.

"Another, please, just like hers." I dip my head toward my mother.

"Dirty?" he says.

"Filthy, obviously."

Mum laughs and pats me on the shoulder.

"That's my girl," she says for the bartender's benefit. He gives her a noncommittal smile.

Dinner is a hot slippery muddle. Croquettes, fluke crudo, creamed corn, and duck. We order too much and eat it all anyway. The tension is loosened by a bath of wine. My mother talks about our family, by which she means her family, the Rosses. Specifically, the one-year anniversary of my grandmother's death, in which she and her siblings reunited for dinner at my aunt's house.

"So it was nice seeing them all, then?"

"Oh, sure." She slides a fingertip through the sauce at the bottom of her dish, pops the finger in her mouth, and shrugs.

"What?"

"Nothing, really. I guess I just find it a bit worrying on the rare occasions we're all getting along."

"Really?"

"It makes me uneasy."

"Why?"

"You know the rule."

I don't, but I do. In the way that I know all my mother's rules. A series of directives from a haywire GPS I cannot switch off. Guiding me round and round in maddening spirals, urging me into a tree or over the nearest cliff. *Rerouting. Rerouting.*

"Which one?"

"Every family needs a scapegoat."

It's meant to be a warning, possibly an outright threat. In my mother's worldview, every family needs an odd man out. In order for the whole to cohere, one member must bear the blame for all wrongs of the past. For many years, in particular the years leading up to my grandmother's death, Mum felt this role had been unfairly thrust upon her. She railed against it, lamented it bitterly. But now that Granny is dead, the tension among the Ross siblings has cooled. My mother feels she's been miraculously returned to the fold, which makes her happy but also nervous. Because now there's a vacancy to fill. I nod blankly, pretending to misunderstand her, wishing I did. You'll see, she is saying. You'll see.

6

⁓

AFTER my mother moved out, the general view in town was that she was nuts. Not chemically imbalanced, but reckless, shameless, impulsive. A woman possessed of an overly high opinion of herself. Why else would she have left a kind, handsome man with a good job like Jim McLaren? And those poor girls.

How did I know what the gossips in town thought? Because many of them told me. It's amazing the things grown-ups will say to children of divorce. The stone was cast by Mrs. Oliver, the blind Christian housewife whose house we went to for lunch after Mum started her job at the paper.

"Your mother has a lot to answer for," Mrs. Oliver said to me one day as I sat at her kitchen table spooning the remnants of cold pea soup into my juice glass—an ingenious food disposal method if you ever happen to find yourself with a visually impaired babysitter.

"What?" I said, then corrected myself. Mrs. Oliver was a stickler for manners. "Pardon me?"

"I said your mother has a lot to answer for. For breaking her vows. It sets a bad example for you girls."

"It does?"

Mrs. Oliver regarded me with her blank glass eyes.

"You're a big girl now, Leah. I trust you'll make better choices for yourself."

She was sidestepping my question. I was beginning to notice this was something grown-ups often did. My mother might have a lot to answer for, but if I asked her a question, at least she answered it.

"Mind you take care of your father. He's a good man."

There were so many surprises in Mrs. Oliver's little speech I could barely take them all in. First was the revelation that, by splitting up with Dad, my mother had broken some kind of sacred covenant. The idea that there might be an actual penalty involved filled me with worry. What Mrs. Oliver seemed to be implying was that a punishment would be levied upon Mum socially, possibly even in the eyes of God. This I knew for sure because everything that Mrs. Oliver said, every story she told or comment she made, eventually circled back to God.

My gaze drifted over to Meg, who sat at the other end of the table twirling her hair. I caught her eye and winked.

"Thank you so much for lunch, Mrs. Oliver. The soup was delicious. Would you like me to clear the table?"

"Yes, please, dear. You're very welcome," she said, a smile blooming on her face.

"My pleasure, Mrs. O."

Meg grinned and bounced in her seat, swinging her legs under the table. "May we please be excused?"

"Of course, girls."

Mrs. O accompanied us to the hallway and stood as we pulled on our coats and boots. Just as we were leaving, I poked out my tongue and waved both my middle fingers in her face. Meg stuffed a mitten in her mouth to keep from laughing out loud.

In the years after the divorce, my mother moved constantly, frenetically, from rental to rental, crisscrossing Cobourg. Dad sold the house on Hamilton Avenue and moved to a bungalow on the other side of town that my parents had bought years before as an investment property. They divided the money equitably without argument, but for some reason Mum was always broke. My sister and I changed primary schools three times in a town three miles wide. Her last house is where we stayed longest, almost a year, a white stucco Victorian miller's cottage overlooking Pratt's Pond on the north edge of town. The plan was that my sister and I would take the bus to school and back, but in the end we almost always missed it and did the half-hour walk each way at a jog, lunch boxes rattling in our school bags, through the snowy, muddy woods behind the courthouse, over the town creek and across the highway past the Baskin-Robbins and into the suburb on the west side of town.

Since becoming a general reporter for the *Cobourg Daily Star*, Mum had gone from being an aloof, bookish housewife to expert village gossip. In those years Mum could inform you who'd won the pumpkin-growing contest at the Roseneath fall fair, which kids on the Junior A hockey team were out for the season with concussions, and whose dad was recently convicted of domestic assault. A couple of times a week she slept with a police scanner beside her jewelry box on her old pine dresser; the device crackled and bleated through the night. If there was a four-alarm fire or a six-car pileup, she'd pull on her ski jacket, and slip out without waking us.

I learned how to use a can opener and heat soup on the stove for dinner. In the morning, if Mum wasn't around, I packed our lunches and made sure Meg brushed her teeth before school.

The cottage at Pratt's Pond had character, Mum said, which meant it had a fireplace and hardwood floors and roses that climbed the half-rotted trellis beside the door. Character also meant there were mouse droppings in the cutlery drawer, peeling paint and limited hot water. In the winter, frost formed inside our bedroom windows and an arctic chill whistled down the chimney and snuffed out the fire, filling the room with soot. The living room rug was singed from sparks. Fire screens were another thing Mum didn't believe in.

I wasn't sure what my mother did believe in apart from Penguin classics and Mozart but the list of things in which she did not was growing longer by the day: curtains; carpeting; having more than one television; saltshakers; houseplants; books with bumpy covers; radio stations that weren't CBC or Classical FM; chicken balls; sugared cereal; sentimental greeting cards; handwashing after peeing or before eating; air-conditioning; scented lotions; houses without bookshelves; piano lessons; people who went for a drive instead of a walk; taking escalators or elevators when stairs were an option; chiming doorbells; anything that was just for guests; Highland dancing; Brownies and Girl Guides. My sister was dismayingly committed to the latter. At Meg's flying-up ceremony, we stood at the back. As the rest of the parents made tearful home videos on their camcorders, Mum made me giggle by whispering that the whole thing was in fact a colonial cult.

I liked the cottage at Pratt's Pond apart from the fact it was constantly freezing. Even in winter the thermostat was fixed at 15 degrees Celsius. I learned not to complain; there was no point. I developed an after-school routine that involved coming into the house, taking off my snowsuit, then changing immediately into a series of layers: leotards under jogging pants and socks and an itchy Irish knit sweater over a turtleneck and sweatshirt. I slept in a ski toque. In the mornings I stayed under the covers as long as possible, practiced blowing smoke rings in the frozen air.

Meg and I got home from school around four, but Mum didn't get off work until six or seven, often much later. I'd turn up the heat to 20 degrees and often forget, which would make Mum irate when she returned, exhausted from a long reporting shift at the paper.

"If we're not careful, we'll have to move again," she'd threaten. "We can't afford to live in a steam bath. I'm not rich like your father."

Dad wasn't rich, not by a long shot, the point was that he made more money than Mum, which was why at his house we had babysitters. At the age of eleven, I was still unable to distinguish my mother's facts from her fantasies. The facts were mostly complaints, ruminations: she was poor (but with panache!), she hated her job (though she also loved it), she wanted a boyfriend (but commitment sucks the life right out of you). The fantasies were harder to grasp.

When she was home, we'd sit up late talking even if I had school the next day. She didn't believe in bedtimes.

"Ugh, I'm sick of this town, aren't you?" she'd say, pouring herself a J&B on the rocks. I'd agree uncertainly.

"Maybe we should just move to Provence?" she'd add.

Many nights we'd sit in front of the fire reading our books or talking about our future life in the South of France—Avignon or Antibes? (it seems clear now she must have been reading Peter Mayle)—while my sister slept under the coffee table or wedged in the space between the wall and the love seat. We thought it was hilarious how Meg fell asleep in situ. Mum and I had a running list of all the weird places my sister had slept half the night: flung over the arm of a chair. On the upstairs landing. Under the kitchen table. In the empty bathtub. In a cupboard with her stuffed pig, Hamlet. Around ten o'clock we'd rouse her for the zombie shuffle up to bed. After that, we'd continue talking of France.

"But what will we do in Provence?" I'd wonder.

"Whatever we want!" Mum would say. "But mostly write and paint. The quality of light is unparalleled. We'll ride around on our bicycles and eat baguettes and unpasteurized cheese, which is so delicious, it's illegal in Canada."

"Won't we have to speak French?"

"We already do!"

"Not really."

"*Pas vraiment!*"

"Seriously, Mum, where would I go to school?"

Mum would give an exasperated laugh and sweep her hand through the air in a dismissive zigzag motion. "It wouldn't matter. Don't you see? We'd be *poor with panache.*"

The South of France, Mum assured me, was the best place for creative souls like us. We talked about it all the time, and the more seriously we discussed it, the more anxious I became.

"But what would you do for a job?"

"I'd go freelance. Write a roman à clef about my divorce, like Nora Ephron."

"What's that?"

"Thinly veiled fiction."

"So, like, a novel?"

"Please stop saying 'like,' Leah. You sound like a Valley Girl."

"Somebody would pay you to do that?"

"Do what?"

"To write a book about your life?"

"Oh, I don't know. Can we please just read?"

Since the divorce I'd become increasingly concerned about my mother's finances. Even though she worked all the time and got support from my dad, we could never afford anything. She was always saying we'd have to go live in a cinder block, by which she meant one of the grim pebble-dash high-rises in the social housing project on the north end of Division Street inexplicably known as the "depot."

"You can't imagine how ashamed I was," she'd often sigh, remembering the initial rupture. "All I took was three plates, three forks, three knives, three spoons, three juice glasses—just three of everything for me and you girls. *From my own kitchen.* That's how awful I felt for leaving your father."

My mother was no longer guilt-ridden; she was rueful. By this time my father had sold the place on Hamilton and moved in with his new girlfriend, Diane, a special ed teacher with no children of her own. She was quiet and shy, fastidiously tidy—the opposite of Mum. She had a collection of vintage Barbies she let me and my sister play with so long as we folded up all the clothes before returning them to their correct cases. Dad and Diane bought a new house, a Victorian right on the park with seven bedrooms and a wraparound porch. After the split, the single women in town put on lipstick and got in line, my mother said. It was so much easier for men to move on after divorce, especially men like my dad. It's true people seemed to like my father—not just women but pretty much everyone. He fit seamlessly in Cobourg. My mother and I were the odd girls out: bookish, prickly, overly opinionated. People like us weren't meant for a small Ontario town, she said.

Night after night we returned to the subject of our imagined life in Provence. We'd be penniless, but it wouldn't matter, because it was warm all year round in the South of France. My mother wouldn't be stuck in this dreary backwater, wasting her talent filing reports on the last meeting of the board of education. I'd learn French in five seconds flat because I was so clever. Every morning I'd bicycle to school in a cotton sundress after breakfasting on a baguette and Époisses.

"When would we see Dad?"

Mum rolled her eyes. "Obviously, your father would come to visit."

"I can't really imagine Dad in Provence."

Mum burst out laughing as if I'd just made a witty joke. "Oh, Leah, nor can I."

What I'd meant to say is that I couldn't imagine Provence at all.

A<small>T</small> Pratt's Pond I had a hamster, a fat orange male I named Adrian Mole. He was the last in a line of sickly pet rodents. Meg and I had two hamsters before that, females named Emily and Charlotte after the Brontë sisters. They were "teddy bears," which meant they were cuter and fluffier than normal hamsters and also sufficiently inbred that they died in quick succession, which Mum said was fitting, given their namesakes. Charlotte seemed to suffocate under the shavings, her eyes gummed up with pus. Emily, an albino with bright, beady eyes, lasted longer but succumbed to dehydration while we were at Dad's. Secretly I fretted that Mum had forgotten to fill her water bottle.

Adrian, however, was a survivor, in part because he was fat from overfeeding and inherited two water bottles instead of one. I trained him to live through anything, even being alone on the weeks I was away from him. The more contemptuous my mother became toward Adrian—the feeding, the smell, the sound of him running in his wheel at night, all of it drove her nuts—the more my affection deepened. Mum found it impossible to understand, perhaps because I agreed with her on everything else. But Adrian was the exception: he was mine and I adored him. Once I smuggled him to school in the front pocket of my hoodie. He sat quietly, a warm lump on my lap, nibbling sunflower seeds through class.

Because of the deaths of Emily and Charlotte, Meg was rewarded with a calico kitten for her birthday. We played with Lucy relentlessly. Apart from watching two channels of black-and-white TV, it was the only thing to do when Mum was at work. There were no other kids to play with at Pratt's Pond. Meg and I spent hours inventing new and elaborate forms of kitten baiting, unraveling whole balls of yarn in a miles-long trail around the house, then sitting on the sofa and winding the thread back slowly as Lucy flung herself from room to room, claws skidding across the hardwood, unable to gain purchase. I spent my allowance on a huge bag of catnip that we stuffed into socks and taunted her with, shrieking with laughter as she rolled about drunk.

Lucy grew into a big fluffy cat with glittering green eyes who lived in a perpetual state of psychosis. She was seductive and affectionate, with a great plume of a tail, but also violent and unpredictable. Her invisible enemies were everywhere, and Lucy launched herself at them, lunging without warning. Ankles and feet were ruthlessly attacked. We learned not to dangle our hands carelessly over the edge of a sofa. My mother adored Lucy, in part because she was a champion mouser. Only Adrian saw her for the stone-cold killer she was. Lucy lurked over his cage whenever she could sneak into my room, often knocking it off my dresser in the hope it might spring open. More than once, I pried him tenderly from her jaws.

One afternoon I arrived home from school to find Adrian's cage empty, wire hatch flung open. I searched the room for clues. I roared downstairs and found Lucy crouched in the living room, staring at the crack between the floor and baseboard. Her tail swept the floor in extravagant arcs.

For three days I searched relentlessly, with the intermittent help of my sister. By the end of the week everyone but me had given up hope. Mum, who had been vaguely sympathetic at first, grew irritable.

In the evenings she would settle for hours on the sofa under the orange wool throw blanket, which had, as long as I could remember, shrouded her like a magic cloak—one that discouraged children from asking for anything that involved her needing to stand up. During that week her evening stillness was immutable as I paced the house with my flashlight, flipping over cushions and peering down heating vents.

"You know," she finally said one night, looking up from whatever she was reading—most likely a novel by Anita Brookner or a *New Yorker* review of a movie she hoped Richard, the man from Toronto she'd recently met through the personal ads, might take her to in the city— "has it ever occurred to you that maybe he wanted to be free?"

I shook my head. "Adrian liked his home."

"Pumpkin, no animal likes a cage. Rodents aren't even mammals, you know. They're very low down on the food chain."

"But he was happy."

"He didn't keep us all up all night running in that stupid plastic wheel because he was happy, did he? He was restless."

"He was just getting exercise! And you said he was smart. Remember that time—"

"I said he was smart *for a hamster*."

I flopped down on the sofa beside her and inhaled the woody scent of the thin Cuban cigars she'd recently taken to smoking. Just one a night, she said, though even one a night soon gave her a cough that sounded like a gravel pit being dredged before breakfast. For years I'd mercilessly policed Dad's chain-smoking, but made an exception for my mother's cigars on aesthetic grounds. I liked their rich, herbaceous smell and the square green boxes they came in, edged in gold and emblazoned with art-nouveau font. I fashioned them into beds for my collection of miniature dolls, tucking them under tissue-paper blankets.

For what might have been the hundredth time that week, I made my mother promise she would have one last look for Adrian after I went to bed.

"Yes okay fine," she said.

"Cross your heart and hope to die, stick a needle in your eye?"

"What? No! Why would I do that?"

"It's a *vow*, Mum."

I showed her how to draw the cross over her heart and pinch her thumb and index finger together to insert an invisible needle directly into her cornea. She laughed and pulled a face.

"Now say it," I said.

"Say what?"

"Say what you'll do if you find him."

"I'll put him back in his cage."

I extended the hook of my little finger for her to pinkie swear. We sat in silence for a while after that, Mum reading and smoking, me staring at the fire, toes intertwined for warmth under the throw blanket. The wind blew down the chimney, causing sparks to pop and fizz into the room in a mini meteor shower. I watched the sparks fizzle out on the rug. Mum didn't look up.

Just before bed, I went to the kitchen for a glass of water and heard Lucy pawing at the door. When I opened it, she hopped inside, shook the snow from her fur, then proudly deposited a gift on the floor, looking pleased with herself. Adrian's half-frozen body. I picked him up and ran to the living room to show my mother.

"He must have gotten outside somehow! Oh god, what should we do?"

My mother's mouth twitched. She craned her neck slightly to peer at his chest, which palpitated in my palm. His eyes and whiskers were gummed up with what looked like pine sap but was probably hamster pus. Mum sighed.

"Oh, Leah, I don't think he's going to make it. The best thing to do would be to put him out of his misery."

"What? No!"

"Maybe you should call your father?"

I'd once watched my dad place an injured sparrow behind the tire of his Celica and reverse. He was gentle with animals, but he'd worked weekends at a funeral home in high school and wasn't squeamish about death. He said it was cruel to let an animal suffer. Adrian was suffering; I could see that.

"There must be something we can do." My mind raced. I thought of the lifesaving course I'd taken at camp where they taught us what to do with hypothermia victims, which was to get naked together in a sleeping bag. I took him to bed and cupped him in my hands for hours as I lay, trying not to fall asleep in case I crushed him.

The next morning before school, I placed him back in his cage, fluffing up a comfy bed of soft, dry shavings. Then I filled up his water bottle and put a few pellets in his food dish along with a couple of matchstick-sized carrot slices. I thought of trying to feed him milk through an eyedropper as I'd seen a vet on a nature program do with a baby bird, but we didn't have one. I put his cage over the heating vent.

After school, he was no better.

"I just can't figure it out. How would he have got out?" I said to Mum when she got home that night. "It makes no sense."

"Oh, Leah, does it really matter?" My mother's voice sounded brittle.

I looked up and she fixed her eyes on her novel. She tugged on the hairs at the crown of her head. I watched her shoulders clench, then almost imperceptibly her body seemed to shrink into itself. She was wishing away the force of my attention, repelling my gaze in her mind. But there was something else. She was radiating something. What was it? Shame? Yes, but also a slow-boiling resentment. Guilt was being alchemized into resentment before my eyes. The realization that she had attempted to murder Adrian was powerful, wrenching.

"You threw him outside, didn't you?"

She looked up at me and sighed. "Pumpkin, you know I'm a light sleeper. It wasn't just the wheel going round and round; it was when he started chewing on the bars. It drove me crazy. It seemed like he wanted to escape."

"Outside in winter?"

"Leah, I wasn't thinking straight. I just thought he should be free, so I picked him up and opened the back door and let him go. It was more a gentle toss than a chuck."

"You're unbelievable."

"What do you want me to say, Leah? I'm sorry. I'm a horrible mother. Are you happy now?"

"I loved him and you *killed* him."

"I emancipated him, it just didn't work out. There's a difference."

"You wanted him to die!"

She considered this. "Look, that's true, but it wasn't my primary intention. I just . . . needed to sleep. When you're my age and you have a job, you'll see."

"You're twisted," I hissed. "I know you killed all of them. All our pets. Not just Adrian."

"The dogs were put to sleep by Dr. Chase. Come on, Leah, he was just a hamster."

"He *is* just a hamster. *IS*. His name is Adrian Mole and he's up there right now, fighting for his life!"

"Sorry, *is*. You're right, it was thoughtless. I'm evil and heartless and you're a perfect angel. Are you happy now?"

"I'm going to spend *years* in therapy because of you. *YEARS AND YEARS!* Do you know that?"

As it turned out, I did spend years in therapy. Most of it was in my twenties in Toronto, with a Jungian named Judy whom I'd sought out after I developed a dangerous habit of fainting in crowded rooms. Judy did old-school analysis, paid for by the benefits plan at the paper where I worked as a columnist. Judy devoted nearly a year to analyzing my early childhood. For a while she'd hypnotize me and tap on one knee and then the other while in a monotone I'd recount the time Mum forgot me at camp, or the hours spent alone as a child, babysitting my sister, longing for my mother to come home, wondering where she was. We tapped out the story of Adrian's attempted murder. The empty fridge. The sign on the fridge:

COMMITMENT SUCKS THE LIFE RIGHT OUT OF YOU.

I didn't mind talking about my childhood, but I didn't get the tapping thing. It seemed ludicrously unscientific. Judy admitted the process was a mystery but promised it worked. The theory was that the tapping helped the psyche to digest painful memories from the past by stimulating the left and right brain in tandem. The memories of my mother, she said, were why I felt so confused in the present.

"You need to process your trauma," she insisted.

I scoffed at the word *trauma*. I told Judy she was overstating it. My mother was the one who'd been raped as a child. My trauma, if she insisted on calling it that, was nothing compared with my mother's. And everything that happened afterward—the divorce, the years of benign neglect, her leaving us for the city, the awful tortured affairs—it was all his fault, the Horseman's. My mother couldn't help it, I explained. When I told Judy *that* story, my mother's story, her eyes grew large and intensely focused. For the rest of the session she asked question after question and furiously scribbled down the answers in her leather-bound pad. At the end, she leaned forward and said, "Now we're getting somewhere."

"But it's not my story," I complained.

"That's not how trauma works," Judy said. "It can be shared. Passed down. Especially between mothers and daughters who lack boundaries."

This seemed a stretch. But I trusted Judy. Miraculously, for a while, the tapping cure did seem to work. I came out of our sessions feeling strangely refreshed. Maybe it was voodoo, but who cared, if it worked? My life felt, if not exactly calm and within my control, less like a series of crises I was lurching through, one after the other. The black bars at the periphery of my vision receded, then disappeared altogether.

In our final session before I moved to London, Judy looked at me very seriously and said, "Leah, I want you to know that, whatever happens, you'll always be my patient."

The years that followed were a lonely time, exacerbated by a tumult of work and a series of long-distance relationships. I often took comfort in Judy's words. I even called her up once or twice, less to talk than to hear her repeat her promise over the phone, confirming the fact that I did, in fact, belong to her. Belonging to Judy felt almost as constant as belonging to my mother—except with Judy I could breathe.

A few years later, my mother met Judy at a dinner party hosted by a mutual friend, and for a time they became close friends. My mother had no idea Judy had been my therapist but Judy knew exactly who my mother was. The mutual friend who introduced them was the same woman who'd referred me to Judy in the first place. My mother told her new best friend everything, of course, but she needn't have. Judy knew her story in granular detail.

At first Mum didn't understand the connection. When I finally put it together over the phone, we both laughed in horror. The whole thing felt like a sick practical joke. When Mum later confronted Judy about it she was surprised to find her completely unapologetic and baffled at my mother's sense of betrayal. Judy told her calmly that in fact it would have been a violation of confidentiality for her to disclose the connection. As far as I know they did not discuss what to my mind was the real issue, which is whether Judy should have knowingly befriended the mother of a patient at all.

As for Adrian Mole, he died the morning after the cat dragged him in from the snowbank. I wrapped his body in Mum's favorite silk scarf then placed him in a Kleenex box full of shavings. The funeral was moving but brief. Meg and I tried to bury him at the base of the climbing rose in the flowerbed, but the ground was frozen, so I hid him at the back of the freezer under some chicken breasts. We meant to give him a proper burial in the spring. But we moved again and forgot.

7

On our first morning in New York, Mum and I order bagels and coffee for breakfast in the hotel diner, which overlooks an in-house sound studio where a guy in a bow tie is recording a podcast.

My mother is astonished the diner only has disposable cutlery. So American, she says, repurposing her plastic knife as a coffee spoon. She's leading a civil disobedience campaign to rid her village of single-use plastic and she's purged her home in accordance with her principles. Beeswax wraps instead of cellophane. Glass jars. Steel water bottles. A ban on nonvintage Tupperware. Her latest action, she explains, is to un-package all her fruits and vegetables at the supermarket and leave the wrapping on the floor to send a message.

"Don't they find it annoying?"

I imagine an elderly woman in a smock at the Creemore grocery store on her hands and knees gathering up the packaging for my mother's shallots and avocados after a long day stacking shelves. Mum rolls her eyes.

"That's the point. If they complain to their managers, the managers will complain to the suppliers. It's grassroots action."

A few months ago, Mum tells me, she and members of her anti-plastic group filled the empty water fountain in the village square with thousands of crumpled water bottles and covered them with photos of dead fish and seabirds. The local paper ran a story on it and she was asked to participate in a local panel discussion about how to start a movement. Talking about her activism puts Mum in a good mood, so I decide it's a good time to bring up the book I'm writing. The one about us.

"Which book?" she says, inspecting the underside of her everything bagel. She knows which book. "Oh, yes, *that* book. How's it going?"

I tell her that, as mentioned, I've been soldiering on with the book project, our former collaboration, without her. Of course, it's developing into a different book, one I hope might be as good as—more interesting and complicated than—the one we'd initially imagined. The writing is going well. I've even found a publisher. I am buttering my bagel as I talk, keeping my tone casual. My mother absorbs the information in an offhand way. In fact—am I imagining this?—she seems happy for me. Not overjoyed or effusive but genuinely pleased, like a supportive but mildly distracted friend to whom I've just imparted a bit of good news. She blinks, smiles, then says, "Well, good for you, kiddo. Congratulations. You've done it."

I monitor her tone for sarcasm and decide there isn't any. Then I come out with it. I ask my mother if I can have her blessing to write my book. It takes every shred of courage I have, but somehow I manage to pose the question. Afterward, I brace, quivering for the answer like a nerd who's just asked a cheerleader to the prom.

She blinks, then shrugs in a manner that suggests she thinks the question is a bit over-the-top, a virtue signal. I expect her to say something oblique like *I suppose you'll do what you want anyway, so what does it matter what I say?* But she surprises me by looking at me very seriously and gently patting my forearm. "Consider it my gift to you," she says. "For everything that's happened."

Is that a tang of vinegar in the oil? Doesn't matter, I decide. She's given her blessing; she can't take it back. Something cracks in my chest, and my body floods with relief. Outside, on Lexington, workmen in yellow hard hats are dredging a sewer line. In my head I begin counting backward from ten. I only get to six before she asks the predictable question.

"So how much was the advance?"

✦ ✦ ✦

THE summer before I turned twelve, my mother found a solution to our semi-itinerant borderline poverty. She would become "caretaker" of Vogrie, a crumbling Victorian farmhouse on 250 wooded acres north of town. Vogrie was the place where Mum was transformed into her post-divorce self, shedding her former housewife identity like a husk. She tweaked her name from Cessie to the more whimsical and antique Cecily. Vogrie was the place where we both came of age. Her love affair with Scotch and cigars deepened. I learned to masturbate. She discovered how to make Richard jealous by casually dating other men. We both read constantly, promiscuously, stories of tortured marriages and sexual awakenings, an ongoing relay of dog-eared paperbacks: *By Grand Central Station I Sat Down and Wept*, *The Women's Room* by Marilyn French, Doris Lessing's *The Golden Notebook*, everything by Erica Jong, the whole of Updike's Rabbit series. At Dad's I read the same books my friends at school read: *Flowers in the Attic*, *Carrie*, the Sweet Valley High novels, and *Tiger Eyes*. They were books my mother disapproved of not for their racy content but because they were easy to understand, which meant they were trash.

My mother rented Vogrie for a nominal sum; her position was officially caretaker. The house was a rambling, dilapidated treasure chest of art and antiquities. All of it would one day be donated to major museums or auctioned off, but at the time it was our playground. It had seven huge bedrooms, two separate wings, a kitchen staircase up to the haunted maids' quarters, a box room filled with dusty evening gowns from the twenties and thirties. The place had been the marital home of a pair of childless, wealthy historians, Gilbert Bagnani and his wife, Stewart, former professors at Trent University, to whom the house was now in trust. The elderly widow lived in Toronto and came to visit for a few weeks each summer.

Vogrie wasn't ours, but we thought of it that way. Mum would live there off and on for years, and even after she moved to Toronto, she would use it on weekends. The place was crammed to the rafters with stuff—some of it priceless, much of it worthless, the treasures indistinguishable from the tat. There was an original Chagall sketch that hung crooked in the kitchen, just below the ancient rudimentary buzzer system for long-vanished servants. Above the library fireplace was a large Rubens. (Or possibly a student of Rubens? No one seemed sure.) It was covered in soot from the fireplace, which didn't draw well. The library was the size of my school gymnasium, built with twenty-foot-high ceilings to accommodate a pair of tarnished gilt doorframes imported from Florence. There were so many rooms, they each had a name. The William Ronald Room was christened in honor of a Canadian expressionist who had painted two garish pinwheel-like murals on the wall one Christmas in the 1960s. The Strachan Room contained the impossibly tiny sleigh bed of the late fat bishop of Toronto. The Oriental Room was improbably devoted to the spoils of the ancient Egyptian crocodile king, whose tomb the Bagnanis had excavated together in the early days of their courtship.

I loved it when the widow came to visit. Stewart was frail and stooped but funny and vigorously sociable. We were both lonely and liked to talk. I trotted around behind her like a toy dog as she explained the provenance of this William Morris tapestry or that childhood portrait of her painted as Peaseblossom, a fairy from *A Midsummer Night's Dream*. She told me and my sister we were welcome to play with the sarcophagi in the Oriental Room so long as we weren't afraid of curses. On the mantel was a large, intricately carved ivory pagoda under a bell jar; we eventually lifted it to the floor and used it as a doll's house. She just laughed when we dressed up for dinner in the Egyptian collar necklaces, cuffs, bangles, and rings made of glinting gems inlaid with turquoise carvings of beetles and birds set in gold so pure and soft, you could indent it with your thumbnail. There were closets full of shedding mink stoles, opera glasses, and velvet top hats that popped out if you tapped them with the tip of a cane. We pulled enormous leather-bound first editions from the library shelves in the hope of finding pirate maps and threw them aside shrieking at the wood lice. A whole Christmas holiday was spent giving each other rides on the vertiginous ladder that rattled the length of the library until it finally tore free from its casters, hanging at a slant, never to be repaired.

The magic of Vogrie was less about the abundance of treasure than the sheer decadence of filth. The place was quite literally alive—with rodents and insects and snakes who shed their skins in the root cellar. There were bat nurseries in the chimneys and the young ones often looped clumsily through the rafters at night. At breakfast my sister and I took turns pressing down the toaster to see how many mice would pop out. The water was pumped to the house from a sand-filtered artesian well that thumped and moaned like a dying sex-mad dog. When the pump was broken, which it often was, we crouched in the stream beside the house filling pasta pots or crystal decanters—whatever was at hand—with drinking water for the day. After meals, we washed dishes in the stream, groaning as we scoured the plates with freezing fingers because Mum said soap was bad for the earth.

There were lots of dishes to be done, because there were always lots of people. Technically, Vogrie was meant to be a kind of intellectual study and writing retreat. Favored PhD students or blocked professors on sabbatical would often turn up unannounced and stay for days, taking over some random bedroom, filling it with books and papers, emerging at odd hours begging for an ear of corn or a corkscrew. On the weekends, my mother entertained a succession of friends in rolling overnight dinner parties. Most people left after a few days, but some lingered on as unofficial housemates, so long as my mother approved.

It was my job to tour all arriving guests through the house while my mother chopped and sweated onions or moved from room to room, hoisting trays and glasses, bumping open doors with her hip. In my memory she is always wearing high-waisted Edwin jeans with a bright silk blouse of orange or red or blue. My mother was still in her thirties at the time, a beautiful woman who insisted that prettiness had skipped her over. Unlike her sisters, she'd been denied my grandmother's doll-like face. She had my grandfather's Roman nose, fair, freckled skin, flyaway blond hair, and a strong, compact body. Her parts were unremarkable individually, but together they resulted in a strange combustion. The energy was all in her eyes. They were large for her face, mascara eroding their edges, a dark and plaintive blue.

Everything about Vogrie seemed to suit my mother at that time.

She wore the mess of the place like a costume, reveled in the mess, encouraged guests to play the full-sized Steinway grand, a piano so out of tune everything played on it sounded like a ragtime reel in a Wild West saloon. She was particularly amused by one of the pantries off the kitchen, filled with nothing but a broken freezer and piles of disused egg cartons bound together with rubber bands—literally hundreds of thousands of them, stacked to the ceiling, infested with mouse nests. Once, when I asked Stewart what the egg cartons were for, she lifted her chin and said frostily that she grew up during the war.

Of course, there were also ghosts, real or imagined, who moved through the house in the years we were there. In the end, there were too many to count. The most companionable was a poltergeist called Nellie who, according to her mossy tombstone in the forest, died in childhood in the 1850s. That was it—no other details. I wondered why this was. Were her parents too grief-stricken to bother, or was her life so short there was no point in explaining it with dates? It seemed an unforgivable oversight to me, given the unfathomable length and complexity of my own childhood, which I understood at Vogrie was rapidly coming to a close.

After weeks of exploring in the woods, I'd managed to locate the old family cemetery at the bottom of the drumlin about a mile from the main house. That was where I found Nellie's grave. It was a shady spot, on the bank of a stream in a grazing meadow, grown over with brambles like Sleeping Beauty's castle, but a child, even a big one like me, could slip under the thorns and reach the gate, which easily creaked open. On hot days I'd go there and read for hours on a damp towel I pretended was a picnic blanket, using Nellie's old stone as a backrest. At dusk I'd wander back to the house, to the predinner croquet tournaments, the sound of jazz and tinkling glasses, to the adults and their laughter and requests for towels and toothpaste.

Vogrie was the strangest, most chaotic place I've ever lived, which is saying something. It was the least ours and yet also the place we felt most at home. Maybe it was the fact there was no point in trying to clean it. Perhaps it was the transience of the place that spoke to us. The house and the wild forest around it—250 acres, most of it unexplored bush—seemed to belong to no one at all. The house itself was a liminal space in which my sister and I were safe but never chaperoned, left to our devices but never alone. I have always loved places that conceal other places, the promise of other worlds and lives layered in a palimpsest. Forests with deep hidden gorges, mountains threaded with invisible caves, houses with secret passageways, hidden staircases, dark wardrobes, and ladders that pull down from the ceiling leading to attic dormers where a small girl can hide with her book. In reality Vogrie wasn't terribly grand. It was a dilapidated Ontario farmhouse which had once been owned by a couple of intellectual hoarders. But for me it was a glittering, self-contained universe, a cobwebbed palace of infinite escapes.

One of the grad students who came to stay never left. For a time Mark became my mother's best friend and confidant. He was tall and intense, a crane-necked twenty-something PhD student from South America who described himself as an Anglo-Argentine aristocrat. The first term I could not make sense of and the second I'd never heard applied to anything but Siamese cats in a Disney movie. Like my mother, Mark was lovelorn, missing his Brazilian girlfriend, Sarah. On the weekends when Mum was too sad to get out of bed because of her latest romantic bust-up with Richard, Mark would bring her trays of toast and tea and shoo me away from her bedroom door.

"Your mother is *resting*," he'd say in his mid-Atlantic accent then look at me knowingly, as if surely I was old enough to understand what he meant. In truth I had no idea. The notion my mother might be so heartbroken she couldn't even drag herself out of bed had never occurred to me—nor had the idea that she might not want to talk about it. Unlike the hard-drinking parents of some of my school friends, Mum never slept in on the weekends. She didn't even nap. What was she doing in there? I couldn't work it out, but I knew better than to press the point with Mark, who could be snappy. What I felt more than anything on the days when he barred me from her room was violently jealous.

Until Mark came along, I had been my mother's primary confidante. I'd never known anything else and that was the way I liked it. I saw it as my right to tiptoe into the crepuscular confines of her bedroom then slip under the quilt and ask her in a gentle whisper what the bastard had gone and done this time. If she cried, I knew how to soothe her tears. I knew just how to rub her back and massage Vaseline into the cracks on her heels which sometimes bled in winter. I was good at making toast and tea, though to be honest it had never occurred to me to take it to her bedroom on a tray. Here's another thing that never occurred to me: that by barring me from my mother's bedroom Mark was protecting both of us.

8

THE summer I was ten I spent the entire summer at two different all-girls' camps: Oconto for the month of July, a big old-fashioned camp on a lake in the woods where we wore uniforms, slept in canvas tents on wooden platforms, and went on long canoe trips. In August, it was Saddlewood, a horse-riding camp house on the grounds of a country boarding school. By then I'd been going to camp since age seven and loved everything about it. My parents loved it, too, not least because my grandmother paid the fees. I loved the ritual and order of the days. At Oconto, the 6 a.m. polar dip followed by the flag raising and recitation of *Salutation to the Dawn*, the clang of the dining hall bell, the chanting and clapping. I was even fond of the terrible food—powdered mashed potatoes, steamed hot dogs, Hamburger Helper, and tuna casserole topped with soggy chips—which we all complained about while washing down third and fourth helpings with plastic pitchers of red-dye Kool-Aid. On Sunday night after sundown we had "vespers," a candlelit procession to the ethereal woodland chapel during which we recited poems then sang folk songs in the dark. Every night after lights-out, one of the counselors played taps on a bugle from the tip of Eagle Point, the sad, slow notes reverberating across the lake.

Many girls got homesick, especially the young ones. At camp homesickness was not a vague nostalgic yearning, the way I'd heard adults describe it, but instead a pathological viral illness that could infect a girl, or group of girls, at any time, striking without reason or warning. A generalized melancholic hysteria comprised its major symptoms and almost nightly one or more of us would be violently ripped from sleep by sudden inexplicable fits of sobbing and wailing. The counselor on night watch would appear almost instantly (apart from watching for scavenging bears, this was her entire job), then rouse the stricken girl from her bed and quietly usher her by flashlight to the infirmary where, it was rumored, you were given hot chocolate and read a story from *The Many Adventures of Winnie the Pooh*.

Disappointingly, I did not get homesick. Not once. Partly it was a matter of place and specificity. In the years after the divorce we moved so often I had no home in particular to long for. On the rare occasion I felt despondent in the night, no image flashed into my mind as the place where I *ought* to be. I loved my parents but like most children of divorce I was used to being away from them. They both moved that summer while I was away—my mother to a bedsit in Peterborough where she slept during the week while working at the city paper (returning to Vogrie at weekends), and my father to a new house with his girlfriend, Diane.

To me camp was better than home. It was like an orphanage in the woods on a lake run by charismatic teenaged tomboys, the kind of girls who knew how to whittle a spoon, dance the Charleston, and rig a sailboat—a place where kids were competent and in charge. I developed raging tween crushes on all my counselors, in particular the loud ones with short hair and dirty necks who swaggered around at dawn rousing us from our bunks with portable stereos on their shoulders blasting "Don't Stop Believin'" by Journey. I spent a lot of time braiding intricate gimp bracelets in their favorite colors and worrying I might be a lesbian.

My favorite thing about camp was the singing. We sang as we walked and sang as we swam; we sang as we paddled and sang carrying canoes over our heads on mile-long portages across land. Our repertoire was the normal campfire songbook ("Johnny Appleseed," "Kumbaya," "Boomdidiada") plus some pop songs such as "As Tears Go By" by the Rolling Stones and Joni Mitchell's "Both Sides Now," which we called

"Clouds." The camp anthem was a mash-up called "Fish." It combined "Sh-Boom (Life Could Be a Dream)" by the Crew Cuts with Billie Holiday's "Blue Moon" and the *Show Boat* theme "Can't Help Lovin' Dat Man" in a glorious, galloping four-way round underlaid by the shuffling chorus of *sh-boom sh-boom tra-la-la-la-la-la.* "Fish" was our theme song; we sang it morning, noon, and night with unselfconscious abandon. Out of historical context, it was the song's fatalism that appealed, the idea that, for women, romantic love was an act of self-sacrifice to be suffered for the sake of the common good, like childbirth or war. *Fish got to swim, birds got to fly, / I gotta love one man till I die.*

Every day after lunch we ran down to the post office, which on Fridays doubled as a candy store known as the TUC shop (an acronym for Treats Under Control). Some of the girls got post every day, fat sentimental letters from anguished mothers and shoeboxes wrapped in brown paper, decorated with hearts and rainbows and tied up with string. The care packages contained treasures—comic books, homemade muffins, acne cream, batteries, and Polaroids of their siblings they tacked up beside their bunks. My post was more infrequent, maybe a letter a week, which I nonetheless read with relish. Those lucky enough to get post were meant to open and read it on the rocks outside the TUC shop to avoid making their less-fortunate tentmates jealous or homesick.

I still have a postcard Mum sent me that summer. On the front was a late self-portrait of Van Gogh, the one with the blue background and the fur hunting cap pulled down low to his brow. I sat on the rock staring at the flat, anguished saucers of his eyes; the soiled bandage cupping his right cheek. I smiled, reminded of the story my mother liked to repeat, about how Van Gogh had been terribly poor when he painted it. So poor he went mad, cut off his ear, and posted it to a friend, then died without ever having sold a painting, his genius unrecognized during his lifetime. If only he'd lived to see his despair commodified as a postcard! I flipped it over and smiled at the sight of my mother's loopy blue ballpoint cursive. Just then a girl named Brandi who was in my tennis group offered me a homemade oatmeal cookie from her care package. She smiled and explained it had come all the way from Calgary, then she peered down at the inscription on my postcard. I flinched and fought the urge to hide it but I was still chewing her mother's cookie which was exceptionally good, salty-sweet and pleasantly moist in the middle. I didn't want to be rude.

Brandi scrunched up her freckled nose. "Is that meant to be funny?" she said.

"It's kind of like an inside joke." I shrugged and read the inscription again, a smile buttering itself across my face.

The weather is here. Wish you were beautiful!
Love, Mum

On the last day at Oconto, Dad and Diane came to pick me up. The plan was for us to go back to Cobourg. I would spend two days furiously doing laundry, then be delivered to Saddlewood. Diane, it turned out, went to my camp when she was young and now wanted to see it again. Dad hoisted my hockey bag full of filthy clothes on his back then deposited it in the trunk of the Grand Marquis. When I offered to give them a tour Diane smiled.

"Thank you, Leah, but I already know my way around," she said in a voice so soft it was almost a murmur.

What can I say about Diane? She was placid and soft-spoken, with a long, unreadable face, a vague presence in oxblood penny loafers and long corduroy skirt. That day at camp she seemed to slope across the grass of the archery course, as my dad and I lagged behind. I was talking excitedly, holding his hand, the words tumbling out of me in a breathless jumble. I needed Dad to know about all the badges I'd earned, the new friends I'd made, the big black rattlesnakes I'd seen sunning themselves on the rocks during the canoe trip. Diane wasn't listening; she was lost in her own world. "Nothing has changed," she kept saying in her whisper-voice, expression immobile. "It's all exactly the same." Same swim dock, same tennis courts, same red war canoes, same stand of jack pines, same island across the bay. Diane observed all this softly, as if to herself, in a serene, magnetic way that eventually drew my father's attention away from me and my scampering puppy-like enthusiasm.

"It's like stepping back in time," she marveled, gazing up at the dining hall bell as Dad stroked the back of her pressed linen blouse. *What were you expecting*, I thought, affecting an extravagant yawn, *the lost city of Atlantis?*

Diane insisted on showing us the cabin she stayed in as a chickadee and the tent she moved to as a robin. She showed us the place where the outhouses used to be before the flush toilets were built. In the dining hall, on the memorabilia wall, we found her face in a black-and-white group shot underneath the camp crest—a tiny pigeon-toed smudge of a girl in a bucket hat. Even as a child, her expression seemed blank, unreadable as a freshly painted wall.

"Can you believe I was your age once?" she asked me.

"Nope," I said. Dad guffawed and Diane covered her mouth, shielding her perfect teeth from view.

On the walk back to the car, Dad reached his arm around Diane's waist, then tenderly brushed a fleck of dried leaf from her shoulder. Something about the way he touched her made me want to launch myself into space like a missile and explode in a spray of light. "Shotgun!" I hollered, then dashed toward the car. No one bothered to race me. I would not be sitting in front.

Back on the highway, heading west, Diane twisted round in the passenger seat and extended her left hand until it floated, disembodied and immobile, a few inches from my face. On her third finger was a ring that looked, I immediately thought, just like the one Prince Charles recently gave Lady Diana. I stared at the dark sapphire and its winking ring of diamonds, silently masticating my cherry Chiclet. Eventually, Dad tilted the rearview mirror and lowered his Ray-Ban aviators to meet my gaze. His expression was stern but urgent, almost pleading; he was willing me to be polite.

"Let me guess," I said, "you're getting married?"

Diane nodded. A closed-lipped smile stretched across her face.

"So who's the lucky guy?"

Dad's eyes flared at me in the rearview mirror.

"Kidding!" I said. "That's awesome. So can I be a flower girl? Pretty please?"

Dad gave me a conspiratorial wink then readjusted the mirror. "I think that can probably be arranged," he said, then reached over to squeeze Diane's knee under the pleats of her denim skirt.

"Let's not get ahead of ourselves," she said. I stared out the window blinking back tears as the bullrushes streaked past. I pictured myself in a puff-sleeved dress with a crinoline and a crown of rosebuds, scattering flower petals on the floor of a church.

A⊤ Saddlewood, we wore riding clothes instead of uniforms. T-shirts tucked into breeches, knee-high boots, and velvet hard hats decorated with forked black ribbons that hung over our ponytails like snake tongues. We thwacked the rumps of our lazy school ponies with leather crops, urging them over pole jumps in the heat.

The rest of the year the camp was called Bethany Hills Girls School. Some of the campers went to boarding school but not this one. They'd made a rule against it after a few parents began leaving their daughters here all year round.

My horse that summer was a gentle buckskin gelding called Dusty, with whom I fell instantly in love. When I wasn't riding him I was brushing him in circles and combing the burrs from his mane and tail then bathing him with a sponge dipped in a bucket of cool water. When Dusty was out to pasture, I tended to his tack, washing the bridle and saddle with glycerin soap before massaging it with the oil from the skin of a mink. During rest hour I'd drag my sleeping bag out to the field and sketch my oblivious horse as he grazed on clover and ragweed. While my cabinmates swam in the brackish unheated pool, I'd lie on my bunk and read books on stable management, preparing for the day when I'd be able to load Dusty into the trailer and take him home with me the way the private school girls from Toronto did with their thoroughbreds.

On the last day, there was a much-anticipated horse show. I spent hours grooming Dusty to a golden shine. I combed out his tail and twisted his black mane into plaits. I wasn't a particularly gifted or competitive rider, but the day of the show Dusty rose to the occasion. He lowered his head like a proper show horse, took the bit in the tender part of his mouth and leapt at my urging. One by one we sailed over the poles. To my astonishment we placed first in jumping and third in dressage. At the awards ceremony, the judges hung two enormous ruffled ribbons, one red, one green, on Dusty's bridle.

Afterward I stayed mounted, guiding Dusty out of the ring to the parking lot behind the stables. I stood up on tiptoe in the stirrups and anxiously scanned the crowd of parents and campers for my mother.

I dismounted and hugged my friends goodbye, returning their false promises to write. Standing with Dusty and waving as we watched their grinning faces recede in the rear windows of a succession of station wagons and SUVs.

I took my time with Dusty in the stable, untacked and groomed him, lifting the salt grit of dust and dried sweat from his flanks as he munched on a bucket of honeyed oats. I leaned my face into the curve of his neck, inhaling the piney smell of his sweat. Mum told me horses seem smarter than dogs, because they are bigger and stronger, but in fact they are stupid. It's this stupidity, she said, that makes them submit to the saddle. Dogs have been known to howl for days at their dead masters' graves, but a dog would never consent to be ridden, even by a child. *But who would want to ride a dog anyway?* I wondered silently, resuming my ongoing conversation with her in my head.

I led Dusty in his halter out to the paddock and pressed my forehead against his flank, hoping for a final nuzzle. His pack was grazing in the shade of an oak tree, maybe a hundred yards off. At the sight of them he pulled away from me violently. I let go of the halter and watched in dismay as he broke into an eager trot. The other school ponies greeted him lazily I thought, flicking their tails in a careless blasé manner as if to say, Oh you again. I waited for him to look back—just once—but he dipped his head and began ripping up a patch of daisies.

When I returned to the campus it was eerily quiet, like an Old West ghost town. I sat on my stripped vinyl bunk and rested my feet on my packed hockey bag and began to reread my favorite book, *Emily of New Moon*. A Bon Jovi song wafted through the window screen, punctuated by sudden shrieks of laughter: the start of the annual staff party.

I fell asleep for what could have been a minute or an hour, and when I opened my eyes, the light was waning. I walked the path to the dining hall, admiring the elasticity of my late August shadow on the grass, then slipped in the kitchen door, finding the rotary wall phone where I dialed the number for Vogrie. A man with a strange mid-Atlantic accent answered.

"Hallo?" he said. "Hal-loo?"

I paused, unsure if I'd been wrong about the number. Then, in the background, I recognized the familiar tinkling sound of jazz piano, ice cubes, laughter.

"Hi, can you please get my mum?"

"What?"

"Cessie?"

"Sorry, whom?"

"Cessie Mc—Ross. She's the caretaker?"

"Oh, gosh, you mean *Cecily*! Yes, sorry, dear, I thought—never mind. Hang on." He drops the receiver with a clatter.

An hour or so later, the battered blue Mazda sped up the camp's long drive, gravel crunching under its tires. I was waiting near the gate under the willow tree with my hockey bag and ribbons, my velvet riding cap perched primly on my lap. The Mazda skidded to a stop and Mum burst from the car like a streak of light; she left the door open, the engine idling. She was wearing clothes I'd never seen before: a mandarin-orange silk blouse tucked into a matching skirt that is long, with deep pleats. Her hair glowed tawny in the waning light.

I held up my ribbons, grinned lamely, but she breathlessly brushed them aside, and folded me into a hug so tight and familiar, I wished I could move into it and sign a ten-year lease. The vanilla shampoo scent of her hair is mixed with the perfume Richard likes, White Linen by Estée Lauder. Beneath that, candle wax, lemons, and a whisper of cigar smoke.

She was crying, of course. But for once I didn't mind.

"I'm such an idiot," she said. "I just completely blanked. I'd written it down somewhere, but then—*poof!*" She made a one-handed gesture of a fist exploding just above her ear. "Will you ever forgive me, Pumpkin?"

She studied my face with eyes that silently implored me not to tell my father—she didn't need to say this—nor did I need to promise her I wouldn't.

Once on the road, Mum was chatty, full of questions about camp and Dusty, whom I'd described in my letters. There were so many things I had to tell her, but we'd been apart for so long, my mind filled with static. I couldn't form a coherent thought. So I skipped over everything else and instead told her the big news, the front-page splash, which was Dad and Diane's engagement. Mum looked at me goggle-eyed then turned back to the road and fell silent, chewing the inside of her cheek. I recounted the whole story, how they'd picked me up at Oconto, then dropped the bomb. The Princess Diana ring, the waggling finger, Diane's unsmiling face and whispery voice. My mother thought it was hilarious when I imitated Diane's blank expression or the way she'd say, "That's funny," instead of laughing at Dad's corny jokes.

"Well, I'm happy for them," Mum said finally, eyes fixed on the road. "Aren't you?"

I shrugged. "I guess so. If Dad's happy."

Normally I monitored my mother's feelings so closely they often seemed inseparable from my own. It occurred to me for the first time that I'd never considered the question of my father's feelings, let alone his happiness. For a moment I tried to. I shut my eyes and tried to picture the thoughts inside his head but it seemed silly somehow. Ludicrous. Like wondering whether a tree is happy. Or a car.

"At least she's got money," Mum said with a shrug. "Do you think she wants children of her own? I hope your father's told her about the vasectomy."

I was confused. Diane was a special ed teacher. I didn't know about inheritances or vasectomies yet, so I changed the subject.

"She's desperate for me to be a flower girl."

My mother made a guttural sound, which I parroted then pretended to barf. "Like, gag me with a spoon."

We laughed as Mum geared up the Mazda, persuading the hatchback to find purchase on the dusty back road. By the time we crested the hill, both of us were in stitches at the idea of me in a princess dress, walking down the aisle scattering rose petals from a basket. The valley spread out before us and I blinked, dazzled by the depth of the view after so long in the flat familiar confines of camp.

"Wait," Mum said suddenly. "Do you *want* to be a flower girl? It's okay if you do. I won't mind."

"Ugh, gross. Are you kidding?"

She smiled, then reached over and squeezed my knee.

EVERY weekend at Vogrie is the same but different: the churn of grown-ups in and out. Adults in the kitchen unpacking bags of groceries and wine. Adults reading and talking and asking where they might find some kindling for the fire. I can't keep track of whether they are friends of Mum's or people from the university or both. It doesn't matter. No one notices me, because quiet children are invisible to adults in deep conversation, and at Vogrie all conversations are deep and adult. On this particular weekend, someone brings dogs. My sister chases them through the hall wearing a flapper dress over her pajamas, leaving a bread crumb trail of loose beads. "Yee-haw!" she cries, herding the dogs with a bamboo riding crop. In the sitting room, my mother reclines on a dilapidated satin sofa beside the dying afternoon fire. Her friend Gloria, whom I do recognize, is on the opposite chair. Gloria is tall with red hair and she has an important job with the CBC. She's older than my mother, and the ex-girlfriend of Richard, the man from the city my mother is in love with who is not exactly her boyfriend. Richard himself sits at the end of the sofa, stroking my mother's bare feet and smoking a cigar as she and Gloria talk.

The reasons why Richard is not my mother's boyfriend are complicated and murky. Sometimes he has another girlfriend; other times he says he doesn't believe in commitment, except that he does—just not with my mother. He doesn't take her out in public as much as she would like, which she suspects is because he's ashamed of her. The last time she broke up with him, it was because she saw him in a crowd shot at an awards ceremony with a beautiful blond TV presenter. Richard says he rarely takes her out because she lives way out in the country and works split shifts at the paper, which means she is usually not available, which she admits is also true.

Despite not being her boyfriend, Richard is around a lot. If he doesn't have an event in the city, he comes to Vogrie on the weekends. Like everyone else, he's enchanted by the house. When my mother breaks up with him, he always manages to persuade her to take him back, not with abject apologies or declarations of love or promises of anything. He just keeps calling and pretending nothing's happened until he catches her at a weak moment. I'm not sure what she sees in him. He's paunchy, with unruly gray hair and basset-hound jowls, though I suppose Mum is right that he has a nice mouth. He's a great kisser, but he's less exciting in bed. He's never even given her an orgasm. Not even one! She fakes it every time. Apparently he likes it when she gives him a blow job with her pearls in her mouth, which I think is just weird. He drives a silver Lincoln and wears a cardigan with piano keys running down the front because he's really into jazz. He's actually much nicer to me than most of the grown-ups, curious and attentive, which I resent.

"Well, hello there, young lady," Richard says when he sees me hovering in the doorway.

My mother smiles, then goes back to listening to Gloria, who is halfway through a long story.

"How was your walk?"

"I went to the graveyard," I say. "On the way, I found an old bird's nest. It must have fallen out of a tree. There were no eggs in it."

No one is listening but Richard. He beckons me into the room.

"How exciting. Can I see it?"

I shrug and duck out of the doorway.

ONE morning when Mark is away from Vogrie and Richard isn't visiting, my mother calls me to her bedroom. It's large and bright, at the front of the house, with two floor-to-ceiling Gothic windows that look out over the front lawn and, beyond that, a field of soybeans. It's called the Empire Room, which has something to do with the period of the furniture. There's a big double sleigh bed and a small vanity with a stool and a three-sided mirror and an old-fashioned silver brush made of horsehair that no one ever uses except my sister and me when we're playing princesses.

Mum points to an ad she has circled in the newspaper classifieds.

White professional male, 40s, attractive, slim, 6 ft., seeks similar-aged or younger female for companionship, conversation, lingering dinners and laughter. Must be well-read, lively and slim, open-minded and passionate about ideas. A love of travel and live jazz a bonus if not a must. Let's meet and see where this goes, shall we?

I'm confused. I look at the date and see it's this morning's paper. But the ad—it can't be. It's the same ad, almost verbatim, that my mother replied to two years earlier, just after she left my father. I helped her write the letter. Then, when Richard had called, I helped her choose what to wear for their first date in the city.

"I don't understand," I say, though I do. It's obvious. Not only is Richard seeing other women in the city, which my mother already knows, he is actively trying to meet new ones. "Mum, he's a jerk."

"I know," she sobs. "I know, I know, I know. But I just can't stop. Something about it . . . it just *feels right*. I can't explain why."

That night, I go to bed in my room, the Withers Room, which is across the hall from my mother's. Meg sleeps one door over, in Bishop Strachan's child-sized bed. I fall into a restless, twisting sleep and wake up disoriented, my nightgown drenched. At first I think I must have a fever, then I realize I'm not in the right place. My mother is with me. She's sobbing, one of those horrible hiccuping long cries where she can't stop. Her tears are making everything wet. Somehow I've ended up in her bed again, but I can't remember how.

"I never should have left your father," Mum whispers. "I was so stupid. It was a terrible thing to do. Now I've ruined all our lives."

"No you haven't," I tell her again. "Everything is going to be fine."

"I feel like something terrible is going to happen, Leah."

"Shhh. Everything is going to be fine."

I rub my mother's back until the tears stop and her breath evens out into sleep; then I creep back to my own bed.

The next morning, I help my mother answer Richard's latest ad. We sit at the kitchen table agonizing over every sentence, making sure it's alluring enough to press his buttons but not in a way that reveals its author. She puts down the address of a girlfriend in the city. When his response is forwarded, she writes back and coyly suggests they meet for dinner. Then she gathers up all the clothes he's left with her here in a bin bag and has a taxi deliver it to his house with a note telling him what a schmuck he is.

"Imagine the look on his face!" I say when she recounts all this to me on the phone at my father's.

Within a month, they're back together.

ONE night at Vogrie, I hear a terrible noise that seems to come from the hall, a guttural moan followed by a rhythmic *thump-thump-thump*. I think it's Nellie, the girl ghost, straying from the nursery beside the old maid's room, flinging objects about like a poltergeist in a horror film. Then I hear a small muffled shriek—my mother's—and sit up in bed. Richard is here. What's he doing to her? I imagine him torturing her with whips and chains, his terrible lips twisting into a sadistic smile.

"*Oh, fuck! Oh god!*" My mother's voice. Blood throbs hot in my ears.

I put a foot on the pine floorboard and flinch from the cold. My bed seems to rock like a boat. Then there are more sounds, a cacophony of sounds, animal but also somehow my mother's, and they are dreadful, the sounds of anguish, fear, unbearable pain. I should go to her, rescue her, but how?

"*Oh, oh!*"

I'm also not stupid. I know everything about sex, or at least I think I do. Mum's told me most of it, and I've read *Fear of Flying*, *The Women's Room*, and even *The Joy of Sex*, which has pictures. But I've never actually heard it. In my imagination there would be sighs and murmurs, gentle laughter, maybe a flute? Not all this grunting and moaning and swearing. I burrow into the mattress and pull the pillow over my head, fighting back tears. Then I remember: *she's faking.*

RICHARD had a son, a dropout named Jake who lay in bed all day on the top floor of Richard's Summerhill town house drinking beer and smoking rollies. Richard was disappointed by his son's fecklessness but justified it by adopting a fatalistic view, as if Jake's failure was inevitable and by extension, no reflection on himself. One night over dinner at Vogrie, Richard, slightly drunk, bet me that I wouldn't go to university. I laughed at the ridiculousness of what I now see he probably meant as a kind of contrarian gambit—a clumsy exercise in reverse psychology. Or maybe he intended it as a hex? I was only twelve at the time and a decent student, ambitious enough that I was happy to lay a blind bet on my future self. If he lost, Richard promised he'd buy me my first computer. If I lost, his prize would be the satisfaction of proving a loser wrong. "Bring it on," I probably said, and we shook across the table as my mother laughed and rolled her eyes.

ONE weekend Richard arrives at Vogrie with Anya, his new wife. The marriage, my mother has explained in advance, was one of convenience. Anya had been assigned as Richard's translator on a work trip and impulsively Richard had proposed—not because he loved her but because he wanted to free her from the shackles of a grim totalitarian state. Anya is predictably gorgeous, slim, with luscious red hair, tight jeans, and enormous, unfashionable glasses she manages to make cool. She and my mother become instant friends, in part because Anya makes it very clear at every opportunity that she has no interest in Richard romantically or sexually. This is thrilling to me not just because of the implicit insult to Richard but also the potential influence it might exert over my mother. After she leaves, my mother tells me in a whisper that Anya has had almost a dozen abortions because back home that was the only form of birth control.

Another weekend, Anya brings her two young sons, Ivan and Anton.

They speak not a word of English, but my sister and I are instructed to play with them and we try. Ivan impresses us by plonking out Chopin on the tuneless library piano, then spends hours poring over dusty leather-bound volumes of antique maps, yelping with delight, tracing the shapes of countries, as the world takes shape for the first time in his mind. Anton, the younger, is more difficult to like. He is my sister's age (eight) but much smaller and prone to dark sulking and feverish fits of rage.

On Saturday we all drive in to Cobourg to buy groceries. As we walk into the over-lit superstore, Anton suddenly becomes hysterical. He sinks to his knees sobbing, pounding his head, shrieking and covering his eyes. Anya falls over him, shielding his face from the store's fluorescent lights. Later my mother explains: he'd been overstimulated by the sight of so much fresh food. "So much stuff," is how she puts it. I'm not sure why I'm telling you about Anton except that I've thought about him, about his panic attack in the grocery store and the way Anya threw herself over him, for years.

S TEPMOTHERS are scapegoats not just in fairy tales but more often in real life. Too often we bear the brunt of the residual anger and guilt of the refugees of divorce. I know this firsthand because for the past decade I've been one myself. No matter how pure our intentions it's almost impossible to escape suspicion and, occasionally, outright scorn. It's assumed we are selfish, that we have an agenda, one that's at odds with those whose interests are aligned by blood. For many women, the stereotype of the evil stepmother can be a corrosive trap. But I must say, Diane made the best of it. She rose to the occasion. She took the role and made it her own.

The house my father bought with Diane was a gingerbread-trimmed Victorian on the prettiest street in Cobourg, across from a leafy park that gave way to the sprawling town beach. It had five huge bedrooms, a formal dining room, a living room, and a downstairs library and sunroom. The day we moved in, Diane convened our first ever "family meeting," which she opened by informing my sister and me that we were "absolutely forbidden under any circumstances" to set foot anywhere but the kitchen and the attic. Our bedrooms were not actual rooms but uninsulated gables on the third floor connected by a playroom that doubled as my father's study; his messy desk tucked out of view behind a Chinese screen. The three large bedrooms on the second floor, Diane explained, were to be rented out to paying guests, as she planned to start a bed-and-breakfast. But Diane quickly discovered she didn't like the hassle of strangers traipsing through her immaculate house, so instead they were repurposed. One became her unused "sewing room"; another housed the overflow of her vast preppy wardrobe of pastel polo shirts, L.L.Bean sweaters, and pleated corduroy skirts. The room that overlooked the park, which I coveted desperately for its soaring ceilings and bay window reading nook, was used to display Diane's collection of antique stuffed teddy bears. There were, quite literally, hundreds of them, many dating back to the last century, with jointed arms, matted fur, and black button eyes I imagined being stitched on by dour Victorian parlor maids. They covered the dust-ruffled queen-sized bed and bookshelves, the rocking chair, windowsills, and lined cushioned bench of the coveted reading nook. On weekends, Diane carefully rearranged her bears in various tableaus—mother bear pushing her cubs in a doll-sized antique pram, teddies playing tennis and golf or hoisting rods over their shoulders for fishing. She dusted them with a handheld vacuum. When she was finished, she took a Polaroid and noted the date on the back, a warning, she explained, for "meddling little hands."

At that first family meeting, Diane handed us each a copy of a twenty-page *Book of Rules*. It had been typed out in a twee cursive font, photocopied, then stapled together. The fifth copy was bound and laminated and would be placed on the kitchen shelf "for reference." Diane explained all this as my father sat beside her, hands fiddling with the pack of cigarettes he'd agreed to stop smoking in the house. At Diane's prompting, Dad cleared his throat and asked if my sister and I wouldn't mind taking turns reading out the rules. I scoffed, but in the end we obliged. Many of the rules were sensible, the dictums of a strict but reasonable household that were nonetheless anathema to my sister and me: Make the beds each day. Clear and wipe the table after meals. Load and unload the dishwasher. No swearing or saying *Shut up.* It wasn't so ridiculous, I see now, that Diane wanted to teach us the value of order and impose some structure on what was, after all, her own home.

But as Meg and I read on that day, it became clear that either Diane had gotten a bit carried away in the writing or we had entered a strange and draconian new world. Inexplicably, we were allotted just two showers a week, five minutes in length, no exceptions—a rule Diane enforced by placing an egg timer on the back of the toilet in our bathroom, where it crouched, ticking off the seconds like a nasty green toad. At the age of twelve, having got my period a year before, nipples swelling and throbbing, I wanted nothing more than a long, hot shower every day before bed. But on Tuesdays and Thursdays at five minutes on the dot, Diane would stroll into the steamed-up bathroom, having removed the door lock the week we moved in, and flush the toilet to scald me out.

"On school days," the *Book of Rules* reads (I still have a copy), "both girls depart for school no later than 8:45. Prior to departure, the girls will arrive downstairs in the kitchen dressed and ready for school, hair brushed, face and hands clean by 8:15 *otherwise forget eating breakfast.*" Diane meant it. The italics are her own. She was breathtakingly consistent, meting out punishments with the smug satisfaction of a bureaucrat. My sister and I quickly learned she had no qualms about sending us to school hungry if we turned up to the breakfast table with gritty fingernails. After forgetting a load of damp clothes in the dryer, I was forbidden from going on a class trip to the zoo. Diane once told me that her standards were lax compared with her own mother's. "I had to make my bed with hospital corners and I wasn't allowed to sit on it during the day" she said in a tone that fell short of self-pity and admiration. Her father was the surgeon general of the town hospital and drove around town in a vintage Rolls-Royce.

Like my mother, Diane had a lot of childhood stories involving ponies and foreign holidays and swimming pools. Unlike my mother, Diane didn't need to work but she firmly believed in making the world a better place. She taught children with severe learning disabilities at a special school. She described it not as a job but "a vocation." She once took my sister and me on a tour. It must have been after hours because the school was empty. At the back of Diane's classroom, where the boot rack and coat hooks should have been, was instead a large door that opened into a custom-built padded closet. I remember her demonstrating for us how the deadbolt worked.

While I mostly obeyed Diane's rules, I also contrived ways to convey my contempt for her authority. Loathing my stepmother, I discovered, was pleasurable in a number of ways: it deflected blame from my sister, proved my loyalty to Mum, and allowed me to cultivate a frosty adolescent hauteur whilst remaining affectionate toward my father. Dad did his best to keep the peace, attempting to placate me privately while also remaining outwardly supportive of Diane, who was, of course, invariably in the right. Her rules were so elaborate and numerous, it made rebelling easy. At least once or twice a week I'd find myself called up on some minor infraction, which I seized as an opportunity to point out the ludicrousness of Diane's pedantry. During these scenes Dad would implore me to "please stop pushing it," then stand silently, rubbing his forehead, as Diane pulled out what we now simply referred to as *The Book* and commenced her ritual of shame. First I'd be made to read out the rule in question; then Diane would deliver her calm and sonorous monologue on why it was "completely unacceptable" and "deeply disappointing" that I had, yet again, failed to refill the wood bin or rake the leaves or forgotten to clean the toilet bowl and wipe the sink on a Wednesday, which was my day to do so, as it was clearly written right here in black and white, page 7, subsection 14b. "Is it really necessary for you to be perennially reminded of the rules?" she would ask again and again. The question was rhetorical, of course. The pause between her asking it and my extravagant eye roll was followed by a sigh. These expressions of feeling, Diane would explain, were rude and contemptuous and they would not be tolerated. These were the foothills on which I'd die a thousand stubborn deaths.

Diane, for her part, never once put a foot wrong. I don't remember her ever raising her voice or displaying a whiff of emotion. She'd just stand there, hands thrust deep into the pockets of her skirt, looking tired and disappointed. The consequences meted out—Diane disliked the word *punishment*—were never violent or rash but administered grudgingly with regret. They involved the temporary withdrawal of routine "privileges" or pleasures: the unplugging of the playroom TV or the cancellation of birthday parties and sleepovers. What she desired wasn't my suffering but something more valuable, which she would never have: my submission.

To make sense of my situation in those years, I devised a system of binaries: Mum was creative and original, while Diane was dull and pedestrian; Mum was free-flowing, uncontainable, a curious child of the universe, while Diane was rigid, earthbound, drearily conventional. The year I turned twelve, I gave my father and Diane a pine corner shelf I'd made in woodworking class. It turned out beautifully, to my surprise. I stained and varnished it and presented it to them at Christmas.

For my mother, I wrote a prose poem. I read it out for the guests at her small candlelit birthday supper at the table in the kitchen at Vogrie. Everyone cried, even Richard.

All I remember now is the title: "For Them I Made a Corner Shelf. For You I Wrote a Poem."

9

After breakfast that first day in New York, my mother and I walk the High Line then weave through Chelsea Market, poking into shops and galleries. I hold up a T-shirt that says, I SPENT MY THIN YEARS THINKING I WAS FAT. Mum says she spent her youth thinking she was old. She laughs, then we both do.

We go out for a fancy brunch at a private members' club where we sit in tufted leather chairs and order eighteen-dollar Bloody Marys chilled with fat balls of ice and garnished with six different kinds of pickled vegetables on toothpicks. The buffet is a royal wedding feast: platters of prawns the size of baby fists; avocados stuffed with crab; oysters on the half shell; a quail inside a chicken inside a duck inside a turkey, carved by a man in a puffy white hat. There are eight different kinds of salad. I would move to New York, I tell my mother once we have sat down, just for the salad.

After we eat, I show Mum a video Rob has just sent me of the boys getting ready for school. "Hullo, poo-poo head Mummy!" Solomon says, then they take turns poking out their tongues at the screen. "Don't forget to buy us presents!"

I talk to my mother about how much easier Frankie seems than his older brothers did as toddlers, then find myself wondering aloud if this is in fact a self-involved misperception? Perhaps as "experienced" parents we're like zoo animals—hostages who've grown so accustomed to the routines and rhythms of captivity we no longer remember the pleasures of the wild. Mum laughs and agrees that yes, it's probably the latter.

Irrespective of the reason, I say, things are getting better—easier somehow. Rob has started getting up with the boys in the mornings and making breakfast. It's amazing how this minor adjustment in our division of labor, him doing one meal a day, waking me gently with coffee in bed, has made a tangible difference in our marriage. He's more engaged. I'm less resentful. Ultimately, I think we might make a good team, I say to my mother, who raises an eyebrow. The Bloody Mary is humming in my veins making me loquacious. Reckless and giddy with sentiment. It's been difficult since Frankie's birth. My mother knows this. His entrance was early and violent. The last bit involved a vacuum and scalpel, forceps and a wailing alarm that summoned a crowd of trainee doctors who piled into the birth room like a somber Broadway chorus line. They blocked the view of the limp bluish creature on the table to whom an obstetrician was affixing a doll-sized mask attached to a tiny plastic air pump. Rob sat to my left, gripping my trembling hand. For most of an hour we sat there watching the residents watch the consultant doing things we could not see to our son. I will never forget how calm and studious they were, like a flock of intelligent and curious birds. Necks craning, shoulders shifting under smooth white coats as they jotted down notes and looked on with interest, guessing at the outcome.

Three years and two surgeries later Frank and I have both recovered. I am working again and Frankie, well. He's a bespectacled leftie with barely there dimples and a smile that swallows his head. As a baby he slept like a lamb. Later he gave up the breast, then his bottle, his nappies, followed by his crib and stroller with an insouciant shrug. He roared into nursery, then big school without so much as a wave or a kiss. His first word was *More!* Spoken in reference to garlic mashed potatoes, it sums up his approach to life. His absurdly boundless enthusiasm delights his brothers and father, but to me, the person who was both the driver and vehicle in the car wreck of his birth, Frank seems a genuine boy wonder. I decide to tell my mother a secret—a private cherished conviction I haven't shared with anyone, not even Rob, out of superstition. I don't want to jinx it.

Frank seems proof of something I'd not thought possible: that joy can be born of trauma. That sometimes, without apparent effort, suffering and horror can be sloughed off the human psyche like water shaken from a dog. I have no idea why or how it happened, just that this is how it is with Frank. As I confide in my mother my eyes prickle and a tightness gathers in my throat. It's the jet lag, I say, wiping my nose on my sleeve. I shake my head, laughing, overwhelmed by sudden joy.

Across the table my mother regards me coolly.

After a pause she says, "You know Basil's an early bird. Five a.m., every morning, like clockwork."

I nod slowly, uncertain where she's going with this.

"He cooks every meal and brings me coffee in bed. Every. Single. Morning."

"That's lovely," I say.

My mother has told me this before of course; the question is, why is she repeating it now? I do a quick mental rifle through our conversation before realizing she's still stuck at the part where I told her about Rob making breakfast.

"He's so nurturing," she continues. "He takes such good care of me. It's wonderful. I remind myself every day not to exploit it. His goodness, I mean."

"I'm so happy for you, Mum. I'm so glad you have each other."

There's a pause, then she says, "You know, my therapist thinks it was hard for you when we got married. Harder than you like to admit. She thinks . . ." My mother drifts into silence then mutters that it doesn't matter.

"Go on," I say.

"I just wish you and Basil were closer. I love you both so much."

I nod again slowly, saying nothing. Mum closes her eyes and twitches her head to one side, wincing slightly as if responding to a sound only she can hear. I get up from the table and walk over to the buffet, where I scoop up shredded kale with a heavy silver serving spoon and deposit it onto my plate. I lift a cut crystal jug, tilting it toward the glass with great care, so the water dribbles out slowly like a leaking tap. When I return to the table, Mum is on her phone scrolling through Instagram. She taps Like on a photo of my aunt Kate's yellow Labrador plunging into a murky farmer's pond. Mum and Basil's dog, a guileless, deaf shih tzu named Banjo, had to be put down a few weeks earlier. Since marrying Basil, she's become a born-again pet lover. After Banjo's death Mum posted a photo of him staring wistfully out the window at a snowbank, with a caption by George Eliot: "Only in the agony of parting do we look into the depths of love."

After a minute or so her gaze lifts from the stream of images on her phone and drifts across the table to rest on me. "So is it all going in your book, then? Is that what it's going to be: *Mommie Dearest?*"

I tell my mother she can read the book first. I tell her I want her to be okay with it. Speaking quickly, too quickly, I say that this is very important to me. She is quiet, still as a statue, patiently hearing me out.

"What I want . . . ," I begin to say, casting around for the words I'd had in my mind on the plane. "My intention . . ."

"Is what exactly?"

I reach for my mother's hand, but she flinches and pulls it away.

"I want the book to be an act of devotion."

I make this declaration because it's what I'd planned to say and also because it is true. But the words, once uttered, make contact with the air between us and are spoilt, detached from my intention. Corrupt. This is the most dazzling of my mother's powers: her ability to scramble meaning with a word and a glance. Simple statements are muddled up into menacing riddles, truths become self-serving lies. Oil sours to vinegar, water to wine. In such moments I understand it doesn't matter what I say, what I write or do. What matters, perhaps the only thing that has ever mattered, is this. The way she can look at me and decide.

My mother gathers herself, folds and refolds her napkin before setting it crisply back on the softness of her lap. Then she leans across the table and hisses: "Do you really think you're so much better than me? *Do you?* Because you're not. You may not know it now, but you're a mother. Just wait. *You'll see.*"

"See what?"

"That mothers are to blame for everything. That children are bottomless pits. That the resentment is relentless. You can never win."

I know I should end the conversation here. Change the subject. Feign the need to pee. That's what my sister would do. But my sister wouldn't find herself here in the first place. Meg is a sensible senior bureaucrat with a government pension plan and a stable marriage who FaceTimes our mother every Sunday night just before supper and speaks to her for ten minutes before putting her kids on to make funny faces into the phone before they accidentally hang up. My sister would never be drawn into a conversation like this, let alone write a book about herself or our mother. She finds my work incomprehensible, a kind of madness, and maybe she's right.

"To answer your question, no I don't think I'm a better mother but I do think I'm different."

"Oh, really. How so?"

"Well, for one thing, I plan to live with my children. At least until they go to university."

This is a mistake. I've gone too far. The reality of my mother's departure, her flight and absence, is not in dispute. Especially not where my sister is concerned. While I eventually followed my mother to the city, my sister stayed in Cobourg and did not live with her again after the age of eight. It's the truth, but it's an unmentionable truth, or at least unmentionable by me in this particular manner and context. Technically my mother and I are allowed to talk about anything, no subject is off the table—the Horseman, her leaving, the affair with Richard—but only if we adhere to a strict set of unwritten rules. The first is that my mother must be the one to bring it up. The second is that when she does bring it up, ruefully, it is my job to console her, to say it's okay, that she tried her best, played the hand she was dealt. "Don't beat yourself up," I'm meant to say, "the past is the past and look, Meg and I both turned out all right, didn't we?" That's the script. Those are my lines. But now we are off script, further off than we've ever been. We are skating the vertiginous edge of an unmarked mountain pass in a conversational whiteout. My mother takes a slow, deliberate breath and straightens her back. She has something else to tell me. Something important.

"Leah, I don't want to hurt your feelings," she begins. "I was never going to mention this. I swore to myself I wouldn't, but at this point I think you should know something. It wasn't my choice not to live with your sister."

My mother says this almost casually, making it clear that she is imparting what is for her an obvious truth that I have unfortunately, through no fault of my own, been unable to grasp because I have lacked a full picture of the facts.

"I asked Meg to move in with us repeatedly when she was in high school, but she always said no," my mother explains.

I think of my sister. Her little blond head. My sister with her tantrums and her whooping cough, her middle-of-the-night earaches.

"Oh come on, Mum. Don't put this on her. She was just a kid."

Mum shakes her head like I'm still not getting it. She leans forward and positions her face nearer mine, chin tilted up in defiance, pale thin brows raised above the dark frames of her glasses.

"I wasn't going to tell you this," she repeats. "But since you brought it up, the real reason Meg didn't live with us was because of you. Because of what you did to her."

I am unable to speak or breathe.

"Yes, you. *You* were the reason. You bullied her and did . . . other things. Terrible things."

My mother sits back in her leather chair and lets this sink in. I close my eyes and dip my head to one side, shaking it gently as if I am trying to drain the confusion, like sea water from my ear. I have no idea what she's talking about. *What terrible things?* I want to ask, but I can't. I cannot.

"You have a lot to answer for, Leah, you know that?"

I press my face into my napkin, which feels slippery and synthetic, cool against my cheek. I allow myself only one thought. Just one. *I will not cry.*

From the age of twelve, I saw my sister only occasionally. Holidays, the odd weekend back in Cobourg—our visits became more infrequent as the years progressed. We are close now, for a long time that's what I told people. There was a period in our twenties and thirties when I'm

sure that's what we were, though we never lived in the same city, anything less than a full day's drive apart. Now there are oceans and time
zones between us, jobs and babies and partners, all of this on top of the
past. We call each other once or twice a year. Birthdays and Christmas
mostly. Missed calls that turn into a petering trail of cheerful texts.
What I believe is that we are as close as can be expected given the distance, the absence, the passage of time. We wish each other nothing
but love. This is what I tell myself. But maybe my mother is right and
my sister feels differently? Maybe she has always secretly felt this way,
harbored a silent grudge because I hurt her, traumatized her in some
way I cannot remember when I was only a child myself?

No, *no*, I tell myself. *It's not true. It can't be true.* Or can it?

There is no point in unpicking it. What matters is there is a debt to
be paid. One from me to my little sister. For things to be right, it must
be paid. It does not matter why or how. I cannot blame everything on
my mother. I lift my face from the silky coolness of my napkin and
draw a slow breath. I look at my mother evenly.

"I'm so sorry, Mum," I say. "I'm sorry you had to go through that
because of me."

She flicks her hand away from the earring she's been twisting. "It's
between you and your sister," she snaps. Then, in a deliberate and mol-
lified tone she adds, "Look Pumpkin, I don't actually know what happened. I wasn't even there."

For the rest of the weekend in New York, my mother's brunch dis-
closure sat in my pocket where I worried it like the stolen strawberry
obsidian. I spent hours parsing my memory trying to work out what
it was I might have done to traumatize my sister as a child. If what
Mum said was true, I was to blame for all of it: a mother's loss of her
daughter, a daughter's loss of a mother, a sisterhood betrayed, a family
wrested apart. Hadn't I been a good girl? That's what my mother always
said. Perhaps I was secretly bad and pretending to be good? Or maybe
she knew I was bad and told me I was good in the hope of making me
better? Or had I actually deluded my mother, and everyone—including

myself—into thinking I was good? I mean, I *believed* I was good, but malignant narcissists, sociopaths, and cult leaders are filled with self-regard.

I ruminated for so long eventually I was forced to admit I'd become caught in a kind of thought trap, a fallacy of my own making: If I denied being a witch then clearly I was a witch. If I confessed it would amount to the same thing. This is how false accusations often elicit false confessions.

There was one thing though. It was called the fairy godmother game. I started playing it when Meg was five or six and I was seven or eight, when we were still living in the house on Hamilton Avenue. It continued after our mother left home, and went on intermittently in various houses until we were both too old to play pretend.

At first the fairy godmother only appeared at Dad's house, because that's where the costume trunk lived. But the game was revived at Vogrie in the maid's room, which we believed was haunted by the ghost of Nellie. It was a storage room filled with old boxes, a mothballed assortment of vintage finery. The fairy godmother's costume was less important than the transformation. I'd don layers of dresses and robes, old wigs, lace shawls, the scarves we used for séances, a pair of moldy high heels, or a molting raccoon coat, then on top of it drape myself in all the beads and baubles I could find. The one constant was an umbrella, usually broken. The umbrella was important because that was how the game began. I'd open it—*floof!*—and enter the room where my sister happened to be. She'd stir, twist round on the sofa at the sound of the gust. Opening an umbrella indoors was bad luck. After chewing gum, it was the only thing our mother consistently forbade. It wasn't the transgression that thrilled me so much as what it suggested. Opening the umbrella was like the moment in the ghost story when the door slams shut. A signal the normal rules no longer applied.

Floof!

"Leah?" Meg said uneasily the first time it happened. She was still young enough to be scared of people in costumes, even ones she recognized. "You look weird. Why are you wearing that?"

I improvised the voice on the spot, a velvety singsong mimic of Miss Nancy on *Romper Room* and Glinda the Good Witch from *The Wizard of Oz*. "Oh, my dear sweet girl, *hahaha*." A high, tinkly laugh, my grandmother's giggle. "Well, that's just where you're mistaken. I'm not Leah at all. I do look a bit like her, but in fact I'm your *fairy godmother*."

"Yeah, right," Meg said, turning back to the TV. She resisted at first but I always reeled her in.

I remember playing it at Vogric one time. We were in the library, a perennially cold and gloomy room, even in the height of summer. The library was where the TV lived—a black-and-white job with rabbit ears on which we watched VHS movies. We only had two, *The Fox and the Hound* and Monty Python's *The Meaning of Life*, which we watched until the tapes rubbed out.

"Bug off," Meg said when I swept into the room dolled up in sloppy drag.

"Don't say 'bug,' dear," the FG admonished in the manner of a grown-up. "It's not a swear, but it's still a rude word. I won't tell on you, but you mustn't say it. I imagine you heard it from your sister. It's something Leah would say, isn't it?"

Meg nodded, eyes narrowed, fixed on the screen. I moved round and into her eyeline, then twisted down the volume so she couldn't ignore me.

"Leah is gone now, you see. I've taken over her body—for now. Don't worry, my dear. Your sister will be back in good time. She's fine. You needn't be afraid. You have nothing to fear from me. I'm your *fairy godmother*."

"What—Leah, don't—"

Meg's features drew tight around her turned-up nose. Her hands balled up into tiny fists. High up the chimney there was a scratch and fluttering of wings. We watched a flurry of ash drift down and settle slowly in the hearth. Meg began to keen. She was tipping into terror. Our mother and Richard were out on a long walk. I pulled back, trying to save the game.

"It's all right, it's all right, my dear, sweet girl. Don't cry! You're safe! I'm here to take care of you. Your sister isn't very nice, is she? I watch over you both and I see what she does. How unfair she is. It's terrible. You poor, sweet thing."

Meg's lower lip pushed forward, protruding like the bottom half of a plum. She nodded. "It's true, she's not nice. Well, sometimes—but mostly she's a meanie."

"I know," the FG said. "I watch over you both."

"You do?"

"Well, yes. For instance, yesterday she didn't let you have the last cookie."

Meg nodded vigorously, and as she did, her face began to relax.

"That was terribly unfair of her," said the FG. "And the day before that she didn't let you play pretend with her and Tracey. That was mean."

"I got so mad!"

"I know you did. And she teased you for crying. That was unfair. I was watching. You see?"

Meg's mouth twisted. She didn't smile, but an understanding passed between us.

"I *told* you I was watching, dear girl. But it's all right, because I'm here now, and now we can play. We can play anything you want. Anything. Your wish is my command. I'm nothing like your mean sister."

Meg's eyes widened, brightened, then narrowed again. "But wait— how do I know you're real? How do I know you're not just her trying to trick me?"

I pretended to think and then I did think. I closed my umbrella and tapped it lightly against the floor, three times, a flourish to buy time. When the answer came to me, it was perfect.

"Why don't you ask me for three wishes? Just small ones: I'm not Santa Claus, you know, but I assure you I *am* magic. Now, make me three wishes and I'll grant them in the coming days, when you least expect it. That's how you'll know I'm real."

My sister's wishes were easy. She wanted a Cadbury Creme Egg, a pack of cinnamon Trident, and a Strawberry Shortcake figurine like the one she regretted having traded to a friend at recess. Within the week, she had all three. I laid them in places I knew she was sure to find them: under her pillow, at the top of her sock drawer, stuffed into her snow boot. When she discovered them, I made sure to be there. I liked to see her gasp.

T HE longer the game went on the more distorted the fantasy became.

On one occasion, about a year into the game, the fairy godmother appeared and apologized for being the bearer of bad news. "Don't be upset," she said solemnly, "but I've killed your sister."

Meg's hand flew to her mouth. The FG put a kid-gloved hand on her small shoulder.

"Don't worry, my dear, Leah was very bad. She had to die. But it's only temporary, she'll come back to life. I can bring her back if you want. I told you, I have powers. I'm just inhabiting her body so we can play." I've dispensed with the mask. I no longer need it. She believes.

"No, no," Meg said, her chin twisting with worry. "That's murder. You'll go to jail!"

The FG laughed her beneficent laugh. "Oh, no, no, they can't put me in jail; I'm magic. And besides, I live in Leah's body now. Who would know the difference?"

Meg thought this over.

"She's not very nice to you, is she, dear?"

"Not really," Meg allowed. "I mean, sometimes? But there was this one time she bit me."

The FG was shocked. She shook her fist at the ceiling.

"That's awful, my dear girl. *Positively dreadful*. Perhaps I should kill her permanently . . . so we can be together forever? No one would know."

"No, please," Meg said carefully. I could see the cogs turning over inside her little blond skull. "It's not me; it's Mummy. She'd be sad. She'd miss her."

"Oh, really. Why?"

Meg frowned. "Leah's her favorite."

The FG looked aghast. "Why on earth would that be?"

"I don't know. She just is."

The FG pondered this for a moment. "Well, if your mummy loves your sister so much, why does she only see her on weekends now?"

"I don't know," Meg said. She shrugged then dipped her head. Pressed a quivering chin to her chest. "I don't really know anything. I'm still just little."

The FG's heart clenched. She fell to her knees and scooped the skinny tow-headed girl into her arms. Holding the child on her lap, she rocked her back and forth like a doll, the two of them cradled in the sunken middle of the yellow-flowered sofa.

"Don't worry, don't worry, it's all right," the fairy consoled the child. "You have me now. I'm here. Leah's gone, but I'm here." The FG rocked the little girl as she began to cry. As they both began to cry, softly, together.

When they were both tired of crying they sniffled and wiped their noses on their sleeves and smiled at each other, silently acknowledging their own silliness. They looked at each other fondly then, laughing in sheepish recognition.

Then the FG offered the little girl one more wish.

"I wish you were my sister," the child said.

The fairy grinned.

10

IN my last year of junior high I decide, with my mother's blessing, to
audition for the drama program of a selective arts high school in Toronto. The monologue I will perform is from George Bernard Shaw's
Joan of Arc, the ultimate adolescent girl's cri de coeur, chosen not by me
but by my drama coach, Mary Doig, a wisp of a woman, English, with
large, glittering eyes, who directs the local repertory theater. Twice a
week for the month leading up to the audition Mary Doig comes to the
big house on Church Street that Dad and Diane have bought and helps
me to practice the monologue. She sits in a wooden chair dragged from
the kitchen and stoops under the pitched attic roof, offering subtle but
pointed adjustments to my delivery. She teaches me how to move with
intention while not over-indicating, a skill I never quite master. How
to slow my breath and lift up my arm, palm up, fingers splayed, just
so. She explains the power of a well-hung silence. She instructs me
to close my eyes and draw my focus in slowly, absorbing the darkness
inside and sitting with it for a moment before speaking. "Still yourself," she says. "Gather in before casting out." She teaches me to open
my eyes slowly, as slowly as I can, lifting my lids slowly like heavy
blinds and letting the world materialize at my leisure as if it were my
creation and not the other way around. After that, a gradual release
of breath and then: *Scene.* It is all terribly precious, but at thirteen, in
Cobourg, I am entranced. Bits of the monologue are still seared into

my brain, especially the bit where Joan foretells her own demise, even welcomes it, in light of the injustice of her incarceration: *Bread has no sorrow for me, and water no affliction … all this is worse than the furnace in the bible that was heated seven times.*

Such a dignified little bitch. Never before had it occurred to me that rage and defiance could be virtuous in a small girl. Chin up, head shorn, barefoot in torn boy's underwear, that's how I wanted to perform the monologue. Mary suggested a simple sheath dress instead, my hair tied back.

Like Joan, I was bent on escape, even if it meant self-immolation. I was, I thought, past caring. By this point I loathed Diane with a passion verging on religious fervor. My diaries at the time are full of it—pages and pages of contempt, lustily fueled by weekends with my mother and Richard during which Diane and her fanatical petit bourgeois cleanliness were a constant source of mockery. The strict routine of my day-to-day life on Church Street stood in stark contrast to the unpredictable but largely happy chaos of my visits with Mum at Vogrie. It was during this time that my mother finally moved away from Cobourg to the city, first to Peterborough, where she was a managing editor at the *Peterborough Examiner*, and later to a job at a trade publication in Toronto. Mark took over as official caretaker and Mum used the house as a weekend escape.

If the twelve-year-old me was hurt by her abandoning my sister and me to the clutches of an evil stepmother, my juvenile diaries do not betray even a whiff of it. My mother's flight only heightened my appreciation for our increasingly infrequent time together. It did not occur to me until much later that for all the joylessness of Dad and Diane's house, what it offered was something my mother was not prepared to provide: stability. Structure. Routine. These were things she taught me to treat with derision. Meg, we agreed, was too young to understand. Unlike me, she struggled with her lessons, and every weekday evening in the years on Church Street, Diane spent an hour helping Meg with her homework. I remember fretting to Mum once that Meg was being brainwashed by these nightly sessions. She just laughed.

By the time I was in junior high, things at Church Street were deteriorating fast. There was nowhere to go, but I knew I couldn't stay. One night, after some infraction or other, I finally came out with it and called Diane a bitch to her face. The moment was exhilarating, one of the high points of my childhood. I was standing on the central staircase in the front hall. My father and Diane were on the first floor. My father's face sank into his hands. I waited just long enough to watch Diane's brow lift in disbelief before wheeling around like a coward and dashing upstairs to the attic, where I threw myself facedown and sobbing on my bed. My father followed as he always eventually did, patting my back and shaking his head, saying little except that he loved me and everything would be okay.

A few weeks later, we all went to see a family therapist in his office at the Cobourg General Hospital. The psychologist was a young man, tall and rangy in blue jeans with a mass of dark curls. He was an old friend of Diane's, probably some hospital connection through her father. I remember she called him by his first name, Elias. When the *Book of Rules* came up, Elias's attention was instantly piqued. He pleasantly requested that we bring it in for the next session. Diane agreed; she could barely conceal her pleasure. Finally, a chance to show off the thoughtful, well-bounded system that no one—least of all me—could simply adhere to. I dreaded the next session like death, but when we got there, something amazing happened. Elias sat for several minutes scanning all twenty pages of the *Book of Rules* as we all sat fidgeting in our seats. Then he lifted his face and said, "When you get home tonight, I'd like to ask you all to burn this."

We did. My father lit the fire and made a ceremony of it. One by one, we handed our copies to my father to be pitched into the kitchen woodstove. Even Diane obeyed the doctor's orders. I watched her with adolescent relish, already constructing the anecdote for my mother. Diane's wool slippers were crossed at the ankles under her immaculate corduroy slacks. Her English sheepdog, Bear, huddled at her side like a shadow, sensitive to his mistress's silent displeasure. My father handled the moment with methodical practicality, ripping pages off their staples one by one and crumpling them up in his farm-boy hands. When it came time to hand mine over, I shrugged and said it was lost, a lie that was so much in character, not even Diane bothered to question it. Dad took a match from the box and lit it off the tip of the woodstove. Then a strange silence, as if the air had been sucked from the room, before the rules went up with a dramatic *whoosh*. The burst of light followed by the crackle of twigs giving way. I kept my gaze fixed on the blaze, somber, careful to resist the urge to smile.

Dad broke the first rule by lighting a cigarette off the end of the still-burning match. He took one or two luxurious puffs before slipping on his boots to smoke the rest alone in the snow.

Later that night, I checked to make sure my copy of the *Book of Rules* was still there, at the bottom of my maternal great-grandmother's carved pine jewelry box where I kept my diary, safely protected by a tiny padlock to which only I had a key.

One Saturday morning a week or two later, I found my father sitting in his study. He waved me over to his desk, where he was finishing up a phone call. Putting the phone down, he looked at me and grinned like a schoolboy.

"I think you'll be pleased to know I've just had an offer accepted on a new house. Just for the three of us."

For my last year of junior high it's me, Meg, and Dad at 321 College Street, the little postwar house on a big lot he bought just for us. In the summer we go on a two-week boat trip. I've been promoted to first mate and Meg has moved up from "bosun" to second mate. We cruise around the Thousand Islands, exploring the beginnings of the St. Lawrence River just past the Olympic Harbour in Kingston. Dad gets up at dawn each morning, casts off, and motors for a couple of nautical miles before we even stumble out of the V-berth looking for Froot Loops. I'm in charge of rigging. I pull the headsail out from underneath the foredeck, clip it to the halyards, then stand on the bow hauling it up the mast. The rest of the time I sit in the cockpit watching the sails for luff and winching them in as directed. Dad steers with a can of beer in one hand, cigarette clamped in the other, faded ball cap pulled down tight over his polarized aviators.

That summer my father teaches me to sail. He explains that a first mate's job isn't just to take orders but to watch and anticipate what the skipper might be thinking and, when asked, to offer an informed deputy's counsel.

"Wind's come up from behind us now," Dad says, securing the boom with a hoist of his bicep as I release the port jib sheet, freeing the headsail to flap and writhe as we consider our options. Ropes ping against the mast and halyards, and above that are the shrieks of the gulls. It's cool and cloudy, and the lake is fresh and green as pickle brine. On still, humid days the water is blue but smells like a tuna sandwich pissed on and left in the sun. Dad says it's all the industrial spill-off that flows up from Rochester, New York, poisoning the tiny carp that decorate the swells like silver sequins and wash up in drifts on the beach. It's 1988 and the fresh water isn't as fresh as it sounds. Dad says the sea is clearer—he's sailed all over the Caribbean and made it through the Bermuda Triangle without a motor or a radio—as he flicks his butt off the stern. I watch as the speckled filter of his Craven "A" is tossed up and swallowed in the froth.

"Jibe starboard on a port tack, then try a broad reach?" I say.

Dad squints and pulls down the brim of his ball cap. "That, or we could try a dead run."

"The spinnaker?"

"Not ruling it out."

"You think?"

My eyes flick up to the wind indicator, a black arrow quavering on top of the mast. We've never run a spinnaker before, not with just the three of us. Spinnakers are unpredictable, risky, a great billowing distraction and the cause of most onboard sailing accidents. A pain in the ass to get up and down, they're expensive and easy to rip. They're primarily used for racing, though if you do manage to get one up in soft wind, the effect is like flying in a dream: a smooth, silent glide. Spinnakers capture the wind like a parachute, but where parachutes work against gravity, spinnakers work with it, harnessing so much power, they can send a multi-ton vessel skimming across the waves like a bath toy.

"Air's too light," I say. "Probably won't be enough pressure."

Dad lights another smoke, cupping his hand over his sun-leathered face and sucking till the paper crackles. After the first drag he holds the ember upright like a candle. Watching the smoke swirl off, he takes the measure of the breeze.

"As I say, nothing in life worth doing is easy." Then he flicks a cracked thumbnail toward the hatch, our cue to get down below and start hauling bags up from the V-berth. Once the cabin is awash in turquoise nylon and the tip of the kite is clipped on, I take the helm while Dad and Meg work on the foredeck, trimming the leads and getting the spinnaker ready to set.

"Okay, honey," he shouts, "position yourself wide and watch the luff. Fall off a bit, that's right, lower, lower yet . . . Okay, now, Meg, on the count of three, *HOIST!*"

As Dad pulls in the sheets, working arm over arm, Meg feeds him the sail, untwisting the nylon as she goes. I watch the luff and curl, feeling for the crosswind, as Meg scrambles back to the cockpit, a jumble of bare feet and skinny limbs, last summer's hand-me-down blue Speedo hanging loose off her hips, the elastic faded and shot.

The chute is flapping, twisting, puffing up and suddenly deflating. "Come up! Come up!" Dad cries over the cacophony, his figure obscured by the writhing nylon curtain. "FOR CHRISSAKE, LEAH, I SAID COME UP!"

I flinch at the sound of Dad's skipper voice. I turn to find Meg, but she's slipped down below. Bracing myself, I use the entire weight of my body to turn the boat into the port crosswind. At first there is just grinding resistance, but something shifts. The boat seems to judder, buckling in on itself like a rope sagging before it's snapped tight. With a single dramatic gust, the chute billows out, taut and curved full, a giant pregnant wind belly. The world goes silent as we skim like a paper cup across the murky green-gray waves. Meg clambers into the cockpit eating a half-melted Creamsicle and squints in surprise at the sight of me at the helm. From the foredeck, Dad hoots and punches the air. "*Now we're cooking!*" he shouts. "*Remember this feeling, girls—it's the closest you'll ever get to flying!*"

11

<small>～○～</small>

AN artist moves into Vogrie. Her name is Viv and she's in her late twenties. She's not much taller than me but stronger, with a frosted layer cut, clattery earrings, and two dogs—a Staffordshire terrier named Caesar with a massive slobbery grin and Cleo, a collie mix who looks just like the dog from *Annie*. Like their mistress, Caesar and Cleo are noisy, sociable, and prone to sudden bursts of excitement. In addition to dogs and art supplies, Viv arrives with a decent stereo and for the first time Vogrie is filled with music. She transforms the William Ronald Room into her studio, which we all agree is appropriate for a painter—though Viv doesn't call herself that. "I'm just an illustrator," she laughs, adding that she chose the Ronald Room not for the murals but because it faces north.

Everyone loves Viv except Mark. They bicker like students in a dormitory, sniping about dishes and groceries and mixed-up bits of laundry. One day, after some minor slight, Viv leaves Mark a note threatening to pee in his bed. Everyone thinks this is hilarious except Mark. A few weeks later he packs up and moves to Brazil. Because my mother now has a job in the city, Viv is now Vogrie's official caretaker.

I become fascinated by Viv's work, which doesn't look like work at all but a kind of hyper-focused form of adult play. Every day for several hours a day, including weekends, she sits at a spinning stool before a wooden easel propped up on a desk, absorbed in her illustrations.

The pictures she paints are almost always of animals: talking giraffes and smartly dressed pigs, cunning cats and jellyfish that smile. The window she faces overlooks what we call the "garage" but is in fact a half-collapsed milking shed. Mum says it's the least remarkable view in the house, but the light, Viv explains, is abundant and diffuse, which makes it easier for her to judge the quality of her work. I chat to her so much during the day that eventually I take to lounging on the daybed in her studio reading impressive novels like *Madame Bovary* and *Doctor Zhivago*, which she never asks about. Sometimes I pretend I'm an old-fashioned lady and Viv is painting my portrait, but in truth I am the one observing her. I like the careful way she unscrews the tiny tubes of paint, squeezes a dot of color on a wooden board, then dips in her brush and blends it to just the shade she wants. The water jars on the windowsill go from clear to foggy as she works. When the water turns the color of thunderclouds, I carry them across the hall to the big farm kitchen and stand at the sink letting the oily liquid spill through my fingers, imagining I am an artist's assistant.

Viv doesn't read novels or listen to Classical FM. She's a metal head, the first one I've met who doesn't have a mullet. AC/DC, Journey, Guns N' Roses, and Mötley Crüe are her favorites. It's from Viv that I learn that U2 is lame and the Beastie Boys are white and Ozzy Osbourne did, in fact, bite the head off a bat and is also a nice suburban dad. She also teaches me that the spots over a dog's eyes are a trick to make them look awake and that watercolor is a forgiving medium and asparagus makes your pee stink, while beets make it pink. Into every children's book she illustrates, she sneaks in at least one drawing of Caesar. In one, his face appears instead of the queen's on a postage stamp; in another you can just see his pointy white tail peeking out from underneath a closet door. I ask Viv if these fragments of Caesar are her "personal motif," a term I have recently picked up from Mum. Viv just laughs and says I'm reading too much into it.

Now that we're back to seeing Mum every second weekend, I am desperate to live at Vogrie full-time and convince my sister to take up the cause. When we nervously suggest moving in, Mum is delighted. "Of course!" she says. "I'd love that. But won't your father mind?"

He does. "How will you get to school?" he asks when I tell him the plan. "Who's going to take care of you when your mother works nights?"

"The bus. And Viv will be there," I say, having already thought it through. It tips the balance. After a few days of lobbying, Dad agrees to the plan.

We set a date to move. I mark a triumphant X on the kitchen calendar. A week away from the date I walk across the park to the liquor store, collect as many free boxes as I can carry, and begin to pack up my attic room. Dad doesn't offer to help and Meg seems oblivious. Two days before the move, something comes up on Mum's end, so I unpack and mark another X. This happens three times. Mum's excuses are plausibly vague. She's got people coming to stay or things are crazy at work. Next weekend would be better. The final time she leaves it to my father.

It's a Thursday night and we are having dinner in the sunroom. I'm fizzing with anticipation, because tomorrow is Friday and Mum will pick us up in the U-Haul van I reminded her to rent on the phone. Dad sits at the dinner table ignoring his pork chops and applesauce. He wipes the milk from the bottom of his mustache with the back of his hand.

"Listen, girls, about the move: I had a call from your mother today," Dad begins, then relays whatever bland complication has resulted in Mum letting us down for what we all know will be the final time. Eventually he trails off shaking his head.

"But she said!" Meg protests.

"She *solemnly promised*," I add unnecessarily.

Meg excuses herself from the table to watch TV. It's my night to do the dishes and I approach the task with silent, mechanical fury. When I am done I pester my father with questions. I am convinced that he has somehow misconstrued my mother's words, failed to understand her intentions, which I am sure can only be pure.

Dad is patient at first, carefully concealing the rage that's building inside him. I prod him long enough that eventually he erupts, throws up his hands in frustration and rises from the table.

"Leah, it's your mother we're talking about here," he says, as if that isn't obvious.

Your mother. That's what he calls her. Mum, by contrast, calls Dad "my ex," which I like better because it seems mature, like I'm her girl-friend and we're gossiping about a guy she used to date. Thinking of what Mum might do in this situation, I roll my eyes and snort. Dad shakes his head at my preteen insolence and pulls a cigarette and lighter from the pack in his pocket. He starts toward the back door, then changes his mind, swivels to face me, and leans in close, putting a big hand on my shoulder.

"Look, honey," he murmurs under his breath so Meg won't hear. "The truth is if I understood half the things that woman's said or done, I'd probably still be married to her."

AFTER the canceled move, Dad offers to drive us out to Vogrie every other Friday night himself. Mum interprets this as a chivalrous ges-ture, but really it's because it irritates him that Mum is always late to pick us up. On our arrival, if Viv's battered Jeep is in the drive, which it usually is, Dad doesn't bother to get out of the car. He musses our hair and waves goodbye, then reverses back down the wooded drive. On this particular Friday it's a cool day in April, but the windows and doors are thrown open. "Hells Bells" by AC/DC is on full blast. Caesar, Cleo, and Tweezle—the new potbellied pig Viv has acquired to our delight and our mother's horror—bound toward us yapping from the side of the house and jump up on us with muddy feet.

The sour odor of pig feces assaults us from the mudroom. Meg and I moan and plug our noses. The floor of the big central hall is littered with puddles of piss and droppings. I kick one with my toe and it skit-ters across the floor like a pebble, so old it's nearly petrified.

Viv is not in her studio. Eventually we find her in the formal dining room. She's sitting at the head of the big polished mahogany table under the glowering, barrel-chested portrait of Bishop Strachan. A guitar solo is roaring out of the boom box on the sideboard, tucked between the punch bowl and the soup tureen. The room is fogged with smoke, which is odd, because Viv doesn't smoke, or didn't until now.

She's wearing the big raccoon coat and a green satin turban from the box room, the one held together by a mother-of-pearl brooch. Underneath that is a black lace dress I don't recognize.

"What's with the costume?" Meg asks.

"*Shut up*," I hiss, having instantly decided Viv looks fabulous.

She hasn't noticed us yet because she's absorbed in her task, writing frantically on a large pad of yellow foolscap. The yellow sheets are everywhere, some of it stacked into piles, some of it scrunched up into balls. Thousands of pages, all of them covered in loopy urgent scrawl. Without looking up, Viv takes a slug from a two-liter bottle of Cherry Coke and plucks one of several burning cigarettes from a large crystal salad bowl she's transformed into an overflowing ashtray. I want to get her attention, so I rap on the table as if it's a door.

Viv startles, then jumps up from the table, gaunt and wild-eyed in her turban. "Oh, hi there! HELLO, GIRLS! I'm so glad you're here!" She turns down the music and rushes over to hug me and then my sister. She's lost a lot of weight; even through the raccoon coat I can feel the prickle of her bones.

"It smells in here," Meg says. I glare at her.

"Have you seen our mum?" I ask, trying to be nonchalant.

"Who?" Viv looks slightly agog, then smacks her forehead. "Of course—Cecily! Right. I forgot she was coming this weekend. Cool, cool, more the merrier. You know I love a crowd!"

"She must have got stuck in traffic," I say, maintaining the pretense that we are in fact having a normal conversation.

Viv's eyes are blazing, her mind is somewhere else. "Did I tell you girls I'm writing a novel? Three novels, actually; it's a trilogy. Do you want to read it?"

"Nope!" Meg shouts, then runs out to find Tweezle.

"Sure," I say.

"Are you thirsty?" Viv says, offering me the bottle of Cherry Coke. "I wish I had something else, but it's the only thing I can stomach these days. The funny thing is I've completely lost my appetite."

"I'm okay."

Viv sinks back into her chair and resumes writing furiously with her purple felt-tip pen. Her elbow is angled wide and her eyes are half-closed, like a medium from the movies.

"I like your dress," I offer.

Viv looks up and laughs. "Oh god, this. Thanks! It was an impulse buy—Givenchy." She jumps up and twirls, causing the skirt to ripple around her like Ginger Rogers, except that underneath, instead of high heels, is a pair of muddy rubber boots. "It's too long for me, really. I don't know what I was thinking. I should have taken it back right away, but now it's too late!"

The intricate lace is frayed at the hems and pocked with tiny cigarette burns.

"Do you want it?" Viv says. "You're taller than me!"

"Really?"

"No, actually, I'm kidding." She laughs. "That would be crazy. Guess how much it cost?"

"I don't know. A hundred dollars?"

Viv hoots and points toward the ceiling.

"Three hundred?"

"Seven thousand dollars, plus tax!"

"Wow," I say. "Was it on sale?"

"No! I just thought, fuck it, you only live once, right? I put it on my Visa. I've never done anything like that before, and I have to say, it felt *amazing*." Viv spins around the table, twirling round and round before falling back into the chair unsteadily, where she sits admiring the fabric. She lifts it to her face like a veil and inhales. "Maybe I could get it altered. What do you think?"

"Sounds like a plan."

I start to inch out of the room, but Viv suddenly claps a hand over her mouth.

"Oh, shit! By the way, there's no water."

"Really? Since when?"

"A couple of weeks maybe? It just dried up. Poof!"

"It's probably the pump for the artesian well," I say. "It's easy to fix. Mark taught me how."

"Oh, wow, you're amazing. But, seriously, don't bother. I've actually kind of enjoyed it. I do the dishes in the stream and go to the bathroom outside. I'm like a pioneer woman. Laura Ingalls Wilder in a fur coat!"

Viv hoots at her own joke and takes another long swig of Cherry Coke.

The dogs are barking now. I can hear Mum's Mazda crunching up the drive. By the time I get out the back door, she's climbing out, fluffing her hair, looking harassed and exhausted, in need of a Scotch.

"Sorry I'm late, Pumpkin," Mum begins. "Honest to god, the *traffic—*"

I hold up a hand to cut her off. "There's something wrong," I say.

Mum looks around, suddenly panicked. "Where's Meg?"

"She's fine. She's in the library playing with Tweezle."

"That fucking pig. What is it, then? Is Viv home?"

"Yes, but she's being weird."

Mum laughs. "Yeah, so what else is new?"

"Hells Bells" starts up again in the dining room and Mum's gaze drifts over to the house.

"You'll see."

12

AFTER splitting the lobotomizing New York brunch bill, Mum and I hail a taxi back to our tiny room in the hipster hotel. We are unusually silent in the cab, exhausted from all that's been said and not said. Both of us are in need of a long nap in a dark room, ideally separate rooms, without bunk beds. But we don't say this—or anything—because my mother and I are gluttons for punishment. We are determined to stick to our plan, which is—improbably enough—to record ourselves in further conversation. We came up with the notion while planning our trip to New York. It's meant to be a kind of ideas session for a podcast, another collaboration we devised as a sort of surrogate project after Mum decided she didn't want to be involved in the investigation into the Horseman. In the weeks leading up to this trip, we began sending each other reading recommendations, books and essays on attachment theory and maternal ambivalence. In spite of our differences, my mother and I are endlessly united by our obsessive, often rather niche philosophical and literary preoccupations. Our relationship is at its best when we discuss what we are reading or have read or what the other ought to read, and then apply those ideas to our own writing and experience. The idea with the recording session was to use our New York reunion constructively and creatively to have an honest and wide-ranging talk about motherhood, daughterhood, and love—our favorite painful topics.

In the room, Mum kicks off her shoes and reclines on the lower bunk while I perch at the end of the bed, place my phone on the nightstand, and press Record. Perhaps out of emotional fatigue, our dialogue quickly assumes a familiar form: my mother reflects on her experience while I probe her with leading questions. It's supposed to be a talk about big ideas, but when I listen to the tape later, I realize our conversation is mostly about her—and us—a narrative both of us have spent the better part of our lives trying and failing to understand.

CR: Leaving you girls wasn't my intention. I thought I'd just go off and do this for now and then we'd be all together, but then it didn't work out that way . . . I mean, I suppose I could have stayed in Cobourg forever and ever and ever and ever and ever. I could have done that, but I wanted to *be something*. That's why I moved to the city. A lot of the reason I was doing it was for you girls. To show you something. Give you a role model.

LM: Do you still think that?

CR: No. I think I was rationalizing. [*Pause.*] Leah, I was torn. I really was.

LM: Was there also a part of you that wanted to escape us? Because I have a lot of sympathy for that. I mean, here I am in New York. With you. Away from my children. I have to say, it's nice.

[*Laughter.*]

CR: But to do what I did. To move away. To leave completely. This is the worst thing a mother can do . . . But I was reading all these books. Betty Friedan and Marilyn French and Doris Lessing and Erica Jong. I felt like it was finally *my turn*. [*Pause.*] And you came to live with me in the end anyway.

WITHIN a year of Dad breaking up with Diane, Dad meets MJ, a chatty, effervescent woman several years his junior. MJ grew up in Cobourg before moving out west where she now works as head of events at a fancy hotel in the Rockies. They meet at the yacht club: it's a setup; Dad is skippering his rich friend's racing boat and MJ is persuaded to crew. She's in her early thirties, a few years younger than Dad, but in many ways more worldly. She has boyishly cropped hair, pink varnished nails, and a pleasing angular face that bears a startling resemblance to my sister's. She's relentlessly cheerful, practical, and prim in a way that does not preclude cocktails and dancing. As the British would say, she's a woman who does what it says on the tin. My father, who has never experienced the romantic attentions of an even-tempered woman who enjoys spoiling him, is instantly smitten. After a few weeks of dating, he sits me and Meg down in the kitchen and explains to us that MJ is planning to fly back to Banff the following weekend to resume her job. Then he asks us very earnestly if he can have our permission to propose. We ask to see the ring. The date is set for February. We will not be flower girls but full-fledged bridesmaids. MJ quits and moves back to Cobourg. Because she is Catholic she will live at her mother's house until after the wedding.

That summer I am offered a wait-listed place at a drama school in Toronto. A few months before the wedding, I move to the city to live with Mum. I tell everyone I want to be an actress. In the drama program I will study method acting, vocal projection, improvisation, and the art of unbearable adolescent pretension. I tell everyone this is my dream, but really it's a means to an end. The school—prestigious, selective, and tuition-free—is how I contrived to live with my mother again. She can't refuse.

On the first day of school, Mum drives me all the way up to North York. "Enjoy your first and last time being chauffeured to high school," she says as we sit waiting for a light on Yonge Street. Watching me fidget, she adds, "The subway is faster."

Mum pulls up across the road from the school so fast, the Mazda hops up on the curb and stalls, just a few feet from two dark-haired girls in identical jean jackets who glance at us and step away, holding fresh binders to their chests. I cringe and sink down in the passenger seat, feeling simultaneously invisible and conspicuous.

"Here we are," Mum says. "First day of the rest of your life."

I nod, right hand clutching the car door handle, left hand threaded through the loop of my army surplus bag. I gaze out the window for a few seconds, taking in my future classmates. The school looks like an international airport compared with the bus stop of my small-town junior high. The students seem bigger, too, as if they've expanded like goldfish to fit a larger bowl. There are hundreds of them, clumped together on the front lawn, falling over each other, arms interlinked, laughing, shrieking, smoking, sharing secrets I'll never know. I try to parse the groups. The hippies in Indian cotton nightgowns and jeans, boys in frilly pirate shirts, their eyes and lips painted black. There are punks with green-spiked Mohawks, swan-necked dancers smoking in bomber jackets, skinheads with Doc Martens, laces color coded to their politics. There is every kind of kid you can imagine, but not a single one of them—*not even one*—is wearing what my mother has assured me is a "classic ensemble" of a navy blue peacoat, mint-green polo, pleated khakis, and deck shoes. It is 8:35 in the morning on the Tuesday after Labor Day in 1989. I have a half-grown-out perm, an army surplus backpack, a pencil case, five bucks for lunch, and not a single friend in the world.

"I love you so much, little Leah," Mum says. "You're brave and I'm proud of you." She plants a firm, dry kiss on my cheek, then pushes my left shoulder back, a wordless reminder that poor posture adds ten pounds.

DRAMA, my major and first class, runs for two hours every morning. It is held in a large underground studio with heavy soundproof curtains that can be drawn across to divide it up into rehearsal spaces. The first day I slouch on the side of a sloped riser waiting for the teacher to arrive as my fellow drama students wander in. Most of them already know each other from the feeder school.

At lunch I avoid the cafeteria and eat my cheese bagel on the concrete ledge in front of the school. I watch a guy with a long blond ponytail sneak up on a group of ballerinas and slip an ice cube down the back of the prettiest one's leotard. She shrieks, and then the dancers laugh and kick him with their flat pink slippers. I resolve to start smoking.

A girl with an unusually long neck sits down beside me. She's tall and lean, broad at the shoulder and hip. She wears violet lipstick, so dark it's almost blue, a battered tank top and army pants, and a long silk scarf, printed in floral, is wound several times around her neck. Her hair is dark orange, long but shaved at the sides, and a banjo is slung around her shoulders on a thick canvas strap. She rolls her head around twice then touches her toes, humming to herself. When she raises her arms to stretch, two thatches of ginger hair appear, licking the air like flames.

"Hiya!" she says, and sticks out a hand for me to shake. I miss the moment and instead give an awkward little wave. She laughs and drops her hand with a shrug as if to say, *Suit yourself.* Her fingers are slender, rounded at the ends like a tree frog's, glitter-painted nails chewed to the quick. She has a long, thin head and wide-set eyes.

"I'm Joni," she says, then looks down at the banjo as if she's just noticed it. "I'm actually a visual art major. Sculpture mostly. But I'm way into bluegrass. Probably a phase. Anyway, has anyone ever told you that you have the perfect nose?"

"No."

"Yeah, it's like Elizabeth Taylor's. A cute little ski jump," she chuckles, as if at a private joke. "My aunt got the same one for her sixteenth birthday. My mom's family's from L.A. Nose jobs are a family tradition."

"That's insane."

"You're telling me. The California clitorectomy. Anyway, she regrets it now."

"Why?"

"It's perfect, but it's too narrow and upturned for her round, chubby face. A bit like yours. No offense."

"None taken."

"I'm assuming yours is natural?"

I laugh in disbelief. "Yeah."

Joni explains to me that noses are problematic. She's thought of getting hers done—tastefully, not in an Elizabeth Taylor way, no offense—but she'll have to wait till she's at least eighteen because her mother doesn't believe in cosmetic surgery. She's a feminist filmmaker, divorced from Joni's father, a modernist composer who doesn't believe in binary thinking or monogamy, which is a fancy way of saying that despite being nearly sixty and on his third wife he reserves the right to do what he wants. Joni goes back and forth between her mother's spotless midtown condo and her dad's place in Cabbagetown, which she describes as halfway between a daycare and a flophouse. Soon she can choose where she wants to live full-time and she's already decided to live with her mother. Joni tells me about the complicated dynamic with her stepmom, how her dad tells her everything, even the stuff she doesn't want to know.

"Men are so predictable, don't you think?"

"Yeah," I say, thinking of Dad, his look of pathetic devotion when MJ offers to rustle up a snack.

"It's like I've become his therapist."

"Well, at least he's being honest with you," I say.

Joni shakes her head vigorously. "He shouldn't be talking to me about this stuff. It's basically a nonviolent form of child abuse. It's called enmeshment."

"Enmeshment," I repeat, cradling the word in my mouth like a lozenge.

"The clinical term is 'emotional incest.' It's pretty common among children of divorce. I should stop enabling him, but it's hard."

"How come?"

"Because he's my dad."

We smile at each other, a wary mutual understanding.

A few days later, in the school library, I go to the psychology section and find a textbook where I look up the term *emotional incest*. I am skeptical I'll find it. But I do.

EMOTIONAL OR COVERT INCEST. Def: A type of emotional abuse. It occurs when a parent consistently violates the normal boundaries between themselves and child. Sometimes called "enmeshment." In an emotionally incestuous relationship, a caregiver depends on the child for support. This reverses the norms of parenthood and means that the child has to prioritize the needs of the adult.

I slam the textbook shut, blood pounding in my ears.

13

MUM'S apartment is across the back fence from Richard's four-story town house. It's so close, our backyards nearly touch. I'm not sure whether this is the result of coincidence or design, but in a city of several million the former seems unlikely. My mother is vague on how she came to live a stone's throw from the man who is torturing her, something about our landlord being a friend of a friend of the family.

For the first few weeks, I sleep on the floor of the mudroom and live out of my suitcase, but eventually we move into the flat upstairs, which has a deck and a bedroom plus an open-air loft that serves as my room. There's no privacy, but I don't mind. What I do mind is that our flat now overlooks Richard's place, a minimalist fishbowl with floor-to-ceiling glass windows.

On the weekends, Mum still goes to Vogrie, alone or with Richard if he isn't with his new girlfriend. Her name is Victoria and she has her own weekly TV news show, where she interviews famous guests about the issues of the day. Sometimes my mother turns it on and we watch Victoria. Mum seems in awe of her.

"She's got great hair, hasn't she?" Mum will say. "So much volume."

"She's on TV, Mum," I say. "I'm sure it doesn't look like that in real life."

"I assure you it does," Mum says. "I met her at a party once. Tall.

Great shoulders. High cheekbones. She's very well-informed. But I supposed she'd have to be, with a job like that."

"I'll bet she towers over Richard in heels."

Mum shrugs to indicate it's irrelevant. Confident men like Richard enjoy the company of tall, successful, famous women with great shoulders, I can hear her thinking. Women unlike her.

The worst nights are the ones when Victoria is over at Richard's house and Mum sits at our dimly lit kitchen window listening to Joan Armatrading, watching her not-boyfriend opening wine for his first-string girlfriend and practicing jazz standards on his gleaming baby grand piano just like he does on the nights when my mother is there. He orders pizza from Tom's, which he and Victoria eat on the black leather sectional while watching the news. Eventually the living room light goes off and, a floor up, the bedroom light comes on, mercifully eclipsed by a Venetian blind. I've watched this silent picture show myself when my mother is the woman at Richard's. It's eerily similar: the wine, the piano, the pizza, Richard, and a slightly shorter, ultimately interchangeable blonde. One light goes off as the other comes on.

When Victoria is there, my mother is the envious understudy mouthing the lines in the wings. She knows it's a ridiculous role in a badly written play, but she still thinks she'd do it better.

Each day at school that first year, I try on six different versions of myself and discard them like ill-fitting dresses in a heap on the floor. I want to be a girl with clear edges, a clearly delineated figure stark as a lithograph, with no margin for error. Somehow, I manage to attract the attention of an older boy named Dave. He spends hours in the food court teaching me to French-inhale. Parts his pillow lips softly, then lets the smoke drift out like a specter before sucking it back up his nose. I practice for hours but I'm hopeless. Mostly I just like to look at Dave. He is tall and lean like a poplar tree, wide bony shoulders tapering down to the slimmest hips. He tells me his father is from Somalia and his mother is Acadian. An unlikely coupling, they hooked up briefly working on an ocean freighter. Dave's hair is twisted into dozens of tiny horns, the beginning of dreadlocks, which he fiddles with as he talks about his recent recurring role on a TV show. When he lopes through the food court at the mall across from the school, strangers high-five him and shout the tagline for which he's become modestly famous. Dave is always going to auditions, getting his headshots redone, calling his agent from a pay phone to discuss commercial callbacks.

One Friday evening, when my mother is packing up to drive to Vogrie with Richard, Dave comes over with a VHS copy of Spike Lee's *Do the Right Thing.*

"It's a pleasure to meet you, Mrs. Ross," he says smoothly when I introduce him.

"It's Ms. Ross. My mother is Mrs. Ross."

Dave laughs a bit longer than he should. He slaps the wall. He's already high.

"Leah, you didn't tell me your mom was so funny."

"Depends on your sense of humor," I say.

Mum kisses me on the cheek and picks up her weekend bag.

"Well, I'm off. Thanks for keeping my daughter company. She says you're on that teen show."

Dave shrugs. "Just a recurring guest role."

"Still, that's very impressive." My mother's eyes slide over the length of Dave's six-foot-plus frame. "I thought all TV actors were supposed to be short?"

He laughs modestly and I join in, wishing I could physically push my mother out the door.

"Well, you seem like a responsible young man, so can you please make sure my daughter doesn't smoke in the house? The smell gets in the furniture."

"Of course." He coughs. "It's a filthy habit."

After she leaves, we watch *Do the Right Thing* in a haze of hash smoke. By the end, our lungs are scorched raw from cigarettes and bottle tokes. Even on my mother's tiny TV, the movie is so vivid, its message so confusing and intense, that when the credits roll, I can barely speak. My body feels simultaneously weightless and encased in concrete. Dave offers me a Pringle and I shake my head. I want to light a cigarette, but I've forgotten how to lean forward. He wheezes, eyes squinted into slits. "You're *so high*," he says.

We fool around for a bit, slurping each other's faces, fumbling with buttons, his finger prodding and poking the crotch of my white cotton underpants, then suddenly retreating in a way that suggests he's too disappointed with what he's found to bother to go further.

"You're not a virgin, are you?" he says.

"Maybe," I say uncertainly. "I mean, is that bad?"

Dave shrugs, not looking at me, then stretches himself out on the sofa and yawns. "I just don't want you to fall in love with me or anything. I'm not looking for anything intense."

I tell him, "Me neither," that I'm trying to focus on school. I suggest watching *Saturday Night Live*. I'm anxious for him to stay. It occurs to me I've never been alone overnight before. But Dave stands up and stretches, saying he'd better get home and hit the hay. He has an audition first thing tomorrow.

WHEN my mother comes home on Sunday night, she hums a Cole Porter standard as she moves around the small galley kitchen, fixing herself a Scotch on the rocks, pouring dry-roasted peanuts into a saucer. Things must have gone well with Richard, I think. Maybe he's on the outs with Victoria? Or, no . . . I bet it's that she's excited about her second date with Grahame, a public relations executive she recently met for dinner through the Personals section.

My mother occasionally sees other men in the hope of a distraction from the agony of Richard. There was Jeff, the artist from Saskatoon who later moved to New York and dumped her. There was a famous children's author she had a one-night stand with years ago who inscribed all my favorite rhyming picture books. For a while there was another Richard, a nicer one—we called him Richard Two—a divorced, ebullient English professor at Trent with two daughters the same age as me and Meg. He invited us away on weekend visits to his island cottage on Georgian Bay, where we all ran around naked, skinny-dipping in the day and night. My mother was so madly in love with Richard Two that for a while she broke it off with Richard One. But then she had her tubes tied and he broke it off. There was also the brother of our landlady, a lawyer twenty years older than my mother, whom she tried to like because of his "patrician lineage" but in the end dismissed as a bore.

My mother cannot tolerate dull men. She says she just wants someone to take care of her, preferably a tall man who reads books and knows how to boil a pot of pasta, but what she really wants is a man who does not bore her. Dull men, it turns out, are not just steady, small-town furniture salesmen like my father. They come in all shapes and sizes, but the thing that unites them is their openhearted interest in having a healthy relationship with my mother. She does not describe them this way. Instead, she says they are "humorless," a quality that, I am learning, is the opposite of "arch." Arch is sexy and intelligent. Arch men keep my mother off-balance; and off-balance is how she seems to want to be. Teetering, anxious, uncertain just up to the point of desperate—the state she purportedly wants to escape is also the one to which she unwittingly returns. My mother longs for emotional safety but is also somehow suffocated by it. Her teaching is not implicit; it's the motto on the fridge:

COMMITMENT SUCKS THE LIFE RIGHT OUT OF YOU.

During my first year of high school, my mother goes on enough bad dates with humorless men that eventually we devise a plan: if she needs to escape, she calls me from the restaurant pay phone halfway through dinner and hangs up. One ring—that's the code; no need to waste the quarter. Then it's my job to call up the restaurant and say to the waiter who answers, *Hello, I'm calling for my mother? She's the bored-looking blond woman in the blue blouse on a dinner date?*

Grahame is the first date my mother has had in ages where I didn't need to call the restaurant. And now there will be a second. I hope badly, so very badly, that Grahame will be my mother's boyfriend. Then

she wouldn't look out the window at night watching Richard and
Victoria.

So is Dave your boyfriend, then?" my mother asks as we are reading
on opposite ends of the cream-colored sofa.

"God, no," I say, "just a friend."

"Well, he's *very* cute. Very articulate. And *tall*. And those green eyes.
So arresting."

"They're contacts, Mum. Can't you tell?"

"What? No! I don't believe it. Anyway, I liked him. He's impressive."

"He meets with a lot of casting directors."

She looks slightly taken aback. "Meaning what?"

"Meaning he's good at talking to adults. He's literally an actor."

She looks at me pointedly. "So he's like you, then, is he?"

"Mum, I'm just in school. Dave's a *professional.*"

She leans over and ruffles my hair, which makes me grimace. Then
she settles down on the opposite end of the sofa, entwining her feet
with mine under the orange blanket. She reaches for her book, but I
want to talk a bit more. I've been alone since Dave left on Friday night.

"How was Vogrie?"

Mum sighs. "It was fine. I mean, we had a nice time, but Viv . . . she's
getting worse."

"How?"

"She's having another manic episode, I think. Eventually she'll
crash."

I've stopped going to Vogrie. I want to be in the city with my friends.

"Well, she finally got rid of Cleo after she killed that deer," Mum
says, "but Tweezle's still there, shitting all over the house."

"Oh god."

"And that unbearable hard rock music she plays. Richard was *not*
impressed."

"Is Viv okay? Should we do something?"

My mother shrugs. "Well, Stewart's pretty frail. It won't be long
now, so the Trust is moving in. Apparently people from Christie's were

in last week. Viv says they're picking over the place like vultures, itemizing every stick of furniture, making lists. They're even measuring the murals in the Ronald Room to see if they can extract them before the sale."

"They're going to *sell* Vogrie?"

She takes a draft of whisky and fixes me with a withering look. "Oh, come on, Leah, I've told you all this. They were just waiting for Stewart to go."

I start to cry. Mum looks at me dubiously. I can see she thinks I'm being sentimental, but I can't help it. She squeezes my hand.

"Oh, sweetheart, I'm sorry. I thought you knew all this. Things change. What's that saying? Things fall apart."

I cover my face and sob into my hands like a child.

My mother asks why I'm crying and I tell her I'm not sure. When the tears subside, I realize that I'm disappointed. That somehow I thought one day we'd go back there, to Vogrie, and it would be like it was before. At this my mother sighs.

"It's a long life and you get plenty of chances," she says. Then she passes me the bowl of peanuts. "Dinner?"

As a teenager in Toronto I became suspicious of what my mother derisively called "obliviousness," appreciative of black humor and contrarian points of view. I spent many hours listening to my mother gossip about journalists twice my age, people I'd never met but who, over time, became fully formed characters in my mind. From my mother I learned that wisecracks were only wise if they skated dangerously close to some unspoken, painful truth. I learned that squirming discomfort was the natural prelude to laughter in the same way that anxiety and desperation were the natural precursors to love. The way to live what my mother called a "life of the mind" was not contentment or normalcy but the ramping up of emotional tension in the hope of blissful, dramatic release. Optimism and positivity were beneath contempt, part of a facile worldview my mother dismissed as *happy! happy! happy!*

"It's your life," she often said. Other mothers might say this, but the difference with mine was that she meant it.

Our fridge sign went up in 1988, at the beginning of my high school years, our blissful extended reunion. My mother was thirty-six to my thirteen, and yet somehow we were exactly the same age. We often remarked on the way time had swung us into perfect tandem. Our fridge, our motto, the haphazard rhythms of our life, came together, and for a time, at least to me, they seemed almost perfect. But even then, in the first blush of our enmeshment, I was beginning to understand there might be other ways to love.

On Hannah's fridge there was a long poem, handwritten on family stationery. For many years I believed it was authored by her mother.

Go placidly amid the noise and haste, and remember what peace there may be in silence, it began.

Every time I went over to Hannah's house, I stopped to read her mother's poem. There was one line toward the end that invariably made tears spring to my eyes: *Beyond a wholesome discipline, be gentle with yourself. You are a child of the universe, no less than the trees and the stars; you have a right to be here.*

It was not a poem so much as a list of tender suggestions for how to love and live. Reading it moved me, but for reasons I could barely articulate it also felt like a betrayal of my own mother. I did not ask Hannah about it, in the same way I did not ask Hannah why her house was always warm or why her mother helped us with our French homework or why there were shelves with jars full of almonds and trail mix that seemed to magically replenish themselves like the fresh fruit in the bowl on the counter. I understood these things were normal even if they were not normal for me—for us.

I'd abandoned my father's cozy, predictable home to follow my mother to the city. I'd left behind a warm, well-stocked kitchen where kind people made corny jokes and spoke without double meanings—everything I would eventually want for my own children. Not that I considered this at the time. The small-town world I'd left was familiar and safe, even occasionally moving, but my mother taught me it was also dangerous. Stability and commitment. The predictable rhythms of life. These were the traps that unimaginative people confused with love. They were obvious. Unforgivable. The platitudes that filled your eyes with tears just before they sucked the life right out of you.

14

On a gloomy frigid morning in the winter of grade nine, I walk up to Dave in the food court and inquire in an offhand manner if he'd like to have sex with me. "I'm not trying to be your girlfriend or anything," I add, in case it isn't obvious.

Dave puts down the script pages he's reading, which he calls sides. He's preparing for a callback for a role as a teenaged gangbanger in a new cop show that's being shot in Toronto. As he considers my proposal, his lips move against each other like he's sucking a candy. When I look at his eyes they are laughing.

"I'd be up for that."

Why do I offer myself to this boy? I wish I could say the impulse came from an earnest desire to secure his affection, no matter how undeserved on his part or misguided on mine, but that wasn't it. I chose Dave not because I loved him but because I didn't. I chose him for my mother. I wanted to show her that I was pragmatic when it came to matters of the heart.

Later that day, Dave and I take a bus to the suburban edges of the city where he lives on the first floor of a tower block. His mother is at work. He leads me into a small, chilly back bedroom and we lie down on his bed, which, like mine, is a single mattress on a carpeted floor. He fiddles around with a stack of cassette tapes, then selects *Hatful of Hollow* by the Smiths. Without talking or kissing, Dave eases off my jeans and T-shirt then removes his own pants, so he's in just his boxers and T-shirt. "Do you mind?" he asks, indicating his shirt. "I'm a bit cold."

He doesn't wait for an answer. It occurs to me I'm also cold and that I'd like to keep my shirt on, but I can't because I have breasts, which are apparently integral to the process. Dave props himself up on bent arm so he is lying both beside and over me, then leans his face into mine and we kiss. He has beautiful lips, softer than my own, and the inside of his mouth tastes tangy, almost electric. Kissing him reminds me of sucking on tinfoil. Just as I close my eyes and begin to float away somewhere warm, he pulls his head back and runs his thumb across my forehead, staring at my face but not actually making eye contact. I wonder what he's thinking about. Maybe the angle of the light? Whatever it is, I'm certain it has nothing to do with me.

"Do you want anything to drink? All I have is water."

"No, thanks," I say.

Dave nods soberly and sits on the edge of the bed. He produces a condom from somewhere and rips it open with his teeth, holding the wrapper in his mouth and squinting as he concentrates on the surprisingly complicated process of putting it on. It occurs to me he must need glasses, that his contacts are only cosmetic. This thought makes me pity him slightly, but not enough to stave off the cord of dread pulling itself tight around my chest.

Dave's penis is the first one I've seen up close. It's terrifying—the girth of a baby's forearm, purplish, neatly circumcised, and angled to one side like a toadstool. When he pushes it inside me, the pain is explosive: I whimper like a puppy. I knew it would hurt, I'd expected to bleed, but I can't imagine how anyone could even pretend to enjoy something so spectacularly awful. Dave tries to kiss me but I turn my head away. He pauses to ask if I'm okay.

"Yeah, fine," I say. Coy smile, gritted teeth.

He continues to move in and out of me, gingerly at first, then faster and deeper. I stare at a movie poster on his wall. *Police Academy 2.* He stops again and looks at me. Either it's over or I'm doing something wrong.

"Sorry to be rude," he says, "but do you mind if I turn over the tape?"

"No."

"Music helps me to focus."

"Okay."

He leans across and presses a button on the stereo beside his bed, then puts on the B side of *Hatful of Hollow*.

W HEN I get home that evening, my mother is reading on the sofa, the tinkle of Bill Evans in the background. On her lap is Brie, a fluffy orange rescue kitten she surprised me with on my birthday. Brie purrs and nuzzles, rolls herself over, and grips my mother's wrist like prey, sinking in her tiny white kitty teeth.

"For fuck's sake!" Mum brushes the tiny cat off her lap, sending her flying into the blanket chest we use as a coffee table, where she rebounds, then slinks under the sofa. Mum shakes her wrist then sucks it. "I know she's your birthday present, Leah, but, honestly, you said you'd change the litter."

"I *do* change the litter. Sometimes."

"Well, not enough, I can smell it from here. I don't know what I was thinking. It's a second-floor apartment, and you know I don't believe in indoor cats."

"Maybe we should move?" I say, thinking of Richard's house, the nightly picture show.

"I thought you were sick of moving?"

I shrug.

"I think I'm developing late-onset allergies," my mother says, wiping her eyes.

I kick off my shoes as Mum talks about an article she read about the sinus problems afflicting middle-aged women. Sinking into the small patch of free sofa, I reach for Mum's feet and rub them under the orange blanket the way she likes. She tells me about the low-grade headache she wakes up with most mornings and how she thinks it's a reaction to Brie's dander, which is everywhere because she's cooped up in the apartment and scratching herself all day. I understand that my cat will soon be dead. It seems inevitable. What's surprising, even comforting, is the fact I don't care.

"How was school?" she asks, reaching around to tug a strand of hair at the crown of her head.

"I didn't go," I say. "I lost my virginity instead."

I watch my mother's eyes, which had already begun to slide back to her book, snap open, and lock on mine. It's so rare to command her full attention. My friends' mothers follow their kids around asking questions, issuing curfews, sniffing jackets, checking pockets, and phoning other parents to make sure they are home, but my mother isn't like this. She has better things to do. She trusts me because I'm special. It's hard to surprise her, but I have.

"Oh, Leah, wow. You're still a bit young, don't you think?"

"Not really," I say. "I mean, I'm young, but I'm also mature for my age."

Mum smiles. Confusingly, her eyes are misted with emotion. "Well, okay," she says with a reluctant sigh, as if I'd just insisted on paying for lunch. Then she adds, "It's your life, Pumpkin."

"Don't you want to know how it happened?"

Mum recoils slightly. "I mean, I don't know. Not really."

I shoot her a wounded look.

"Sorry. I mean sure. I guess so."

I tell her it was with Dave. And that it was just like an episode in an after-school special, except he wasn't pressuring me at all. I was totally in control. I tell my mother I just wanted to see what it felt like. "Get it over with, you know, so I didn't have to wonder about it anymore."

A weak smile spreads over her face; the mist recedes. She likes Dave.

"You don't have to worry," I tell her. "He used a condom. I won't get pregnant or AIDS or anything like that, and before you give me a lecture about going on the pill, you should know that won't be necessary, because I'm not doing it again. Ever."

She laughs. "Oh, really? Why not?"

"I found it overrated."

I don't mention how much it hurt. Or the fact that I could barely sit down on the bus. Or that I'd bled into the wad of toilet paper I shoved into the crotch of my underwear. That I was still bleeding.

Mum drains the last of her Scotch, then reaches round and pulls at a strand of hair at the crown of her head. "Well, if you're no longer a virgin, I suppose I might as well ask you for a cigarette."

Smoking is the one thing my mother and I have argued about since I moved in. She quit years before leaving my father, and it's a point of pride that she didn't start again during or after the divorce. Cigars don't count, because they're Richard's. My dad still smokes a pack a day.

"But you don't smoke cigarettes," I say carefully.

"I thought *you* didn't smoke."

"I don't really. I guess you could say I'm a social smoker."

"Well, I am too."

We laugh.

"For heaven's sake, Leah, do you have a cigarette or not?"

We light up two du Mauriers and smoke in silence. On the news, students in Berlin are having a party as they dismantle a boring brick wall.

15

ONE morning over coffee, my mother tells me she's thinking of asking Victoria, Richard's TV presenter girlfriend, to lunch.

"Why?" I ask, knowing there can only be one reason.

"I think she deserves to know the truth. Don't you?"

My stomach lurches. But I pause to consider her question carefully, as I do all my mother's dilemmas. Sometimes I ask her to leave me with a problem so I can think about it for a few hours or overnight.

"He'll be livid," I say.

My mother nods as if to say, *Well, duh.* I understand that she's drawing a line in the sand and daring herself to step over it.

"Do it," I say.

THE following week my mother arrives home with news to report. The lunch with Victoria went well. Astonishingly well, considering. After absorbing the initial shock, Victoria was gracious, even warm. She did not shoot the messenger, my mother explains. On the contrary, they bonded in mutual female rage. I gasp.

"Just like *The Witches of Eastwick.*"

"That's *exactly* what I was thinking!"

We stare at each other, astonished and giddy, laughter bubbling up from hell.

Victoria broke up with Richard after that, as my mother knew she would. My mother broke up with him, too—a less surprising development. An alliance was formed between the two women. They spoke on the phone and met for coffee, wounded veterans sharing stories from the war. Richard did not rage at the damage my mother had done, as I'd hoped he would. I'd had fantasies of finding him on our doorstep and slamming the door in his face. But he did not cause a scene. Instead, he simply stopped calling. As endings go, it was not entirely satisfying. I understood what my mother really wanted was the pleasure of seeing him suffer. And yet, as I assured my mother, it was also the perfect outcome. A beautiful plan, seamlessly executed, devoid of drama or mess. Richard, the man who was never alone, was finally abandoned. My mother had resumed control of her life by making a mess of his. What could be more hopeful?

For weeks after the lunch with Victoria, Richard's house went dark. In the evenings Mum and I mused cattily about where he was. Perhaps he was at a wine bar nursing his broken heart on seventeen-dollar glasses of Barolo? Or had he seen the error of his ways, gone mad with guilt, then checked himself into a sanitarium? Most of the time Mum was convinced he was out on the town looking for his next victim. To me it hardly mattered. All I cared about was that it was finally over. Eventually, over time, my mother's friendship with Victoria cooled. This made my mother anxious, but I assured her it was normal, even healthy. The triangle was broken. She needed to let go.

My mother agreed, but I could tell she was secretly on edge. The resolution of the Richard situation plunged her into an emotional paralysis that was worse than the darkest lows of their affair. She stopped walking to work for exercise. She stopped going to parties. She stopped going out of town on the weekends. She stayed home and tried to read but abandoned book after book. Occasionally I persuaded her to go with me to the movies, where we would sit together, engulfed in the overheated darkness, but afterward she had little to say. She wouldn't ask with relish, as she normally did while the credits were still rolling, "So what do you think it was *about*?" I finally had my mother all to myself, except she wasn't there.

Without the tension of the love triangle, my mother had gone murky, out of focus. A woman who lacked shape or form. Even I began to miss Richard—not the man himself but the excitement and urgency my mother's obsession fueled. As it turned out I needn't have worried.

One night a few months after the breakup, Mum beckoned me over to the window and pointed to the wall of light. There was the old familiar picture show. The bottle of wine and two glasses. Richard at the baby grand. The tall blonde with her marvelous, voluminous hair, reclining on the leather sofa, looking back into the room.

Victoria had taken him back. Of course she had.

"Tomorrow he'll call," my mother said.

"No," I said. "It's too soon."

As it turned out, I was right.

RICHARD waited a week.

A week during which my mother sweated and paced, ate virtually nothing, and talked of little else. When the triangle resumed, it was the same but different. Once Victoria had accepted Richard's transgressions and had forgiven him, my mother's humiliation was complete. He called less often after that. And when he did call she went to him unthinkingly. In a funny way my mother seemed relieved; like an addict who's finally abandoned the pretense of having it all under control, she gave in completely. I could no longer bear to watch over her at the kitchen window when she was at Richard's. When she was home, she no longer pretended not to be watching Richard's house. She cried openly for weeks, at night and in the mornings before work. I began pretending not to notice.

Eventually she stopped bumming my cigarettes and went back to cigars.

"You're not supposed to inhale them," I'd say.

"Then what's the point?"

She developed a dreadful rattling cough like an ill-fated woman in the first act of a Victorian play. I ignored that too.

One night, while I was sitting at the table, failing to concentrate on my math homework, an idea occurred to me.

"Our lease is coming up soon."

My mother's eyes, a dull shade of blue, brightened for the first time in months. *Moving.* I could feel her mind fixing upon the possibility of it. A change of scenery. Her body began to twitch; the old restlessness pulling her back into the room. She looked at me then—really looked—for what felt like the first time in months.

"Little Leah," she said. "How did you get so smart?"

I shrugged, so pleased with myself I could have jumped up and done a pirouette.

"I love you so much, Pumpkin."

"I love you, too, Mum."

16

THAT summer, Mum and I both stay in the city and work. In the evenings we scour the classifieds looking for a new apartment. One weekend, for a break, we drive up to visit family friends at their cottage in Muskoka. The first afternoon, we make a trip into town for ice. Mum fetches a bag from the freezer, then stands in front of the flimsy wire postcard rack, spinning it.

"Which one?" she says.

I have no idea who the postcard is for, only that wherever she goes my mother likes sending them. A montage of sunsets, steamboats, and windswept jack pines blurs past like a picturesque roulette wheel, then comes to rest on a pair of beady-eyed loons bobbing on the water. She shakes her head, shifts the ice bag higher on her hip, and smacks the floor with her flip-flop. I don't care about the card. I'm worried about the bag of ice. Soon it will melt and we'll be forced to buy a bag of water.

"What about this one?" I point to a dock scene with the slogan *Muskoka: Once discovered, never forgotten.*

"God, no. Too needy. We need something pointed. The aim is to send a clear, decisive message."

"Is the point to show that you're having a good time?"

My mother laughs. "Not exactly. And we *are* having a good time, by the way."

I realize the postcard is for Grahame. Everything I know about

Grahame is through my mother, but I feel as if we've been intimately acquainted for years. Grahame has a terrible name and a boring job, but he compensates by being rich. He has thick gray hair and a wide, convex chest that makes him seem bigger, more attractively bearlike, than his unremarkable height (five feet ten inches) might suggest. He subscribes to the *Economist* and orders in sashimi. My mother and Grahame went on three dates last February, the last of which was a spontaneous two-night business trip to Chicago. Unlike Richard, with whom my mother says sex is like forcing an oyster into a parking meter, Grahame is like a jackrabbit in bed. While neither metaphor is clear in my brain—I have not had sex since the tape-flipping episode with Dave—I instinctively understand why my mother prefers the latter. What woman would choose a bivalve over a bunny?

Grahame travels a lot for work, but no matter what five-star hotel he's in, every day he has exactly the same breakfast: whole wheat toast, crunchy peanut butter, and freshly squeezed orange juice.

Mum had liked Grahame *a lot*. And Grahame seemed to like her too. Why else would he have complimented her shoulders? Or looked so relieved when she mentioned having her tubes tied? Or called her up spontaneously at 10 p.m. on a Friday to ask her to fly to Chicago the next morning?

Grahame could have been my mother's boyfriend if he hadn't made the dumb mistake of vanishing into thin air. Not even a voice message. Nothing. Who does that? Just . . . *poof!*

The ice is melting. On the right hip of my mother's Gap clamdiggers I can see a wet patch forming.

"Aha!" She plucks a postcard off the stand, then flashes it toward me, eyes dancing over the edge. On the front is a starving beaver—or is it an otter?—standing on a riverbank beside some bulrushes. Its brown fur is matted into oily points as it sits back on its haunches looking confused.

"What is it?"

"A muskrat. You've seen them; they live in ditches and swamps."

"But why is it on a postcard?"

She flips the card over and squints at the back. Apparently they're native to Ontario. Filthy things. Water rats. Vermin. My mother raises her shoulders to her ears and lets a long theatrical shudder of disgust run through her body.

Bad Grahame. That's what we call him. What a jerk.

"Oh, Mum, it's *perfect*."

"Isn't it just?"

"But what are you going to write?"

She swivels around and saunters over to the post office counter, where she reaches across a portly older woman in a floppy green sun hat for the ballpoint pen on a string. The woman is halfway through sending a stack of parcels and she stares at my mother indignantly and sniffs.

I think my mother is oblivious—she often is—but without looking at the woman she mutters, "Hold your horses, dearie." The lady puffs up, eyes goggling, and shakes her head, which my mother doesn't see because her eyes are fixed on the card. On the back, she writes Grahame's address, which I'm both impressed and disturbed to see she knows by heart, just like his home and work phone numbers, which we have dialed and redialed before thinking better of it and hanging up. On the message space, she scrawls a single sentence in full caps:

THIS IS YOU.

She signs her name, then licks a stamp, fixing the queen's head to the corner with her thumb. With a flick of her wrist, she hands me the card. We both burst out laughing, imagining the smug expression sliding off Grahame's craggily handsome face as he reads the postcard and the name and the penny drops.

"Put it in the mailbox outside, will you, Pumpkin? I'll get us a fresh bag of ice. This one's half-melted."

W E move into our new flat in the fall of grade ten. It's a sub-basement in a purple warehouse building on Beverley Street, across from Grange Park, in the nether land between Chinatown and the garment district.

It's an hour-long subway commute from my school, but I don't mind, because downtown is cool, and Mum can still walk to work. The landlord is a painter named Charlie who made a fortune painting pictures of the queen riding a moose. Our building is an old sweatshop that he converted into six open-concept apartments. All the tenants are single mothers—not the sad, destitute kind, but attractive women with jobs in arts and media who can afford to pay the rent. The park is full of needles, but in the morning the sun shines into our sitting room, silhouetting the old women who gather there to do tai chi. Mum has more friends now, not just the other tenants in the building but people she knows from work. The two of us have worked out a mutually satisfying routine where we stay out of each other's hair during the week, then spend most weekends poking around markets and going to movies. Vogrie seems like a distant memory. Viv is still living there, but the place is on the market. The lithium has made her sluggish and dull. She's working to pay off the debts she racked up during her last manic phase. Like Mum, she no longer loves a crowd.

ONE night that fall, I stay over at Hannah's house and don't bother to call my mother to tell her where I am. I go to school the next day as usual, but on the subway home I'm worried she'll be angry or, worse, terrified. There is a serial rapist loose in the city's north end. The media call him the Scarborough Rapist, but his hunting ground extends farther than that. His targets are mostly young women coming home alone late at night or early morning joggers. He roughs them up if they struggle, not just to subdue them but afterward, too, then leaves them to bleed. There are posters showing police composites of his face in all the bus shelters near my school, and the papers are full of it. A girl has gone missing in Burlington. The thought at the time is that it's probably unrelated. But most of my girlfriends are forbidden from taking the bus after dark. Curfews are being tightened. It's driving everyone crazy. Everyone but me. Instinctively, though, I feel I should offer my mother a plausible excuse, but what possible explanation could I have for staying out all night without calling? I think up outlandish lies and quickly discard them. Why complicate an already bad situation? Nothing occurs to me except the obvious: I forgot. Which is still a white lie. The truth is that Hannah's mother reminded me, but I just didn't feel like it.

By the time I finally slink in the door that evening, guiltily, my mother is already home from work. I am fifteen, there is a rapist on the loose, and I haven't checked in with her in over thirty-six hours. Mum is sitting on the white sofa, reading a book and listening to Bill Evans—an indication she's back with Richard. She can't bear jazz piano when they're on the outs. Increasingly, there are things we don't talk about.

I hang up my coat and put down my bag.

"And how was your day?" she asks after a while.

"Fine," I say warily.

Normally I'd go straight to my room to write down my day in my diary, but instead I drink a glass of water at the sink, then stand at the counter watching her, curled up on a corner of the sofa in the raised sitting area. I'm expecting her to say something, but she doesn't. Her eyes continue to scan the pages as she idly plucks at the hair on the crown of her head.

"Sorry I didn't call."

"Thank you for apologizing." Her tone is flat, unreadable. On the stereo, Evans plunks out his heroin-addled anguish.

"I was at Hannah's."

"I figured. I wasn't worried."

"I'll call you next time."

"That would be nice."

At no point does she look up from her book.

And I do call, for the most part. Except when I don't. It's fine. My mother is not worried. She's never worried. Nothing bad is going to happen to me, her elder daughter. She's already decided the ending. This is our deal: my freedom in exchange for hers.

Intuitively, over time, I have come to understand why my mother is not like other mothers. She will not protect me, because no one protected her from the Horseman. What others might see as neglectful,

I recognize as a gift. She has decided on a different outcome—one in which the eldest daughter prevails. It's her story, of course, a narrative of convenience, but it suits me just fine. I don't want a conventional arrangement. My mother loves me, but she will not manage my life for me. It's *my* life. Lots of mothers say this to their daughters, but the difference with my mother is that she means it.

M y mother calls me from work after school on a Tuesday to say her colleague, the entertainment editor at the magazine where she works, would like to know if I am available to babysit tonight. He and his wife are desperate, she says, because they have a gala to attend and their regular sitter is busy. One kid, about five, six bucks an hour. As it happens, I'm free.

I take the subway to their house, which is far away, all the way out in the east end, in a part of the city I've never been. When I get there, the Editor and his wife are charming. They're older than my mother, mid-forties, and according to Mum very "well-connected" in the city. For the party, they're dressed up in a 1920s theme. The wife, a TV writer, has short hair that curls owlishly around her temples. Her small mouth shimmers like the inside of a clamshell. He is lean and dapper in a tuxedo with a crooked bow tie. Their kid is already in bed, so I sit on the sofa and do my geography homework in front of the TV. I eat some rice cakes from their kitchen, and once the late news is over and the TV turns to fuzz, I poke around the house and try on the mother's high heels and jewelry. Eventually I fall asleep on the sofa reading a book. When they burst in the front door after 2 a.m., apologizing all over themselves, I am disoriented. I gather my things and the Editor offers me a ride home, which I accept. He tells me things as he drives. Stories of the celebrities he's recently interviewed. Madonna. Mick Jagger. A famous director whose name he's surprised I don't know. I am exhausted but also impressed.

My mother reveres the Editor and his wife, both of whom she says are talented writers. I can tell she's slightly intimidated by them as a couple because of how embedded they are in the city's "media scene," a world she aspires to and also resents because it makes her feel left out. My mother has a raging crush on the lead actor in the legal drama the Editor's wife writes on. I babysit for them a handful of times over the next couple of years and it is always the same: friendly small talk at the front door. The false promises to be home early. The late-night drive home listening to the Editor's latest brush with celebrity. Unlike my mother, who does the "front of book" section, he gets to travel.

Babysitting is an okay gig, but it's too tiring for what they pay me. Every time I come away thinking that next time they ask I'll say no. Then one night something different happens. It must be during the film festival, because the clubs and bars on Queen West are still open when the Editor drives me home. As his car nears our building, he notices that Chicago's, the blues bar at the end of our street, is hopping. A saxophone goose-honks over a thumping double bass. People are spilling onto the street in jeans and spangles, smoking and laughing.

"Hey," he says, "shall we continue this over a beer?"

"It's Tuesday," I say, not bothering to add that I'm under the legal drinking age.

"So?"

"Just that it's a school night."

He slaps his head, then shakes it. "Sorry," he says. "Of course. You're just so smart and good to talk to. I was enjoying our conversation."

The Editor drops me off, waits and watches until I'm through the door. I go to bed in my clothes and lie under the duvet, face burning, thinking: *Wow.*

17

ON our second night in New York, Mum and I have plans to meet my friend Violet for dinner at a fish restaurant in the East Village. A waiter takes our coats. The room is painted white and decorated with mermaid art. The booths are wooden and straight-backed. We sit in silence while we wait, examining the specials on heavy laminated menus.

Violet rushes in five minutes late, apologizing profusely, frothing with good humor. She tosses her coat in the empty booth beside us. Mum sits up, pushes back her shoulders, adjusts her pelvis, bracing at the presence of an interloper. Like me, she conceals her shyness with an armor of haughtiness.

My mother extends her small, dry hand and Violet squeezes it, tucking herself into the tiny booth beside me so we are side by side facing Mum, who arranges herself regally in the center of the table, regarding us both coolly.

"Ladies! Darlings! What are we drinking?" Violet says, and grabs the menu. "Mmmm, yes, I'll have one of those. I was so desperately hungover, but I had a three-hour afternoon siesta and rallied against the odds. Oh, look, you're wearing your hair clipped back just like mine. I love it."

I can see my mother is startled by Violet's almost manically charming effervescence. The shift of focus is a mercy; it loosens the tension that's been stretched between us like a taut wire. I am so relieved at the sight of Violet I could cry.

"You look gorgeous, darling; I could eat you," she says, kissing me on both cheeks. "How long has it been since my going-away party? Months! And lucky me, I get to meet your mother: what an absolute honor. My god, the eyes! The resemblance is shocking."

Violet's from London, a couple of years older than me, British, a northern transplant like my husband. She's thin and vivacious, a stylish magpie with a mop of black curls, one of those women whose metabolism seems to run at an exhilarating, mood-lifting double time. She explains to my mother how we met a couple of years ago through mutual friends, a gay couple who live in the Bahamas. She's living in New York now for a lark—a temporary secondment at the Manhattan office of the hair and makeup agency she manages.

Violet is cheerful but no stranger to disappointment. She used to be married, properly married, for twelve years to her university sweetheart, who became a Tory MP. They tried for a baby and failed—six rounds of IVF, countless miscarriages, all culminating in estrangement and an agonizing divorce, one that coincided with the fertility doomsday of her early forties. Her ex now has a baby with his new, much younger Russian bride, a fact she trots out for a laugh, her voice carefree, devoid of bitterness.

"So I'm single now. Perfectly, completely, and utterly free. I didn't expect to end up here, but the funny thing is, I'm happier than I've ever been." Violet's eyes sparkle. My mother looks openly skeptical.

There are other people I could have looked up—friends in New York I've known for longer and haven't seen in years, people I ought to see and reconnect with—but Violet was the only one I could imagine having dinner with my mother on this particular weekend in this particular city. She knows nothing about my past except what I've told her—which, now that I think of it, isn't much.

Violet asks my mother all about her recently published novel and then about retirement, about her husband and the village where she lives, about the snow, about skiing and skating and snowshoeing and other Nordic activities. Mum answers guardedly at first, but soon she's laughing and talking about what a relief it is to be retired, the books she's reading, Basil, the uxorious second husband who takes such good care of her. By the time the second bottle of wine arrives, Mum has settled into her comfort zone and begins dispensing advice on love to Violet.

"It's a long life and you get plenty of chances," she says, patting the tips of Violet's black-varnished nails. "I had a terrible time after my divorce. I thought no one would ever want me again. Then I met Basil. I was fifty when I remarried. I mean, imagine getting remarried to a younger man at fifty? I couldn't believe my luck!"

Violet smiles, gazing benignly at my mother, letting her head fall slightly to one side so that her curls brush my shoulder. She's close to fifty but looks and acts much younger. A woman whom middle age has not succeeded in draining of beauty or energy. I know my mother means well, but I bristle with irritation at her endless talk of marriage. My mother has just listened to Violet's story, and yet she's somehow failed to absorb it.

When it comes to attachment, my mother is torn, pulled in opposite directions by an internal contradiction that makes it difficult for her to feel safe, especially in the company of women. With her sisters, her daughters, even certain friends, my mother perceives every interaction as either a covert threat or an opportunity for one-upmanship. It's as though she were back on the farm again, jockeying for the love of her father, or at the riding club, longing for the monstrous attentions of the Horseman. My mother brought me up to believe that independence was everything, that motherhood and wifehood were a trap. She taught me these lessons, then spent years plotting my wedding and begging me for grandchildren. The dissonance between what my mother claims to want and what she actively desires is a confusion that has followed me through life.

"My husband is so nurturing. I'd be lost without him," Mum is saying to Violet. "I'm just saying, don't give up hope. If it happened to me, it can happen to anyone."

"Well done *you*. I love a happy ending," Violet says, which makes my mother smile. Violet's shoulder presses into mine, just enough to confirm for me the almost imperceptible trace of acid in her tone. My mother takes a sip of wine and nods, satisfied her message has been received. Then she turns her attention back to her plate of grilled hake.

When dinner is done, Mum heads back to the hotel to go to bed, but Violet and I stay on at the restaurant. We order more cocktails as the waitstaff close up around us—vodka and soda for her, gin and tonic for me. When the drinks arrive, I apologize for my mother.

"But why?" Violet says, blinking. "I thought she was divine."

"All the remarriage stuff. I just hope you weren't offended."

Violet laughs and shakes out her curls. "Don't be silly. Aren't all mothers like that, really, when you get right down to it?"

I laugh wearily, then shrug.

"You must need a pick-me-up," Violet says, then taps my knee as she passes me her change purse. I start to object, then smile weakly and begin making my way to the bathroom. I know without asking that the purse will contain a white paper packet wrapped in plastic and filled with high-grade cocaine. It's an awful drug, thrilling, fleeting, like a roller coaster ride that's over before it's started. What it makes you want, more than anything, is more of itself. I never buy it, though when I am offered it, I find it hard to refuse.

Two hours later we are in a low-lit underground piano bar, singing Elton John tunes with an unfunny stand-up comedian we've accidentally befriended. He keeps buying us drinks, which we accept, and offering us drugs, which we decline. Again and again he asks which one of us is married, until eventually Violet shoos him away with a flick of her hand.

"Single men in New York are the worst," she says, grimacing, as the comedian slopes back to his table defeated. "At least Englishmen are up for a bit of banter."

Hours later, we are sprawled in the basement sitting room of Violet's sublet, drinking ginger tea with trembling fingers, waiting for the jitters to subside. I keep threatening to call a cab, and soon I will. But something is holding me back. It's not the fear of being alone but the fear of returning to the hotel room where my mother lies, gently snoring, on her side, slack-jawed, Ativan bottle open on her bedstand.

I want to hear Violet laugh, so to lighten the mood I tell her the story of my childhood. I tell her about the divorce, and Vogrie and Viv the manic-depressive painter and her pot-bellied pig. Then I tell her about theater school and the Chinatown basement and the parties and my mother's disastrous affairs. I describe the past as if I were my mother describing it—affecting a devil-may-care archness, flinging my hands about the room for emphasis. Violet cackles, falling back on the sofa helpless with laughter. Eventually she wipes her eyes with her wrist and lights another cigarette. It's one of those nights that keeps coming to a natural close that both of us are too anxious to acknowledge. The air tightens around us.

"Your mum—she's so *extra*."

I tell Violet we used to be best friends, but since I had the boys, it's been different somehow. Harder. "I've started to question things."

"Like what?"

"All of it, really. The way I grew up. Our closeness. The lack of boundaries. But I can't really be angry at her, or I shouldn't be, because it's not her fault."

Then I tell Violet the story of the Horseman. Just the rough sketch. She is gobsmacked, as everyone is upon first hearing it. I let her absorb the appalling facts then wait for her to ask again, as everyone does, *exactly* how old my mother was when it started.

Then I tell her about the book I am writing. The one that started with the ill-fated search for the Horseman.

"It's a book about victim narratives and what they do to families," I explain to myself as much as to Violet, the words crystallizing into thoughts as I speak them like breath freezing in the air. "It's about all the weird, explosive shit that happens when women tell the truth, especially to each other. You know?"

Violet nods, exhales. Then she remarks brightly on how settled and contented my mother seems.

"You mean smug?"

Violet laughs. "Well, she doesn't exactly radiate damaged victim."

I make a face.

"Well, she *seems* happy."

"She *is* happy. I'm not sure how happy she is with *me*. Do you know what she told me today at brunch?"

Violet looks at me so intently, her pupils seem to pulse.

For a moment I am hypnotized. All the things my mother has ever said seem to flash through my mind, spooling out like scenes from a badly edited home movie. When I was small, she often told me what a well-behaved child I was. *Such a good girl.* Those were the words she used over and over, implanting them in my head, like a mantra. Later, when I was in my teens, my mother marveled at how close we were, how we never fought, attributing it to the fact of my goodness. "You never whined or cried or had tantrums like your sister," she often said, which was not strictly true. I remember acting out. But I accepted it as received truth because it suited us both. After Granny died, my mother started seeing a therapist again, and last summer, while I was visiting her at the cottage with my eldest son—that agonizing, stilted summer visit—Mum mentioned she'd had a revelation. On reflection, she said, her love for me as a child had revealed itself as a kind of narcissism. "I see now, Leah, that your 'goodness' was just an act, a manipulation designed to elicit my love." Then she mentioned the fact I'd gone to theater school. "In a way," she said, "you've always been a little actress."

I do not tell Violet any of these things as I stare into her queer throbbing gaze. But I tell her what my mother said about the terrible things I'd apparently done to my sister.

Violet takes this in then places a firm, dry palm on my knee. I look down, blinking back tears, and notice the black varnish on the nail of her index finger is chipped.

"We fought a lot. I should have been better," I say.

Violet shakes her head.

"I was older, cleverer, more in control. There was this weird game where I dressed up like an evil fairy . . ." My voice quavers. I can't talk about Meg. I can't.

Violet's lips form a single silent *NO.*

"Why not? These things are complicated. Children are complicated."

"Stop!" Violet bangs a fist into the cushion beside her. Her ferocity startles us both. What she says next is serious. Deadly. "Listen to me. She can't put that on you. It's not just that it isn't right—she can't. You were a kid. She was the adult. It was her choice to do whatever it was she did—get divorced, leave your sister behind, shag a married guy, whatever. It's not the end of the world, but they were *her* choices, not yours. She can't blame you for any of it. She can't. That's not how reality works."

"But look—"

Violet glares at me. Her mouth tightens and I see she is furious. I understand that this story reminds her of something else, another story she will not tell me tonight or possibly ever, because, as much as we like each other, we're not actually close. Tomorrow we will trade forlorn joke texts about our hangovers. Violet and I will never mention this conversation again. It will be as if it never happened.

I call an Uber and gather my things unsteadily as Violet empties the ashtray. At the door, she hugs me hard and tight like she means it. I press my head into her wonderful smoky perfumed curls and, as I do, she whispers one last thing in my ear.

"You were just a kid. She's the *mother.*"

18

I⊤ was in the basement apartment on Beverley Street that I met the Peeper. I was fifteen; it was winter. My first winter in Chinatown.

He came to me gently at first. Almost sweetly. He was polite. I say that he came to me, but it wasn't that simple. I summoned him, my body summoned him. It wasn't on purpose. I didn't realize it till the moment he appeared. I was taller by then. My body had rounded out in some places and narrowed in others. All I had to do was stand in a certain way and strange things would happen all around me. On the street. In private. Marvelous, magical occurrences, all of them involving men. I was trying and failing to get the magic under control. It was new and I didn't entirely understand it yet. I'm not putting that forward as an excuse. It's the truth.

I was in my room getting ready for bed one night at Beverley Street. There were no curtains in my room. The window faced onto a tight, dark alley between our building and the one next door where several nights a week an illegal mahjong game raged on into the wee hours, the clattering of tiles and the sharp voices of women talking over each other and erupting into thunderclaps of laughter. The racket exasperated my mother. It kept her up at night. She was nearly forty by then, probably perimenopausal, which is the stage I am in now, so I understand annoyance. But at the time, the mahjong parties didn't really bother me. Soon enough, the rhythms of Cantonese became more familiar, less jagged, predictable. The click and whoosh of the tiles lulled me to sleep.

On this night, however, the alley was silent, a bitter black slice of Toronto winter. My room was dim, lit only by a bedside lamp, tinted pink by the wine-colored nylon scarf I draped over it each night until it started to singe and smoke. I was doing a thing that I did a lot as a child: gazing into the mirror and wondering if I was pretty. It was the big question, the thing that would determine my fate. Was I or wasn't I? People said it wasn't important, but I understood by this point that it was. I'd given up on being tiny; I was too tall for that. But now I was thin, or thinner. I would never be skinny, but prettiness was still a possibility. But the mirror wouldn't tell me the answer. It was a cheap Ikea full-length, which hung askew on my wall beside a Joy Division poster, draped in pottery beads I'd strung myself. I was half-undressed, topless, bothered by the sight of my breasts. They were big, too big for my frame, I'd decided. Pendulous, my mother called them, not meanly; it was true. The left one bigger than the right by an entire cup size. On the stereo was the Smiths' "Reel Around the Fountain." Volume low and crackly on my Radio Shack boom box. My mother was out. It was late. Past midnight.

Tap. Tip-tap.

And there he was. My Peeper in the window. A pleasant face, playful eyes, short blond hair. A thin, dark jogger's warm-up jacket zipped up tight to the chin. Short, or at least not tall. He seemed to be on his tiptoes, so he could lean far enough over the thick basement window ledge to take in the whole of me in the room below, his shoulders quivering with something between effort and excitement, though it might well have been the cold. He may have been standing there for a while, watching. I wasn't sure. But watching wasn't enough. This was why he knocked. He wanted me to see him seeing me; this moment, I realized later, was a crucial turning point in our relationship. And when I did see him, he smiled. Not a menacing smile, but something far more knowing. A smile of complicity.

I opened my mouth to shriek, but just as I did, he raised a hand and pressed a single gloved finger to his lips. As if on command, my mouth clapped shut. This pleased him. He gave a bright little wave and was gone.

In the winter of grade ten, when I am sixteen, my mother goes away on holiday with her best friend Helen, another single editor she works with at the magazine. For ten days they will be in Puerto Escondido, on a wild strip of undeveloped surf beach. My mother is excited; they're meeting Mark Nash, the PhD student from Vogrie. He knows a place where they can stay for a few dollars a day at a remote resort, in huts with sand floors where they sleep on hammocks and eat barbecued whitefish pulled right from the sea. She does not leave a phone number because there are no phones where she's going. I am to stay home alone, which is fine. I am used to being at home alone, during the day or at night, or over the weekends when she goes to the country. I don't blame her for being absent or uncontactable, because I am often absent and uncontactable myself. Like my mother, I'm fine with my own company. I can take care of myself.

But one morning, maybe three or four days into her trip, I get sick. At first it's just a bad sore throat, but then the sore throat gets worse. It hurts to cough, as if the insides of my throat and lungs have been scalded with acid. Maybe it's all the smoking, or singing: I'm in rehearsals for the school show. I skip the rest of my classes and go home on the subway, make myself lemon tea with honey and a capful of my mother's Scotch. I still don't like the taste, but I've noticed she's right: it makes me feel better. I take a handful of Advil, which I carry around in a bottle in my bag and pop like candy because it dulls the persistent ache in my neck and shoulders—the pains I've developed since I traded in food for cigarettes and Diet Coke.

That night I wake up on the sofa bathed in sweat, feeling as if my body were being roasted on a spit. I stumble to my room, where I manage to remove all my clothes before falling into bed, where I am engulfed in a strange, shallow sleep full of waking dreams.

Like this one: The room is still dark. For some reason, I can't move. There is a man in the flat. A strange man. A bad one. I can hear him moving through the flat, shifting things about. He opens the fridge door and closes it, probably because the fridge is empty. He is moving, unhurriedly but inexorably, toward my room. Eventually he opens my bedroom door and stands there awhile, watching me while I pretend to sleep. This dream, which I will have intermittently in different variations throughout my adult life, always ends in the same way. The man moves toward the bed, and as he does, I am suddenly released from whatever invisible bonds have held me back. I spring up, out of sleep, fists flailing, heart pounding. Sometimes I am standing, sometimes shouting.

That's when the phone beside the bed rings. It's Dad. It's early in the morning. He's calling on his way into the city, wondering if I might want to have lunch at the pub near my school after his meeting. This is pretty much the only time we ever see each other now. I no longer go back to Cobourg on weekends; I'm too busy with school and work. I haven't seen or spoken to my sister in months.

"I'd love that," I croak. "But I'm sick."

"You sound terrible, sweetheart," he says. In the background I can hear traffic noise. He's on the 401, on his car phone. "Have you been to the doctor?"

"It's just a cold."

"Did your mother go in to work?"

"She's in Mexico." I know I shouldn't admit this, but I do.

Silence. Traffic noise.

"See you shortly," he says in his skipper voice.

Dad drives straight to the flat on Beverley Street, where he opens the empty fridge, shakes his head, then lights a cigarette and smokes it standing in front of the kitchen sink. He runs the tap to put it out, then looks for a place to throw the butt, but the garbage is overflowing, so he walks down the hall and flushes it down the toilet. Without a word, Dad takes out the bins, then he says he's buying me lunch. I have no interest in food, but he says it's nonnegotiable. I need to eat something.

We drive around the corner to the Bamboo Club, where he orders a club sandwich and I gag down a few spoonfuls of the soup of the day, which is spicy coconut milk. It scalds my chest from the inside out. Over lunch, Dad keeps shaking his head. I can tell he's having an imaginary argument with my mother, the kind he probably still has at 3 a.m. while MJ sleeps soundly beside him in her green satin eye mask. He keeps asking why my mother didn't leave a number. He seems fixated on this detail.

I explain where she is and why we can't reach her, and even if I could, what would I say?

By the time the plates are cleared, Dad is smoking again, asking me one question after the next. Is there no one I could have stayed with? A relative or a friend? Could my grandmother not have moved in for a few days? Or even one of my aunts or uncles? I have no answers to these questions except to say that I'm fine. Even in my weakened state I know better than to say that it's normal for me to be alone. It's been normal since they split. It may not be normal to him, but it is *our* normal. It works for us.

Coffee comes. I try to stir in some Sweet'N Low, but the spoon clatters to the floor. I move to reach for it, but I'm too weak and too tired. Dad shakes his head.

"I'm taking you home with me," he says. "No arguments."

Over the weekend, I lie on the sofa in the TV room of their house in Cobourg while my father's new wife fusses over me with blankets and cold compresses. I barely know her—that's the truth—but this weekend Mary Jane is in her element. She brings me a box of aloe-infused Kleenex and a waste bin. On the coffee table is a wicker basket full of pharmaceuticals: NeoCitran, painkillers, little packets of antacid, chewable children's Tylenol, and the grown-up kind too. Cough syrup with the plastic spoon tucked inside the box. Mary Jane keeps sorting through it and offering to run up to the drugstore, asking if there's anything else I need. She makes me chicken soup, not the kind my mum makes but the kind I like: Lipton's from the packet. Everything is so soft here, quilted, cushioned; the upholstery is trying to suck me up. There's so much food and medicine. The sheer amount of *stuff*—I can't get over it. I think of Anton, Anya's younger son, who became hysterical at the sight of all the food in the grocery store.

On Monday morning, Dad wants to drive me back to the city. I tell him I can take the commuter train and transfer to the subway at Union Station. But he insists, adding he has a meeting later anyway, so I can't argue, though I know he's probably lying. He delivers me to the door of the school and, instead of driving away, he turns off the car and gets out and there, in front of all my friends, folds me into a hug that is so intense, I'm afraid he'll start to cry. I wriggle away from him, embarrassed, but before we part, he grips my arm and I see his eyes are rimmed with red. "Leah, honey," he says, "if you ever need anything, I want you to promise you'll call me, okay?"

"Okay."

"I don't care if it's three in the morning and you're stranded in the middle of a cornfield with a bunch of drunk yahoos or banged up in a Tijuana prison: You call me and I'll come to wherever you are to get you and bring you home. I mean it. Got it, kiddo? Capisce?"

"Yes, Dad." My eyes flick over to where my friends, the drama majors, are standing, blowing the steam off takeout coffees, flicking their morning cigarettes with fingerless gloves.

Dad gets back in the car and I turn away; then, just before he drives off, he sticks his head out the window and shouts something inaudible. Then he shouts it again.

"Call me sometime?"

I laugh and nod. But I don't.

19

THE New Year's Eve open house at 80 Beverley is an annual tradition. All six apartments throw our doors open and people are allowed to mix and mingle, wandering from floor to floor. My mother wears a long, backless green gown with plunging neckline embroidered with delicate golden vines. I pilfered it for her from one of the closets at Vogrie, along with one of the top hats that pop out when you tap them with a stick. Mum and I have spent the day making food and laying it out on the kitchen table as a buffet: angels on horseback and pigs in blankets and blinis with cheap pink caviar.

As soon as it's dark, the guests begin trickling in. At first there's hardly anyone we know; they all float upstairs, bypassing our flat because we're the new tenants. I sense this convergence makes Mum slightly nervous. She fiddles with her hair and fusses around the kitchen, talking to herself in an admonishing voice. "No, no, that won't do," she mutters, adjusting a stack of cocktail napkins. Then: "Come on, Ces, where on earth did you . . . ?" as she rifles through a drawer for a corkscrew. Finally, her friend Helen arrives with her new boyfriend, Rafe. He greets us with kisses then takes their coats to the back room.

I pour Helen a glass of red, then ask her how it's going with Rafe. She sighs, adjusting the silk scarf around her throat.

"Oh, you know. Fine. I'm not getting my hopes up, though."

Helen has enormous brown eyes, pale skin, and fine features. She works as the entertainment editor at the same magazine where Mum does the front of book. Mum says Helen can get away with wearing her hair cropped short because she's so feminine. Not that it matters. Like my mother, Helen is now single in her forties, which means she has a better chance of getting killed in a terrorist attack than finding a husband. Her dream is to adopt a baby girl from China. She was just about to start the process; then she met Rafe.

"So have you told him yet?"

Helen sighs and takes a tiny sip of wine. "I keep trying, but it just seems like such a buzzkill."

"Maybe he'll think it's romantic. You never know."

She snorts. "Yeah, I'm sure it'll get him all hot and bothered."

"You just need to be subtle about it."

Helen gives me a quizzical side-eye. I've been cultivating a sideline as a teenaged agony aunt who dispenses advice to adults on life dilemmas I know nothing about. Sometimes I'm serious—with Mum, for instance—but other times I just make stuff up for the entertainment value.

I remind Helen that Valentine's Day isn't far away. "Maybe you should put on a negligee, light some candles, then scatter rose petals on the bed, and when he comes in, be, like, 'Hey, big boy, I was thinking one day in the not-too-distant future we could get a hotel suite next to an orphanage in Shanghai . . . ?'"

She strokes her chin, pretending to be thoughtful. "Okay, but how do I break it to him about the money? Adoption is expensive. I mean, the poor guy, he works in publishing."

"First you need to give him a hand job in a bubble bath; then, once he's super-relaxed, appeal to his practical side. Say something like 'Look, *I know* you had your heart set on giving me a five-carat diamond and a massive wedding in the Bahamas, but instead I was thinking we could use the money to pay an adoption agency to hook us up with a foundling we could save from life under totalitarian rule.'"

She laughs. "I like it."

"I mean, what forty-three-year-old bachelor doesn't fantasize about foreign adoption?"

"I'm worried he's a closet commitment-phobe."

We look over at Rafe, who is wearing an apron that says *Kiss the Cook* and helping my mother by sprinkling chives over a platter of deviled eggs.

"Anyway, it doesn't matter," Helen says. "I'm doing it with or without him. I want the real thing. Unconditional love. Just look at you two."

"Who?"

"You and Cecily. You're so close. I'm envious."

The Editor and his wife arrive. Helen and I walk over to greet them and the Editor's wife presents my mother with a potted amaryllis, which she graciously accepts, complimenting the Editor's wife on her manners; one of my mother's rules is that polite guests never bring cut flowers because it creates a hassle for the hostess.

The Editor and I brush cheeks while silently pursing our lips, which my mother says is the Toronto version of a European kiss. I ask him what he'd like to drink and he requests a beer, so I fetch one for him and another for myself. We clink bottles.

"I like your dress," he says.

I'm wearing a see-through gauze sack dress—an old slip, really. Like my mother's gown, it came from Vogrie and smells of mothballs. But it shows off my new tortured collarbones.

"It's vintage."

"Isn't that just a fancy word for old?"

I roll my eyes. Across the room, Rafe is trying to contain the froth of a just-opened bottle of cava.

"When do people become vintage?" the Editor asks.

I cock my head, pondering this. "For women? Forty."

"And men?"

"Maybe seventy? Eighty if you're rich. It's fucking unfair."

He laughs. "Don't let your mother hear you talking like that. She's a feminist."

"So am I," I say with genuine indignation. "But I'm also a realist."

He likes this. In fact, he *loves* it. I can tell by the way his lips are wrestling with each other, fighting to conceal a smile.

"I guess we're finally having that beer, then?"

"What beer?"

The alcohol is humming in my veins, steadying me to the point where I am able to stand there, perfectly still, staring at him coolly.

"How would I know what's appropriate?" I shrug. "I'm still in high school."

The Editor rocks back on his heels laughing, then coughing.

"You don't talk like a schoolgirl," he says.

"How many teenagers do you hang out with?"

He shakes his head, puts a hand to his brow. "That's not what I— Christ. This conversation isn't going well, is it? What I mean to say is that you're exceptionally wise for your age."

I laugh. "You sound like my mother."

Someone comes over and compliments the Editor on his recent interview with Noam Chomsky and asks what he was like in person. I wander upstairs to Asna's apartment, where I take a margarita off a tray, then run into Dale, Sarah's son from LA. Sarah lives on the third floor. Dale's father kicked him out.

"Yo," he says, flicking his Lakers cap.

"Having fun yet?"

Dale shrugs and adjusts his balls, which float somewhere in the eviscerated sack of his low-slung jeans, each leg of which could easily accommodate the weedy whole of him. He's sixteen, but unlike me he's not in school. His fed-up Dad apparently put him on a flight to Toronto after he got into unspecified trouble with the LAPD. Mum said it involved a gun. Within a week of arriving, Dale was hanging out with the squeegee punks in the park, the kids with the green and purple mohawks who beg for spare change on the corner clumped around pit bulls. They're not so bad, he insists, even if their music is shit.

"Smoke?" he says. I accept a Camel and let him light it with his Zippo. "Seen my house bitch?"

He means Beila, Asna's teenaged daughter. She's an inverse reflection of her glamorous Lebanese mother: sour and awkward, painfully shy. Apart from glowering at me on the communal stairs, Beila has refused to acknowledge my presence since we moved in last fall. Mum says it must be hard for her, as if being the daughter of a beauty like

Asna would put anyone in a permanent bad mood. According to Dale, he's been having sex with Beila since the first week he arrived.

"Nope," I say, draining my margarita and lifting another from a passing tray. "Aren't you drinking?"

"Nah, parole thang."

I gasp. Dale gives a wheezy laugh. "Take a fuckin' joke. I be bangin' on the grind, yo."

"Dale, I literally have no idea what you're saying."

"Yo bitch, I'm fuckin' flying. Can't you tell?"

He leans in so close, the brim of his cap brushes my forehead. His eyes are flat and empty, pupils like hockey pucks. I attempt a French inhale and fail, sputtering. Dale grins.

Across the kitchen, I notice our landlord, Charlie, whispering a joke into the ear of a tiny witchy-looking woman in a felt hat, who I'm pretty sure is a famous novelist. I make a mental note to mention this celebrity sighting to my mother. When I turn back to Dale, I can see he still wants to talk about drugs.

"Shit's good, yo."

"What exactly are you on?"

"Mini Mitsubishi."

Again I have no idea what he means, but I can tell with a little cajoling he will give me some. I touch his forearm and smile. *Sharing is caring*, I say with my eyes.

"Put your hand in my pocket," he instructs.

"Isn't that kind of obvious?"

"Just do it."

I roll my eyes and stick my hand in his jeans. The pocket is dry, and apparently bottomless. I feel around a bit until my fingers accidentally skim the limp tentacle of his cock. He groans, jaw juddering, pretending to come.

"God, you're gross." I dip my hand into a nearby wine cooler and wipe it on the front of my dress.

"You should blow me for this," he says, pressing an aspirin-sized pill into the palm of my hand. "Beila would."

"I bet."

"I know you think she's a bitch, but she's better brought up than you."

"Sounds like it."

"At least her mother locks the door at night."

I clap my palm to my mouth, dry-swallowing the pill.

I make my way to the third-floor apartment, which is occupied by a potter named Terry and her adult daughter, Alexa, a PhD candidate in anthropology who used to be Alex. There are candles burning everywhere, orange shadows quaver on the walls. A small, reverent crowd has gathered on the floor in front of Alexa, who is playing guitar and doing a low-key-but-impressive Stevie Nicks impersonation. When she sees me, she nods and tosses her hair. I sit cross-legged on the carpet in front of Alexa, watching her play for the better part of an hour. The veins in her hands are mesmerizing.

"Do you mind if I take a break?" she says finally. "My throat's a bit dry."

I jump up and fetch her a beer from a nearby cooler. Alexa doesn't seem to know what to do with it, so I open it on my forearm.

She hoots. "Where'd you learn that, little girl?"

"In a ravine."

LATER I'm downstairs, on the bottom floor, drinking fizzy wine and chatting to Dennis, the boyfriend of my mother's work friend Robert. Dennis has a boring job in government, which he compensates for by being insanely funny.

"So. How did you do it?" he asks, sliding his wire spectacles down his nose, then standing back to appraise my body.

"Do what?"

"Don't tell me you're bulimic?"

"Gross, no. I had a threesome at a pool party and then my best friend broke up with me and for a while I lost my appetite."

Dennis's hands fly to his throat in mock horror. "Oh god. Are you a baby lesbian?"

"I'm pretty sure it was a onetime thing."

"So why did she dump you?"

"She said I was 'too intense,' which is true, but really I think she was weirded out by all the gossip. Anyway, I miss her."

"I get it, honey. High school sucks."

Dennis's gaze slides wistfully across the room to Robert, who is pulling a gold Speedo over the Editor's wife's head so he can take a Polaroid. "Sometimes I wish Robert would break up with me. Just for a few weeks. It would slim me right down."

"You look great!"

"Not from behind. I've got fat-ass disease. It's a rare genetic condition that afflicts just under twenty percent of monogamous gay men."

Laughing makes my vision skitter. Light smears across the walls. Someone has put on "Sympathy for the Devil." The kitchen island is vibrating; platters of food seem to lift and hover, shuddering just over the surface. More worryingly: my jaw is wired shut.

"It's incurable," Dennis continues. "Since I was like, even younger than you, I've only been able to weigh myself naked first thing in the morning after an enormous shit."

"Let's dance!" I grab Dennis's hand and tug him toward where my mother is.

"With *you*?" He wags his head and politely withdraws. "Sorry, hon, gay dad at the prom is a bad look."

"Oh, come on, you're *gorgeous*." I reach round and help myself to a handful of Dennis's corduroy rump. He shrieks and bats me away, then sees something across the room that makes him freeze. He whirls round and claps his hands over my eyes. "Oh, no, oh, dear god. *Don't look*. You're much too young to see this."

I peel his fingers off my eyelids and peer into the pot smoke scrim of the raised sitting room. It's like a stage, and upon it my mother is up and whirling in circles, green gown flying around her legs, head lifted, back arched, arms flung wide and wanting, as if begging the heavens for rain. There are others dancing around her, but she might as well be the only one in the room. Behind her, cross-legged on the sofa, the Editor sits bent over, head down, shaking from side to side, absorbed in the mystery of his bongos.

I shrug, baffled.

Dennis laughs. "I thought you'd be embarrassed."

"Why?"

"Hello? She's your mother."

I make a face at Dennis then run to join my mother. She smiles and we spin round and round each other for song after song, sweaty and laughing, the Editor goading us on with his drums. Someone turns off the music and my mother and I count down to midnight, then kiss each other right on the lips just like we did when I was little.

EVENTUALLY I tell my mother about the Peeper. I don't want to alarm her, but I have no one else to tell. We are drinking coffee from the French press, strong, bitter espresso. The *Globe and Mail* is spread out on the table. Mum is reading a story in the arts section. The CBC news is on the radio.

"I've got a stalker," I say.

At first she doesn't hear me. Then she looks up as if waking from a dream. "A what?"

"A Peeping Tom, I mean. Anyway, I thought you should know."

"What does he look like?"

"He's actually kind of handsome. Blond. A jogger, I think."

"Probably harmless," Mum says. "A voyeur. Has he ever approached you?"

"No, no," I say. "He just sort of stands there watching. And if I don't notice he knocks to let me know he's there. But then he runs away."

"A coward pervert?" Mum laughs. "The banality of evil."

This is one of my mother's favorite concepts, like the presence of an absence or life imitating bad art. It always pleases her to point it out. She sighs and folds the paper shut.

"I suppose we'd better get you some blinds. Maybe on the weekend we can walk over to Spadina."

"Don't bother," I say. "I'll just tack up some of the scarves from Vogrie. It'll go better with my room."

The look is meant to be "vintage goth." Joni's idea. We painted it dusky lavender and papered the borders with black-and-white art photographs ripped from Mum's old *New Yorkers*. For my birthday Joni gave me a blue beaded curtain from Kensington Market, which I nailed up in the door frame. My hair gets caught in it but I won't take it down.

Mum shrugs. I'm relieved. I don't want her poking around my window, because she'll notice that I've removed the screen. That's how I sneak out at night to see my new boyfriend. His name is Max. I met him at a midnight madness screening of *The Rocky Horror Picture Show*. He's a violinist.

At night, I am visited by either Max or the Peeper. They seem to alternate. I suppose this is what it's like to be popular.

The Peeper only comes when my light is on, peering through the gauzy scrim of vintage scarves that does not entirely obscure the view inside. Do I know this? I'm sure I do, but I'd rather not think about it. The scarves are always falling down, unpinned from thumbtacks I've used to affix them to the window frame. Especially with me climbing in and out of the window all the time. Sometimes the scarves fall down completely, and he always seems to know. *Tip-tap. Tap.* I look up, he smiles, and then he's gone.

Max, on the other hand, wakes me in the middle of the night when he wants to talk. Sometimes I sneak him into my room. Or we go to the park and push each other high on the swings. We smoke and talk and make out for hours in the cold. It does not occur to me to set limits on Max's visits. There are no cell phones in 1991, no Internet connections. Knocking on windows, sneaking out at night—this is what feral teenagers do.

I SPEND my school days in a blur, snacking from the bottomless ziplock bag of magical fungus I buy from Teddy the drug dealer and pack for lunch each day. Taken in small quantities, mushrooms lift my spirits. The fluorescent classroom lights streak in the corners of my vision. They help me to focus, though at times the emotional effect is intense. In History of the Second World War, Mr. Chessler shows fifteen carefully vetted minutes of the Holocaust documentary *Shoah*, and when he flicks on the lights, my face is a bath of tears. In African Dance, I pump my pelvis to the drumbeat for an hour. The dance teacher whoops. "Nice lines," she says. The mushrooms are indeed magic: they take away my need for food and make it easy to drift through the halls. I swirl them down with cans of cold Diet Coke, bought from the machine in the caf. Teddy the drug dealer is now my friend. He says he's only dealing to save up for a vintage VW so he can drive to Vancouver and see his girlfriend. He charges me ten bucks a gram, fifteen for two. I'm bad at math, but Teddy is worse. His discount is a loss leader. I'm putting him out of business.

One night Max comes to my window and rouses me from a deep sleep.

"Go away," I say. I have early rehearsal tomorrow.

"Dance with me," he says.

My ears prick. Is he being romantic?

"Dance with me. Come on!"

I stare rapturously up at the shadow in the window. "Really?"

"Yes!" he hisses. "*Dance* with me. C'mon."

I pull on a sweatshirt and scramble out the window, my whole body throbbing with excitement. Maybe I will sleep with him, I think. He's madly in love with me; it's a grand gesture. Max's trench coat is backlit by the streetlight. I think I might be in love with him too. He takes my hand and helps me down, and as I descend, I notice he's placed an old kitchen chair in front of the window to make it easier for me to get down. One chair leg is broken and I nearly topple off, but he steadies me like a gentleman.

"Thank you," I say, motioning to the chair.

He shrugs and offers me a smoke, then mumbles, "Token of my affection."

I look up and see another figure, lurking in the shadow of the alley.

"Max!" I hiss, pushing my fingers into his arm. "Look."

"What?" he says. "It's just my friend Dan. I told you."

Dance with me. *Dan's with me.*

I have sex with Max two days later, in a rented practice room at the

Royal Conservatory of Music. To my astonishment, it doesn't hurt at all. Not only do I want to do it again this time, I think I might become good at it. I want to hone my talent. Max and I resolve to practice.

WHEN I sneak out to see him, Max always makes a point of walking me home. He steadies the broken chair, waits at the window, and watches to make sure I press down the cheap plastic lock. He will not leave until I do. I fall back in bed shivering, dry-mouthed, smelling of Turkish tobacco.

One night Max arrives at my window sweating and panting. He explains that he and Dan spotted the Peeper lurking in an alley a couple of streets over. They gave chase, tailing him all the way down the block and across Spadina before he vanished in the loading docks behind Dragon City. I know I should feel grateful, that Max has been heroic, but instead I find the story unsettling. Until then I'd believed the Peeper was mine somehow. Like an imaginary friend, he'd seemed a creature of my own invention. Just as surely as I'd summoned him I believed I could make him disappear. This conviction, I understand, is the reason I never feel scared like other girls. It's the reason I can walk the alleys alone at night.

LATER that winter I am sleeping in my bed at Beverley Street when a sound penetrates the crypt of my adolescent coma. A knock, followed by a crack—or is it the shifting?—of something plastic, the tinkle of keys or pocket change, a swish of fabric. Not a faint sound. I surface. The swish of effort—someone else's, not mine. The push of effort, hard and near. Frustration. An irritated grunt. The air turns to ice.

"Max?"

The jangling stops. No answer. I sit up, fumble blindly for the switch on the cord of my bedside lamp. I can't find it. The swishing, the jingling again, this time faster, urgent.

The switch. The fucking switch.

Light floods the room.

The Peeper is hanging over the window ledge. The upper half of his torso is in my room and his arms reach for me. At this angle, his arms are cartoonishly long. He's grimacing, distracted by the effort of getting to the place he wants to be. Blue nylon warm-up jacket zipped to the throat, as always. When he sees me, he tries to smile, but he can't. He will, the half smile promises. *Gimme a second.* He's balanced in a way that means if he shifts much farther, he will fall. My bed is beneath him, it's a short drop, maybe four feet. I am on my bed, positioned to cushion his fall. He's not scared, just persistent. Soon he will be on top of me. It's inevitable, the pull of gravity. Instead of falling, he reaches toward me, imploring, beseeching. He's asking me for something, but what? An invitation? A kiss?

His eyes. Those I will never forget. Blue like mine but different. Pale eyes, almost white around the pupils, like a sled dog's. I understand that I *was* imagining things. Before, I mean. The first time he tapped. The Peeper's eyes are not polite. They are playful, but that is not the same thing.

This time I scream. Crazy-shrieking, gulping for air like a girl in a horror movie. He freezes, looking ridiculous. He's still hanging over the sill, keys tinkling cheerily in his pocket. I continue to scream and his face closes. He gives me a wounded look, like he's not mad, just deeply disappointed. But I keep screaming, I can't stop, and he scrambles back out into the alley and I am still screaming after he disappears into the night. I sit up straight in my bed and scream and scream until the room is freezing and I am still screaming when my mother flicks on the overhead light and stumbles toward me in her nightgown, wraps me in a duvet, and says, "Shhhhhh, you're okay. Everything is going to be okay."

THE next day, an officer from 52 Division comes to the apartment and jots down notes in a tiny pad as I describe the Peeper. I tell him about the first time and the last time but leave out all the times in between. I want to keep the story short, uncomplicated. Mum is there and so is our landlord, Charlie. He seems genuinely concerned, but I'm also worried his concern is cloaking something else—a suspicion or a deeper truth. I am, after all, a *bad girl.* The kind who sneaks out at night. Charlie flits about the kitchen making nervous jokes, talking of security and petty crime and recent Vietnamese mafia killings on Spadina. It used to be much worse here, he says. Five years ago the alleys were choked with rats.

The cop is implacable. Mid-twenties. Slight. Face the shape and color of a boneless chicken breast. Does he know I'm lying by omission? I've never interacted with a cop before, apart from the ones who occasionally saunter down into the ravines in the summer to bust up parties and confiscate beer. *All right, kids! Party's over.*

The cop keeps his hat on in the house, nodding as he writes. He asks permission to see my room, then politely removes his shoes. The beaded curtain sways and clicks behind him. Gingerly, he steps up onto my single bed and inspects the window above. His fingers flick at the cheap plastic latch—unbroken—and he rifles vaguely through the heap of fallen translucent scarves on the sill as if it were a sack of wet garbage in which he doesn't expect to find a murder weapon. Then we follow him out to the alley and stand behind him, all of us staring at the three-legged kitchen chair that lies toppled over under my window.

"This yours?" He seems to be directing the question at the chair itself.

"Well, it's certainly not mine," says Charlie.

"The neighbors," Mum says, gesturing to the right. "They keep all sorts of junk hanging around. Also, they play mahjong till the wee hours. Can you do something about that?"

The cop sighs. "Look, it's Chinatown."

"I just thought I'd mention it," Mum says. "I'm not trying to muddy the waters. Though I have made several complaints, to no avail."

"Eventually they'll sell," Charlie says to Mum. Then, to the cop: "The neighborhood is changing."

The policeman nods and flips through his notes. To my mother he says, "You might consider getting your daughter some curtains."

Mum's eyes narrow. I stiffen.

"Well, as a matter of fact, Officer, I offered, but my daughter said she'd prefer to tack up scarves. Far be it from me—"

I'm halfway down the alley and at the front door by the time she finishes the thought.

We all go back inside, because it's cold. The cop stands in the apartment door. The radio attached to his shoulder harness bleats. A woman's voice crackles a string of numbers. The cop pokes at the buttons, squinting at his shoulder, and eventually on the third try he manages to switch it off. He hikes up his navy trousers, weighed down by a belt and holster. I cannot bring myself to look at his gun. Finally, it seems, he's ready to leave.

"We've had a few similar complaints in the area. So if we hear anything, we'll be in touch." Then he turns to me, raises a finger, and gives a wink that is somewhere between a geography teacher and a lounge singer. "You be careful, young lady."

Charlie puts his hands on my shoulders and gives them a squeeze as Mum ushers the cop out. When she returns, we stand there in silence and for one eternal second the three of us—me, Mum, and Charlie—are like a nuclear family.

When I come home from school the next day, a workman is attaching a set of heavy, curved wrought iron bars on the outside of my window, compliments of Charlie. A few days later, Mum comes home from work with a set of blinds and screws them in manually, swearing under her breath.

That night, when Max knocks, I leave through the front door. I take my keys. It makes no difference. My mother doesn't wake, or maybe she's not home. The point is, I walk out the front door.

Why didn't I think of this before?

20

AFTER leaving Violet's, I slip into the New York hipster hotel room just after 3 a.m., easing the door shut behind me. Mum is out cold, curled up on her side. I tug off my clothes and swallow an Ativan from the open bottle on her bedside table. Then I climb the ladder and tumble into a restless, dream-filled sleep.

A few hours later, when a gray dawn light is creeping into the room, I wake up sobbing. These episodes started after Frankie's birth. I'd awake utterly bereft and cry for a minute or two for no apparent reason. My therapist said it was related to the PTSD. That was two years ago now. It rarely happens anymore, but it does happen that morning in New York. My mother stands beside my bunk, her head level with mine. I can see half her face through the slats. She reaches over the bed frame and strokes my head.

"My little Leah," she says. "What's wrong? Are you sick? Why are you crying?"

My sobs are contracting like train cars slamming into each other on the track. Whatever made me cry is slipping away from me, receding into the mist of my subconscious.

"What is it?" Mum says. "You poor thing. How can I help?"

My mind casts about for an explanation. My mother's hand is warm and dry on my forehead. I want to say the right thing to make it last.

My mother's palm on my head, the soft pad of her thumb brushing away my tears.

"It's just a dream," she says, shushing me gently, stroking my head, my hair, my neck. "Go back to sleep, Pumpkin. Go back to sleep. You're okay."

AFTER a breakfast of coffee, Mum and I continue our interview on the lower bunk of our hotel room. We talk for so long, we both end up lying back on the bed, toe to head, like a double therapy session in which each of us is both therapist and patient. We know we should go out, see the sights, that it's silly to spend half a weekend in New York, a city we've both flown into from a great distance, just lounging around talking. But I am hungover because I drank and took drugs last night and she is tired because she's old and far from home. The weather is terrible. And talking is easy. It's what we do best.

CR: Motherhood requires a great deal of self-abnegation. You have to put someone else's interests ahead of your own. You have to. And that's a lot to ask of any person. I thought I was doing what I did for all of us.

LM: Do you still feel that way?

CR: No. I was rationalizing. I mean, I broke up a family, but honestly, Leah, I was suffocating. I couldn't breathe. I *literally* couldn't breathe. I remember we decided to take a little weekend holiday skiing at Blue Mountain. We were all sharing a room. It rained the whole time. It was just awful. We couldn't ski. I locked myself in the bathroom because I couldn't stop crying. I was sobbing and sobbing and sobbing. And crying and crying and crying. It just went on for hours. Eventually, Dad just took you girls out to eat.

LM: What did Dad say?

CR: Your father thought that there was something the matter with me. Mainly because I didn't want to have sex with him anymore, I think. So it was decided I should talk to someone. So I read a magazine profile of Vivian Rakoff, the head of the Clarke Institute, and I wrote him a letter. You know his son is David Rakoff, the writer who died? Tragic. Anyway, his secretary called me up and said Dr. Rakoff would like to see you. So I drove in to Toronto to see him. At the time, he was researching a book on incest in families. And I think he'd misread my letter and thought somehow I'd had a relationship with my father. But once he realized his mistake, he just completely lost interest in me and told me to go home to my children and try to make my marriage work.

LM: Did you tell him about the thing? With your riding instructor?

CR: Yeah, he didn't care. He was, like, Get out of here.

[Mutual laughter.]

ONE night in grade ten, in the basement flat on Beverley Street, Max and I fall asleep on the sofa, limbs tangled, in a state of partial undress. When Mum comes in and finds us, she explodes in sudden rage.

"Get up," she is saying. "Up, up, *up!* I will not have this, Leah. Do you hear me? I will not have it!"

Max and I scramble off the sofa, fumbling with buttons and bra straps, trying to cover ourselves with the blanket. Mum has met Max before. She knows he's my boyfriend, but she doesn't really know him. She walks to the open kitchen, pours herself a Scotch, then sits down at the table, where she leafs through the latest issue of the *New Yorker*, left hand plucking the hair on the crown of her head.

Max leaves.

After he goes, I tell my mother she's embarrassed me. I don't understand why she shouted. He's my boyfriend, I probably said. *I'm in love with him.* But she is not in the mood to explain herself. Or maybe she doesn't feel she needs to.

"Drop it, Leah." This has always been her signal flare. "I'm telling you to *drop it now.*"

A COUPLE of weeks later, I push open the door to the flat on Beverley Street and find my mother sitting at the kitchen table with Helen. It's late afternoon, too early for Mum to be home from work. On the table between the women is an open bottle of wine. Two glasses and an ashtray. The air is blue with smoke. My mother's face is pink and swollen. In front of her is a pile of soiled tissues. She doesn't speak. Helen rubs her hand. I tear off my headphones. The urgency of Shostakovich is swapped suddenly for the lull of Joan Armatrading. Mum looks at me and shakes her head, saying nothing.

"There were layoffs at the magazine today," Helen says, her black eyes probing mine. Helen is my favorite of all my mother's friends.

"I wasn't laid off," Mum says bitterly. "I was fired."

"Ces, it's a fucking *recession*," Helen says. "There were cutbacks."

"Maybe so, but Kevin hates me. You were at the meeting."

I know all about the "meeting." It was a pitch session at the magazine. In Mum's section there's a space that she and Helen have dubbed the "babe box." Each week there's a short illustrated profile of an attractive young woman doing . . . something of note. Ideally in a bathing suit. It doesn't much matter what the thing is. The editor in chief never says this, of course, but everyone gets it. The babe offers a touch of sizzle to an otherwise dry, stolid Canadian news package, written and edited exclusively by men, which is understandable, since its readership comprises primarily people in dentists' offices and retired accountants in Edmonton. But at this particular pitch meeting Mum thought, *Why not mix it up?* Instead of pitching a typical hottie for the babe box, she pitched a short profile of a Canadian Paralympian: a woman, yes, an admirable role model, but also a middle-aged amputee in a wheelchair. Predictably, the editor in chief shrugged and asked, "What else do you have?" So Mum started reading her list of potential babes, each one more ludicrously bimbo-like than the last, until she scraped the bottom of the babe barrel—a mother-daughter burlesque act. The entire staff had laughed. Everyone, that is, except the editor in chief.

"And with that, my goose was cooked." Mum drags a finger across her throat and makes a slitting noise. Then she lights a new cigarette off the butt of her old one.

"Go in on Monday and talk to Wendy in HR," Helen says. "She'll make sure you get a good package."

Mum considers this in silence. The next thing she says is directed at me.

"Obviously we'll have to move. I can't afford to live like this—not as an unemployed single mother." She sweeps her hand around our basement flat.

I pull off my coat and try to hang it on the overloaded rack, but it slips to the floor, landing on top of a jumble of slushy boots. A wave of outrage rises in my chest. I whirl around and shout at my mother. "Why do we always have to move? Why is that always the answer to everything? Why can't we stay put for five seconds and figure it out?"

Mum bursts into tears again. "What? So now it's my fault?"

Helen gets up and puts on the kettle.

"Can't you just get another job like a normal person?"

Mum and I engage in a scornful staring contest. Helen breaks it up.

"Of *course* she will, Leah. Ces, you *will*." Another hand pat. "We're all just reeling at the moment."

Mum pours herself more wine.

"Leah, do you want a glass?" Helen asks.

I glare at Mum. "I have homework?"

"Don't be rude."

I stalk down the hall to my room. I'd slam the door if it wasn't a beaded curtain. I flop down on my bed in my combat boots. I put in my headphones and press Play. Closing my eyes, I luxuriate in the brass-slamming outrage of the symphony's final movement. I imagine Max as a dashing Bolshevik revolutionary wielding his musket in a long wool coat. Behind him, tanks roll through the streets of Petrograd.

A few days later Dad drives into the city and takes me out for one of our regular lunches at the pub near my school. Dad has a burger and a pint. I order a Diet Coke and a Caesar salad, no croutons, dressing on the side. When it arrives, we both laugh at the fact that I've ordered a bowl of lettuce. Dad asks if I want dessert, but I tell him I'm fine. After paying the bill, Dad pulls out his checkbook and writes twelve postdated signed checks for three hundred dollars each. He explains it's the child support he normally pays to Mum. Now he'll pay it to me. "Try to spend it on school stuff," he says. "Or food."

Mum languishes around the flat for weeks, catching up on back issues of the *New Yorker* and complaining how poor we are, highlighting rental listings for cheaper apartments, fretting whether or not Charlie will let us out of our lease. Then one morning something changes. I find her already dressed and reading the arts section of the paper. She's wearing her best jeans and fresh mascara. The kitchen smells of coffee and styling mousse. Her hair has been blow-dried. She offers to poach me an egg, but I decline. She asks how rehearsals for the school show are going and I shrug. She announces in a mildly chuffed tone that she has plans for the following evening. Basil, the head librarian at *Maclean's*, has left a message on our answering machine, asking if he can take her out for dinner.

"So you're going on a date?"

My mother scrunches her face and flaps her hands.

"God, no, he's younger than me. We barely even know each other. I think he just feels sorry for me."

"Mum, you are aware that none of those things actually *preclude* him taking you on a date?"

She thinks it over. "I don't think it's a date. Do you?"

Basil arrives to pick her up on Saturday night carrying two dozen long-stem roses wrapped in pink tissue and tied with a ribbon. The next day I ask Mum if she still actually thinks it wasn't a date. I pump her for details about the evening, but she's unusually circumspect. She shrugs and turns back to Anita Brookner's *Hotel du Lac*.

It takes a while, but eventually my mother decides she approves of Max. She thinks he's handsome because he's tall and dark "like Heathcliff, striding across the moors"—apparently unbothered by the fact that Heathcliff was a sociopathic rapist. The real reason she likes Max is because he's a natural with my mother. He's charming, poised, mildly flirtatious without being untoward. He calls her Ces, using the diminutive. When Max stays for dinner he obliges the adults by giving a short recital. Always the same piece: Bach's Partita no. 3 in E Major. Just the opening bit. He's been practicing it for a recital at the Conservatory, where he studies. He plays it so much in the time we are together that even decades later when I hear it, my scalp tingles.

"If only I was young and beautiful like you, Leah," my mother takes to remarking wistfully during this time. "Then I could find someone to love me too." It doesn't bother me that my mother is openly envious that I have a boyfriend. She's happy for me. Both things can be true.

Mum goes into therapy again and this time she has a breakthrough: Richard and the Horseman, she and her therapist decide, are versions of the same man. Not in real life, obviously, but in her psyche. I already know the Horseman is the reason she married my father and had children so young. He's also the reason she divorced my father. But the Richard revelation is new. It was because of her unprocessed trauma, Mum explains, that she was unable to extract herself from Richard's clutches for so long. Loving him felt familiar, she explains, almost inevitable, mystically fated. Sitting at opposite ends of the filthy, comfy cream sofa, Mum and I marvel for hours over the parallels between Richard and the Horseman. The shame and the agony of an illicit, unrequited love for a callous, undeserving predator. Dark as they are, these talks fill me with hope: my mother is finally moving on.

When Max comes over my mother includes him in conversation about her therapy. He's insightful and sympathetic. His parents are on the verge of divorce. His mother, an art teacher, suffers migraines and cries a lot too. His father is a Marxist law professor and failed tenor in the full grip of midlife crisis. He roams around the house singing *La Traviata* while his eldest son dims the lights and holds a compress to his mother's head. On the nights when Max stays over, we talk to my mother about Richard and the Horseman and try to hide our impatience. Max and I are having a collective teenaged revelation of our own—one that makes us count down the minutes until we can go to bed and fuck.

One morning when Max and I sit down for breakfast, my mother is in a sour mood.

"It sounded like someone was dying last night," she grumbles without looking up from the paper. "Can you two please keep it down?"

21

CR: But then I started seeing this therapist called Diane something. A farmer's wife. I remember driving out to Roseneath for my first appointment and, oh, gosh, it was a beautiful winter's day, bright and sunny, snow on the fields, and I felt so happy and exhilarated, and on the radio in the car Chopin's Piano Concerto no. 2 was playing and I was so filled with great joy. And so I got to her place. It was this very stolid brick farmhouse, you know, two and a half stories, and I remember following her up, up, up the stairs to her office at the top of the house. Then we sat down in this room and I just broke down and sobbed. That's all I did for a whole hour. I couldn't even talk.

LM: Oh, Mum . . .

CR: And then I'd come home and because your father was paying for these sessions, he wanted reports. But it felt like the only thing that was mine. And I didn't want to share it.

LM: You're not supposed to have to share it.

CR: Yes, well, we didn't know that then. And also the idea was that I was doing this for my marriage and so at some point we were meant to go in and see her together. But I deeply, deeply didn't want that to happen, because I was convinced—absolutely convinced—that once we did that, she would suddenly see what a bad person I was and what a good person he was. And I didn't want that to happen. But finally we went and saw her together. And then your dad saw her on his own. And he told me after what she said to him was "All I can do is make it easier for this to happen, because she's already left you."

LM: How did she know that? I mean, how did you come to that conclusion in your sessions?

CR: I don't remember exactly. But I do remember writing a long, long letter for her to read. It was all about what happened with [the Horseman]. I had to write it out, I guess, because I couldn't actually talk about it. I felt like I was coming apart. Like my whole self was covered in tiny fissures. It was the most painful thing I've ever gone through. It was huge, and I did it really badly. I was desperate. It was like falling out of an airplane. I did it all wrong.

LM: Do you think the thing with [the Horseman] was why it all unraveled?

CR: Well, I did for a long time. But my current therapist, she doesn't think so. She thinks I am the way I am because of being the eldest child in a large family with a mother who just didn't have the resources to give me the attention I needed. I mean, I remember just hating it every time another baby came along. I remember just hating all of them. Resenting my siblings so much.

Dad loved Kate the most. She was so fragile and pretty, pretty. Very passive. And when Kate was in her teens and she had a breakdown, what did Dad do? He found a psychiatrist for her to talk to about it. But did he do that for me after everything I went through with [the Horseman]? No. Did anyone ever even ask me how I felt about it? I never even knew if my mother knew! We never had a conversation about it. I think from then on Dad felt I was a bad influence. He was always kind to me, and loving, but there was this feeling that he saw me as corrupt somehow. Maybe he couldn't help it. But I could sense it.

LM: Why do you think he didn't go to the police?

CR: Oh, god, can you imagine? All their friends, the whole town, knowing? No, no, the shame would have been unbearable. I was twelve years old, but I was also physically mature. I looked like a woman. I think because of that alone I would have been blamed.

LM: But he didn't punish you, did he? A lot of men of his era would have.

CR: No, no, my father didn't really punish. He grounded me for three weeks. And he brought my horse back from the riding club. Then he offered to pay me fifteen dollars a week to take care of the horses in our barn, I think as a way of keeping me close to home. But he wasn't paying very close attention. [*Pause.*] It went on for years.

EIGHT weeks after getting fired, Mum finds another job—as the culture editor for *Chatelaine*, a women's magazine that is owned by the same company as *Maclean's*. With the windfall from the severance package, Mum puts a deposit on a small house in the West Annex. Coincidentally, it's a ten-minute walk away from Max's house, and we'll be living on the same street as Basil, the tall, shy librarian who took her out on the date that was apparently not a date, after she was fired. There was no second date, because my mother was too busy trying to extract herself from the affair with Richard.

The lease is up on the flat on Beverley Street two months before the house deal closes, so to save money it's decided Mum will stay with a friend downtown while I move in with Hannah's family, just three subway stops away from school.

Life at the Childs house is utterly exotic. I sleep in the large basement guest room on a double bed with its own private bath. I read the poem on the fridge every day, memorizing my favorite lines. The fridge is stuffed with food. Each night of the week, one of the three sisters cooks dinner. They're all vegetarians except Hannah's father. I help Hannah make lentil curry, which we ladle over brown rice. We pack lunches for school—leftovers or veggie pâté sandwiches, homemade oatmeal flax cookies, and three kinds of fruit. Sometimes I steal up from the basement late at night and gorge on all the food. I put on weight. The house is neither cold nor hot, an even, temperate climate just like the emotional state of its inhabitants, who never seem to cry or shout. Hannah's mother, Miriam, is training to be a psychotherapist. In the early mornings or afternoons when her daughters are not around, Miriam makes me sweet, milky cups of twig tea and listens to me talk about Max. I tell her about the sex. The love. I tell her everything. She listens, smiles, offers no advice, just listens.

Hannah's father travels a lot for his job as a Third World economist. In the fridge is a large Tupperware with *George's Meat* scrawled across the lid in Sharpie. I've only met him twice, most recently when my own mother came for dinner the night she dropped me off. Later, on the phone, Mum mentioned how handsome George was, then added he looked just like a younger version of my grandfather.

In an effort to be polite, I ask Miriam how things are going with George. I tell her I can't imagine what it's like for her. I can't imagine being away from Max even for a few days. I ask if she misses him terribly.

Miriam smiles uncynically and says that long-term relationships go through phases. Sometimes a bit of distance is good for the soul, she says. Marriage isn't only about sex.

When I confide this to Hannah later, as we are doing our French homework, she groans and covers her face. Then, in a tone that's more serious, she says, "Look, I think it's cool that you've bonded with my mum, but I think maybe you should keep your private conversations private, okay?"

I shrug. "Okay."

"You didn't tell her about Rach buying us booze, right?"

"Of course not."

"Or about how me and Adam are planning to eventually . . . you know?"

"No way! I just talk to her about me and Max."

"Okay, cool." Hannah nods.

We go back to copying out French verbs.

THE avocado-green fridge in the house on Yarmouth Gardens is the last place I will tape the tattered A4 sheet bearing our family motto. It's the only property my mother will ever own by herself and also the last place we will live in together. Not long after we move in, Mum quits *Chatelaine* to take a new job as the editor in chief of *Harrowsmith*, a country life magazine published out of a village near Kingston, a two-hour drive away. I will live on my own in the house for my last year of high school. Mum promises to drive home on the weekends she's not in production with the magazine.

Naturally the house on Yarmouth is a charming wreck, a detached unrenovated Edwardian, with two tiny bedrooms and one normal-sized one that fits a double bed. The walls are layered with a palimpsest of flocked wallpaper, which we spend several sweaty days attempting to strip off with a rented hand steamer before giving up and painting over. Mum has bookshelves fitted in the sitting room. The kitchen linoleum and matching appliances are an outdated shade of seventies green Mum declares "olive" because we can't afford new ones. There's a scurry of squirrels in the attic who scrabble about chewing the wiring, evicted the following summer by a lumbering family of raccoons. A deck is built off the kitchen, and for that first heavenly summer before she leaves, we sit for long afternoons drinking white wine and eating asparagus straight from the grill. We talk and read and at twilight raise our faces to the sky, taking in the nightly tightrope performance of the humpbacked mother raccoon tenderly lifting her babies one by one from the crack under the eaves. She sets them on the branches of the Manitoulin maple, then nudges them down to the alley, where she will teach them the art of toppling garbage cans for scraps.

"Did you know that raccoons are the only rodent with opposable thumbs?"

"Yes, Mum, you've told me that."

"Have I really? Sorry."

"We should call an exterminator. It's a fire hazard."

"I know, Pumpkin. We should."

My last year of high school was a big year. It must have been. The truth is, looking back on it today I remember almost nothing about schoolwork apart from a sensation of panic. I suppose I did all the stuff

I was supposed to—crammed for exams, filled out applications, met with guidance counselors, and fretted over my grade point averages— but I don't remember sweating over the work or discussing my options with my mother or anyone else. That I managed to do all of this on my own, quietly and without complaint, seems astonishing to me now, but I suppose at the time it just seemed normal. No one else was go- ing to do it for me. It was, after all, my life. It wasn't that my mother was entirely uninterested. She wanted me to do well, but the matter of whether or not I did was treated by both of us as none of her business. Perhaps it never occurred to me to ask for help. Perhaps I didn't need help? In any case, I got into my school of choice—McGill—with an academic scholarship.

To celebrate, Mum and I go to Montreal for the weekend to visit the campus. For March break that year, she takes me on my first foreign holiday, to an all-inclusive resort in Belize. The place is tiny and rustic, right on the beach. We are pleased it doesn't have a pool—who'd swim in a pool when you have the sea? During the day we read in the shade; in the evenings we sit at the bar eating conch ceviche and drinking sickly pink punch out of plastic cups. We snorkel in shallow reefs and later, rub calamine lotion on each other's sun-blistered backs. When we get back, Mum calls Meg and promises she'll also take her away on holiday in her final year.

Meg remembers, but somehow Mum forgets.

After Mum leaves to start her new job, I'm surprised to find living alone feels very different from just being alone in a house where my mother often is not. The latter is a feeling to which I'm entirely accus- tomed. But when I come home to an empty house, study alone, sleep alone, and get myself up and off to school alone, it is different. I play the music at full blast and eat a pint of cookie dough and ice cream for dinner, then make myself throw up.

When Mum comes home for the weekend, she no longer remarks approvingly on my weight loss. She complains of the smell of vomit in the bathroom. At least once she catches me in the act. When this happens, she does not suggest the outpatient program for eating disorders at Sick Kids, which a handful of my friends have already been through. They give me the pamphlets and I read them carefully. At the library I take out a self-help book called *When Food Is Love*, and follow recommended steps. On the weekends she is home, Mum teaches me how to cook. Nothing fancy. Just six basic recipes, including a classic marinara sauce, risotto with fresh chicken stock, the perfect cheese omelet, a simple vinaigrette (ten parts oil to one part acid; more salt than you think), and the correct way to blanch vegetables. She doesn't bother with meat, because it's expensive and generally easier than you think. Baking she dismisses as too finicky, a form of alchemy, magical in its way but something I can learn later from books.

I understand now what my mother was doing was showing me how to eat by teaching me how to turn food into meals. Mastering basic kitchen skills as a girl helped me to understand food as something I could control without hurting myself. Without words, my mother taught me there were generous and socially acceptable ways to escape reality through the absorbing pleasures of food. In the years that followed, my adolescent eating issues resolved themselves without crisis or treatment. I suppose for the lucky majority of us they do. But I'm not sure this would have happened without my mother's help. It's hard to fear an egg once you've whisked it into a fluff and folded it neatly in the pan.

In our last year of high school, Max and I start a jazz group, the Bathurst Street Trio, with our friend Ed, a pianist. For my "stage look" I cut my hair boy short, paint my lips violet, and adopt a series of snuggly tailored vintage men's suits. We rehearse a short set list from the Great American Songbook in which I manage a passable impression of Ella Fitzgerald. The audience loves us. We gig at jazz clubs around the city and earn a couple of hundred bucks a show, which seems like an astonishing amount of cash.

One night during a break in rehearsal Max catches Ed trying to kiss me. The Bathurst Street Trio disbands but Max and I stay together. In the months that follow, we begin torturing each other. The transition from adoration to anxiety to anguish is gradual but also inevitable, because we are seventeen and understand we have no future. Again and again we break up, only to fall back into the wanton agony we call "love." Looking back now, I suppose we were acting out a version of the adult emotional dramas swirling around us, but at the time it felt like our own private opera of pain. I remember few of the details, except that soon I was miserable, struggling to sleep or think.

On the worst nights, I'd call Mum in the country and sob a hundred miles down the line. She was always patient—exhausted but sympathetic. My mother has always been good at offering comfort and affection when I am in despair. "Oh, my little Leah," she'd say. "I'm worried about you. I'm so worried. Are you sure you're all right on your own? Maybe you should go stay with a friend. Isn't there anyone you can stay with?"

"*He* was my best friend!" I remember wailing to her once.

"No," Mum said. "He's just your first love. *I'm* your best friend. I'll always be your best friend."

Max stops going to high school altogether. He switches to viola that year, in part to escape his esteemed but egomaniacal tutor. For his eighteenth birthday, I give him a watch with leather straps and Roman numerals. It's a Timex, but it's still more than I can afford. I present it to him on the deck one sunny morning and he accepts the gift sullenly, ungraciously. Not because he doesn't like it, but because he sees it for what it is: a desperate reconciliation bribe. He tries it on at my urging. Then takes it off and says he wants to give it back. I refuse, so he slaps the watch down on the table, picks up his viola case, and storms out the gate, in the direction of the park.

I go back into the house and run a cool bath, take off my clothes, and lower myself into it. The bath always stops me crying; it's as if water renders the act redundant. Lowering my head down under the surface mutes the static. The world is calm. But then a force clamps itself over my head, my hair, my shoulders—Max's hands—and violently hauls me up to the surface sputtering.

"*What the hell are you doing?*" he shouts. His face is mottled, his expression desperate. He shudders, reels back, his viola in its case still strapped to his back. Fear—that's what I see on his face. He is terrified.

"Isn't it obvious?" I say coolly, then reach for the shampoo.

As I lather my hair, we gaze at each other. Some wordless challenge hangs in the air. What is it we think we want from each other?

He leaves again, plodding heavily down each individual step rather than going at his usual rate of two at a time. I listen for the cheap slap of the aluminum screen door. I read until the light wanes and the bath is freezing. When I go downstairs to lock up, the watch is gone.

T OWARD the end of the school year, *Harrowsmith* is purchased by a big media consortium and Mum moves back to the city. Her presence in the house seems a return to safety, a sense of home that is both comforting and mildly embarrassing to us both. That last year of high school exposes my loneliness, a terrible, devouring sadness that lives inside me and in its darkest moments renders me helpless, hysterical—a tormented child—rather than the coolly precocious young woman I project to the world. Who am I really? It's unclear and perhaps it never will be. The only thing I understand is that I am not the person my mother needs me to be. Instead we are one and the same: women functioning on the verge of a yawning void. We have glimpsed the darkness of our mutual chaos and it terrifies us both.

We don't talk much about my rolling breakups with Max except to agree that living apart was a disaster. My mother is disappointed in Max. "I thought he'd take better care of you while I was away," she says. Maybe she thought he'd move in and play house? It's a jarring thought, so instead we talk more and more about the Horseman. She fleshes out the details of the story for me now that she has resumed therapy.

Richard has started calling again. Victoria finally disposed of him for good, but now he's living with another woman, with whom he's started a production business. He's no longer just a philandering serial monogamist but an effectively married man. Because of this, Mum and I theorize, he has a vacancy to fill. My mother is the perfect candidate for the position of mistress. She's experienced and familiar with the role.

"How can you even talk to him?" I remember asking her irritably as we sat drinking cold wine on the deck at Yarmouth Gardens that summer before I went to McGill.

Mum shrugs. "It's just dinner."

"Isn't it always 'just dinner' with him?"

"Leah, I'm an *adult*. I'm entitled to have a private life. I'm allowed to have friends."

"You already have friends. You have tons of friends. And, more importantly, you have me."

Mum makes a little noise and reaches out across the table for my hand. When I look over, she drops her gaze. An unseen fist presses on my sternum.

"And now you're leaving me all alone," she whispers, rubbing the top of my hand. "What am I going to do, rattling around on my own in this old house?"

"Mum, it's a three-bedroom worker's cottage."

"That's two more than I need."

"I'll be back for Thanksgiving. Just don't redecorate my room to look like the bridal suite on a cruise ship the second I move out like MJ did, okay?"

Mum laughs and dabs at her nose with a wadded tissue. "Sorry to be a big sap. I just wish you didn't have to go."

"It's just university. I'm not emigrating to Papua New Guinea."

"I know, but everything's going to change."

"You *love* change. Remember the motto?"

Mum frowns and sniffs. Then, in the baby voice my grandmother uses, she says, "*Oh, my widdle Weah. My itsum-dutsum-tutsum.* Please don't go. Won't you just stay here and take care of your pathetic, lonely old mum?"

I rise from my chair and sink to my knees, resting my head on my mother's lap. I wrap my arms around her thighs as she strokes my hair. We stay there for a long moment, both of us breathing and crying and laughing at the absurdity of it. *She'll go back to Richard*, I think. *Of course she will.* And she does.

Years later, I would return to that particular summer evening in my memory. In my mind's eye it became a kind of private religious tableau: our haphazard family of two in the dying hours of one of the dying days of our last summer together. Even though I was the one leaving, my impulse was to press my face into my mother's lap while holding her legs like a bereft toddler. It was only after I had children of my own that I recognized the gesture for what it was: the hug that is meant to hobble.

The language of therapy had not yet fully wormed its way into daily conversation in the 1990s. Apart from Joni, no one spoke of concepts like boundaries or enmeshment; such words existed only in diagnostic textbooks. But even then I was keenly aware of the contradiction between my mother's anxious, keening desire for the love of a man and the tattered sign still taped on our fridge:

COMMITMENT SUCKS THE LIFE RIGHT OUT OF YOU.

Richard, I see now, served a purpose. He reinforced and built upon an existing structure in my mother's mind. The foundation was laid by the Horseman. The blueprints had been drawn up long before either of us was born. Like the bad man before him, Richard became an altar on which my mother debased herself. For so many women, this is what passes for love.

In August, Richard makes good on his promise. Before I leave for McGill, an Apple desktop is delivered to our house on Yarmouth Gardens: payment for the forgotten bet we made all those years ago and shook on over the dinner table at Vogrie. While I know the gift is meant to be a kind of avuncular inside joke, I am irritated at the gesture. Mum seems to find Richard's gift amusing, even sweet, but I am indignant. I resent the implication it carries, that my achievement is somehow the result of his cynicism.

"Who bets an eleven-year-old girl she won't go to university?" I say to my mother.

She flicks her eyes at the ceiling and sighs. Poufs the front of her bangs. "Aren't you being a bit humorless?"

"I'm sending it back."

But I don't.

22

A FEW months later I am in Montreal, sitting on a low leather cushion in a Moroccan restaurant on Mont-Royal, having dinner alone with the Editor. He's in town promoting his first novel, a book I reviewed for the *McGill Daily* after he sent me an advance copy. The novel is a roman à clef, an erotic exculpation of the Editor's hippie years in Greece with a Venezuelan girl named Kiki he later followed to Formentera and shagged extensively on the beach under the influence of hallucinogens. The book is vividly written in parts but also blatantly self-indulgent, a nostalgic fantasy of a man desperate to relive the sexual escapades of his youth. The girl is less an actual character than an extension of the author's ego. I say all this in my review because I am a teenager and it does not occur to me to be anything but honest.

A couple of weeks after the review appears I get a letter from the Editor asking if he can take me out to dinner. He asked my mother for my address. We sit, almost squatting, on brightly patterned leather tufts and eat lamb stewed with apricots on couscous. At first he regards me at a distance; our small talk, which in the past consisted primarily of him telling me colorful anecdotes about Madonna's breasts and Keith Richards's prodigious caffeine intake, is unusually stilted. Finally, after enough wine has been taken, he tells me how hurt he was by my review. I find this curious. It had not occurred to me that a professional writer who flies around the world interviewing celebrities and has published an *actual novel*—albeit a decidedly onanistic one, as I pointed out in my review, having recently come across the word in my thesaurus—could be wounded by the opinion of his freshman babysitter, a volunteer film critic at the campus paper. I'm not sure what he expects me to say, which as it turns out is nothing much. As dinner continues, more wine is taken and his mood lifts. It seems my unflattering review has excited the Editor somehow. Why else would he have gone to the trouble of asking me to dinner? He has taken my uninformed juvenile opinion of his terrible book and turned it into a personal challenge.

He asks me if I've seen *Exotica*, the new film by the writer-director Atom Egoyan, which recently opened the Toronto film festival. It's about a bereaved father who becomes fixated on a teenaged lap dancer in a schoolgirl outfit who turns out to be his daughter's former babysitter. I tell him I have. Twice—once with my mother in Toronto and then again in Montreal with my friend Isabel.

"And what did you think?"

"I thought it was very counterintuitive. Morally speaking."

The Editor smiles. I continue uncertainly.

"At first you assume the main character is just a dirty old man obsessed with this stripper in a schoolgirl outfit like some kind of pervy old pedo-fetishist type, and then when you find out their backstory, it's even creepier, but in the end it's the opposite of that."

"The opposite? Or something else entirely?" He leans forward on his tuft.

I hesitate, feeling a prickle under my arms, the gathering hot lather. I realize the Editor has probably talked about this movie in meetings with senior journalists in the Toronto Media World. Quite possibly he has even talked about it with my mother. His opinion is probably out there, paid for and in print. And I don't even know what it is.

"What did you think?" I say, thinking of my grandmother. *Men like questions.*

He smiles and sighs, as if it pains him slightly to go over it all again.

"I thought it was intriguing. Perhaps a bit strained. But I'm really in-terested to know why *you* liked it so much. What's your take as a woman?"

Woman.

I take a bite of my dinner and pretend to chew thoughtfully. Cous-cous does not need much chewing. If you wash it down with wine, it's like swallowing a handful of tiny pills. I think of Mia Kirshner, the actress who plays the stripper. She's in my year at McGill. I don't know her, but I know of her. Once, she came in late to Introduction to Anthropology and had to take a seat at the front of the lecture hall. Afterward, I heard the third-year hippie guys on the steps of the arts building describing how she'd peeled off layer after layer of mohair sweaters, revealing a tight black cat suit as if for the benefit of the crowd.

"Well, I didn't expect the twist," I say to the Editor. "First, that she'd been his babysitter. Or the fact that his daughter was abducted and murdered. It's like the story takes you into one room, then flicks a switch and everything is unrecognizable, like a song that suddenly goes from major to minor, you know?"

"Yes." The Editor is nodding. "I do."

"All the stuff you think you know about the characters is false and everything the movie seems to be about—sexual exploitation, the male gaze, female subjugation, violence—is not what it's really about at all. Except that actually it *is* about all those things, just not in the way you expect it to be. Like a series of paradoxes hidden inside each other. A palimpsest."

The Editor is smiling. I wait for him to say something but he doesn't seem to have anything to say. Perhaps I have silenced him with my in-cisive critical insights? This seems unlikely.

"Does that make sense?"

Behind his glasses the Editor blinks slowly, so slowly that for a mo-ment I wonder if he is falling asleep, but I can see that he isn't because his mouth is still smiling. Closed lips, fond eyes. He rubs the side of his nose.

"Yes," he says. "Perfect sense. You're a very astute critic, you know that? Apart from when it comes to books."

He waits for me to laugh, which I do.

W e get drunk, very drunk. Stumbling back to my flat, I am astonished that it's possible to get so drunk over dinner. On the walk, the Editor becomes nostalgic for his university days in Montreal. He points out details of the city I'm aware of but have already grown used to even though I've just moved here. The neon cross on the mountain. The wrought-iron spiral staircases. The tenement buildings on Saint-Urbain and Saint-Laurent. Even in my stupor I notice he has an interesting trick of talking about famous people as if he doesn't know them while simultaneously insinuating he does. He wants to know if I've tried the bagels at St-Viateur? Yes, of course, I tell him. Every Saturday morning, if my roommate is not at her boyfriend's, we queue up and eat them steaming from the paper bag. This pleases him.

We stumble-twirl up the stairs to my third-floor walk-up, where he accepts a beer. In the cramped front sitting room the Editor settles himself and flips through my unremarkable CD collection. Without comment he selects the Cranberries and presses Play on the banged-up portable stereo then asks if I have any pot. I apologize, explaining that weed makes me paranoid. He looks astonished. I add that no one calls it pot anymore.

Because there's nothing left to do or say, the Editor kisses me on the low green futon and I let him. I'm surprised how normal, even pleasant, it feels to kiss a man who is old. He has wolfish hair but his mouth reminds me of a rabbit's: searching lips and eager buck teeth. He touches my neck but I keep my hands on my lap, wary of the skin that hangs loose, like a tiny privacy curtain, dividing one side of his throat from the other. As the tension drains from my shoulders, I am flooded by something else, a sensation that is less arousal than relief. His breath makes me think of the pastel pillow mints Mrs. Oliver kept in a dish on her sideboard. Dusty but nice. I open my eyes and find myself staring at his earlobe. It used to be pierced and stares back at me like a snake eye. There is hair growing from the cavern of his ear. I close my eyes, then turn my head to the side.

"I have class tomorrow," I say.

He raises his hands as if I've just pointed a pistol at his chest. "Of course," he says. "I wouldn't want to interfere with your education."

After he leaves, I cringe with the realization that it's Friday. He probably thought I was lying about it being a school night. Then I remember I *was* lying. It does not occur to me to consider whether I'm attracted to him. What's important is that he is attracted to me.

The following week, the Editor calls from his office and asks if I'd like to come to New York with him for the weekend. He's going on a press junket for a major movie opening. He'll send me the ticket, he says. We'll stay at a fancy hotel with a name so famous even I've heard of it. I tell him I'll think about it. "Your mother doesn't need to know," he adds, as if that isn't obvious.

I talk it over with Isabel. Apart from my roommate from drama school, who studies drama at a different university, Isabel is my only friend in Montreal. I met her at the computer terminals in the library, where she helped me set up my first-ever email account. It turned out we were both in first year and had both refused to live in residence or participate in frosh week. Isabel grew up in Trois-Rivières, where she went to Catholic school, the perfectly bilingual daughter of French parents raised in Ontario. Her dad works in hydroelectric. She doesn't add that he's an executive. She has a large, angular face dominated by two enormous dark eyes and wears her hair—*daringly*, my mother would say—in a pixie cut. She has clear ideas about personal style, which mostly involve the color black and being eternally wrapped in a long wool coat belted at the waist. She is offended by Birkenstocks with socks, a fashion crime she describes as utterly beyond the pale. Isabel is having an affair with her film professor, a man named Trevor whom she met in her first tutorial on the first day of first year. The chemistry was instant, she tells me. There was nothing to be done.

Trevor is young, in his late twenties, still working on his PhD. Technically speaking, he's a TA, but we think of him as a professor. What interests us both is the fact that Trevor has fallen madly in love with her. He tells her they need to be very careful, but he also wants Isabel to move out of her student digs and into his one-bedroom flat. She's not so sure. They have sex, loads and loads of sex, which she tells me about in detail over coffees and veggie pâté sandwiches in the basement café of the arts building every day between classes. One day I ask if she's on the pill, and she laughs and tosses her chin as if I've asked her something mildly ridiculous. "He just pulls out," she says. "Or, if he really wants to come inside me, we do it the other way."

My eyes bulge, but Isabel is more incredulous than I am. She knows I've had sex, but it suddenly appears that I'm not as experienced as I'd believed.

"Seriously? You haven't tried anal? Why not?"

I consider the question, rolling it over in my mind like a philosophical proposition. I think of Max. His furry chest. His kind dimpled chin. The sex. Our sex. It's the first time I've ever considered that there might have been something lacking.

"I guess I thought it would hurt?"

What I don't add is that it never even came up, that until this moment I thought anal sex was something only gay men did—not the grown-up ones my mother hangs out with, but the irresponsible, non-monogamous kind.

Isabel grips my wrist. "Oh my god, babe, you have to try it. It's *amazing*. Guys go crazy for it. Literally *all guys*. You just need to relax into it and then it gives you orgasms through your lower back, right up your spine. My boyfriend and I did it *all* through high school. How do you think I stayed a virgin?"

Then, like an actress in a noir film, she winks.

I GO home to Toronto for Thanksgiving. While I'm there, I ask my mother about anal sex. We are sitting in the kitchen of the house on Yarmouth Gardens. She's started a new job, a "job for life," she calls it, as an editor in the Focus section of the *Globe and Mail*. I'm worried she will ask me why I'm asking about anal sex, but she does not. Instead, she calmly regales me with her own experience of anal, which involves several men including my father and basically boils down to this: penis size matters and use lube. I don't get the sense she had any vibrations up her back, but then, my mother isn't Isabel. What stuns me most is simply that she has done it. And that she hasn't bothered to tell me. I know all the particularities of my mother's sex life, or I thought I did. I wonder if everyone is secretly having anal sex all the time and I'm the only one who doesn't know about it.

Max and I have officially broken up, but we still have occasionally tearful phone conversations, which I know means we'll have sex when I'm home. I decide I'm going to try anal with him, in preparation for my weekend in New York with the Editor. We meet up and moon at each other over cappuccinos, then go back to Mum's house. She's out and I have a bottle of lube waiting beside her bed. I instruct Max on what to do, using my mother's expert instructions. Max is hesitant, skeptical, but he's also eighteen and in the presence of a naked girl asking him to put his penis somewhere new. The lube is so cold, I cringe while rubbing it on my rectum. Max politely averts his eyes. I turn my back to him and kneel down on the bed. Bracing my head against the rickety brass frame, I hold on to one of my mother's lace pillows. He fiddles around a bit, prodding.

"I'm not sure it's going to fit," he says after a while.

"Try rubbing my back. I just need to relax."

My breathing slows as Max squeezes my neck and shoulders, working his thumb along my scapula the way he knows I like. With his other hand he rubs the tip of his cock between the cheeks of my ass. I spread my legs wider and gently push myself back, reversing like a car and arching my back so the center of my bum tips up to his face. Max groans. With my right cheek pressed against the pillow, I peer at him under the crook of my armpit. He's grimacing and his eyes are glazed.

"Leah," he whispers. "Don't look at me."

I shut my eyes.

I encourage him with animal sounds. "Remember, go slow."

"Okay, okay. Here goes."

This time when he pushes himself inside me it's like some centrifugal force is sucking his cock up the base of my spine. The pain is incomprehensible, a blitz of raw animal panic. Max falls forward, gripping my waist with both hands. I twist around, jaw snapping.

"*GET IT OUT GET IT OUT OUT OUT OUT!!!*"

He obeys instantly and is deeply apologetic. Fetching a roll of toilet paper from the bathroom, he continues to say sorry, sorry, sorry as he cleans us both up. I cry a bit, softly.

"I'm not sure I've ever wiped your bum before," he says after a while. "Or anyone's bum, really. Is this what it's like to have a baby?"

I laugh. We both laugh. Then Max climbs into bed and we spoon.

"Are you all right?" he says again. "I didn't mean to hurt you."

"It's fine," I say. "Honestly, I'm fine."

Later, when I explain to my mother what happened, adding the stuff Isabel told me about spinal orgasms, she slaps the table and hoots.

"Leah, why would you take sex advice from a girl who went to Catholic school?"

I MEET the Editor for a drink at a downtown oyster bar. We have wine and oysters and then more wine. He is twitchy, eyes darting. "Sorry," he says. "It's just that I have a bit of a profile."

I nod coolly. We drink our wine and discuss his recent profile of Susan Sarandon. He asks if I'm enjoying my classes, which I take as an opening to tell him all about the linguistic anthropology paper I wrote on semiotics. I'm hoping he'll ask me my mark, which Isabel assured me is unheard-of. Instead, he cuts me off in a jocular tone, saying I shouldn't worry too much about that stuff. Marks. When you get out, no one ever asks to see your GPA. No one even really cares if you have a degree.

I'm not sure where he got the idea I want to be a journalist, which I don't. I'm going to be a playwright. I've never thought about it before, but I guess no one cares if you have a degree for that either.

"So have you decided?" he says. "About New York?"

I hesitate. Fumble around, lighting a cigarette. "I want to," I say. "But I'm not sure. There's an issue. You'll probably think I'm silly."

His brow scrunches up with concern. The wrinkles on his forehead remind me of the sandbars in the shallows of the Cobourg beach. I stare at him and for the first time it occurs to me he is older than my father. Significantly older. I wonder why it has not occurred to me before and then realize it's because the mere thought of my father feels like an act of sacrilege in the presence of this man—a man less like my father than any man I've ever met. Which is, perhaps, the whole point of him.

Under the table, the Editor reaches for my hand to show me it's okay.

"I'll come to New York, but on one condition."

The Editor nods in a way that says, *Lay it on me.*

"No anal."

Under the table, the Editor releases my hand. Then he leans back and removes his glasses and, using a napkin, wipes the bridge of his nose. He is nodding, shaking his head. I understand he is trying not to laugh, so I smile, offering him the ludicrousness of my innocence, which I see he finds charming. Not something to be discarded, but a quality with a value of its own.

I think of Isabel's slow, knowing wink. *How do you think I stayed a virgin?*

The Editor is now regarding me with a hangdog expression. His eyes are soft, even moist, as if I have just broken his heart.

"Okay, then," he says, and offers me his hand to shake like a businessman. "It's a deal."

23

THE first night in New York, the Editor orders room service. It arrives on a trolley, just like in the movies, pushed into the room by a man in white gloves and a red jacket with epaulets. He even pulls the lids from the plates with a flourish. The Editor has ordered wine, oysters, and an enormous, unappetizing salad with mayonnaise and apples, which he explains I have to try because it's famous, the house specialty.

After that, we attempt to have sex. He uses a condom; it doesn't seem prudent to mention I am on the pill. It takes a long time and neither of us comes. Afterward, we watch *Letterman*. Then he suggests a walk. He lies in bed and watches me get dressed to go out. I'm putting on the same outfit I wore earlier, the one Isabel helped me pick out: black corduroy miniskirt, short-sleeved mohair sweater, and thick cotton stockings that stop a few inches above my knee, revealing an inch of naked thigh.

"I like your clothes," he says.

I thank him. It's rude to not accept compliments.

"Do you always dress like that?" he asks, then corrects himself. "I mean, like this?"

I think of my daily trudge to campus across Parc du Mont-Royal, the Kodiaks and parka that Isabel urged me to leave behind. "You're going to *New York*," she'd said, as if it wasn't still winter here.

"Not really. I mostly wear jeans."

The Editor is quiet for a moment, then he asks out of nowhere if I like my body. Sure, I lie. He tells me that before he met his wife he dated a woman who told him she'd pay a thousand dollars just to lose ten pounds. It's a detail that will stick in my mind forever—not the fact that his ex-girlfriend said it but the Editor's amazement. The derision in his voice and the wonder in his eyes. I understand he wants me to make him feel there are two sides to the equation: the old, ugly, and ashamed and the beautiful, young, and free. He is asking me to reassure him we are on the same side.

But we're not. Even at eighteen I grasp this with total clarity. I am on his ex-girlfriend's side. His wife's side. My mother's side. I say nothing and continue rolling my stocking up my thigh.

At the Editor's insistence we take separate elevators down to the lobby and meet outside. It's a junket, so he's bound to bump into people, the Editor explains as we begin to walk along the roaring street. The night is clear and dry, the windchill slicing at the exposed bits of my wrists and throat. He explains how the whole junket thing works. The studios pay for everything, flying writers in from all over the world just so they can see the movie and stay in a fancy hotel. Everything is either comped by the studio or, in his case, expensed to the magazine. Some of the journalists are shameless. They bring their dry cleaning and charge it to the room, he says in a tone that makes it clear he would never stoop so low. I ask him where we're going, which makes him stop abruptly. Then, as if the idea has just occurred to him, he says, "Should we go in here?" He points at a flashing neon sign. On it is the cartoon silhouette of a nude woman lying on her stomach. Back arched, head flung back, spike heels kicking the air.

"A strip club?"

The Editor shakes his head and takes my bare hand in his leather glove. Inside, he pushes some cash at a man who sits smoking behind a thick glass window, like the ticket taker at a fairground ride. We walk down a long, confusing hall of mirrors that smells of dry ice and is filled with thudding hip-hop music. I am afraid to touch anything but his glove, which grips my hand, pulling me forward on my tippy high-heeled boots. Finally we come to what he's looking for. He draws aside a curtain and ushers me into a small booth about the size of a confessional. Inside, there's a pane of glass and behind is a room furnished vaguely like an overlit bordello. There's a Chinese screen, a potted fern, and an electric chandelier that's missing several bulbs. A collection of women in various states of undress are draped across velvet daybeds and tufted stools, stretching and yawning like cats who've just woken from a long nap.

The Editor knocks on the glass and a slim Asian woman swivels over. She wears a sequined string bikini bottom, long strings of fake pearls, and a feather in her hair. The effect, perhaps intended, is that of a child playing dress-up. Her face is lightly made up and there is glitter sprinkled round the corners of her eyes. She smiles when she sees me through the glass, her face softening like a doll coming to life. She reaches down and flicks some out-of-view lever, a supple, practiced motion that causes a narrow window to slide open in the glass. The Editor is standing behind me, so close I can feel his breath, damp on my neck.

"Go on," he says. "It's okay."

At first I don't understand, but the woman encourages me by stepping closer to the window and with a flutter of tiny fingers beckons for my hand. I offer it gingerly, trembling. She flinches at my touch, then scrunches up her shoulders and wiggles her hips, pretending to shiver. "Brrrr—cold!" she says, then claps my fingers between her palms and blows on them. When she decides I am sufficiently warmed, she arches her back, thrusting her chest toward me, and with a rustle draws aside the pearls and presses my hand to her breast. I think I might fall over, so I close my eyes, which helps a bit.

"Just pretend you're stroking a kitten," the Editor whispers in my ear, which I do, and find he is right. With this pretense, the throb at the base of my skull subsides and eventually I am able to look. Not at the whole woman, just the bit of her I am touching. Her breast is soft and silky, the sweetest thing I've ever touched. I brush my fingers against her nipple, so much larger and darker than my own, and watch with interest as it changes, some bits retracting, others rising.

I've never thought of a nipple this way, as a rich and yielding universe all its own.

THE summer after my first year at McGill I return to Toronto and get a job as a waitress at an Italian restaurant on Bloor Street. I am living with my mother, but mostly I stay over at my boyfriend Andrew's shared student house around the corner. We are instantly and rather miraculously in love. Inseparable. Andrew is six years older than me, an age difference most of his law school friends find shocking but Andrew seems to find amusing and I don't notice at all. Andrew is planning to finish law school and write his final exams, but he has already decided not to practice. Instead he wants to write.

He must be called to the bar, he explains, because he's the youngest son in a large medical family. His parents are immigrants from Northern Ireland. Two of his siblings have followed his father into medicine and because of this he must become a lawyer. I don't entirely get how this follows, except that he feels he owes his parents something. Andrew writes stories; he's published some of them in journals. They're good, too—better than good. He is talented and smart and handsome and full of potential, but more than anything he is kind. Relentlessly and tirelessly kind.

One day I come home from work after a day shift at the restaurant and find my mother sitting on the deck. I'm planning to shower quickly and change, then head over to Andrew's, where he and his roommates are hosting a barbecue on their front porch.

"We need to talk," my mother says. "I got a call today."

She tells me it was from the Editor.

"He was very upset. He said he didn't know how else to reach you. That you wouldn't return his calls and that when your phone in Montreal was disconnected, he was worried, so he decided to call me. As a last resort."

My mother knows about the Editor, about New York and the dinner that preceded it in Montreal. I've even told her about the long conversations during the car rides home, back when I was his babysitter. I told her these things not because I had to but because I knew she would understand. Unlike my friends at school, I knew she wouldn't act like it was gross, scrunch up her nose and say *But isn't he kind of old?*—as if that wasn't the entire point. I was surprised at how angry she got when I first told her, but I didn't mind because her anger wasn't directed at me. She made a point of calling up the Editor at his office and telling him to piss off. I found this embarrassing but also funny. In any case, it stopped him calling my apartment.

In the end there was no big affair. I just wasn't into it. I *wanted* to be into it—I tried to be—but I just couldn't muster up the enthusiasm. It wasn't the fact that it was seedy; if anything, that was the appeal. Maybe it wasn't sleazy enough? In the end I just stopped returning his calls. People talk about "ghosting" now, as if the Internet made deleting people possible. In fact it was so much easier then. My roommate was almost never home, but when she was, we had a pact: if the Editor calls, I'm not here. He was persistent, but after my mother told him to piss off, he stopped.

I haven't thought of him in months. But now that I do—now that my mother has mentioned him—a certain spikiness rises in my chest. Not anger, exactly, but a simmering irritation that I'm having to think of him at all. Somehow the fact that it's my mother who is the one forcing me to think of him makes this feeling more acute.

"I think it's weird that he called you," I say to her. "Don't you think it's a bit weird?"

Mum flicks her eyes toward the ceiling. "Obviously, Leah, the whole thing is weird. But I didn't create this situation. I'm just telling you he seemed genuinely upset. He was worried because your phone line in Montreal got cut off—"

"It's a student apartment!"

"I know, I know. He said he just wants some kind of closure."

I shake my head and mutter something about being late to meet Andrew. My mother frowns.

"I'm not telling you what to do, Leah. You know I think he's a creep. It's your life. I just—I don't know what I'm trying to say."

This is what we don't talk about: She's seeing Richard again, inter-mittently, after years of refusing to speak to him, and it's making her anxious, restless. She's thinner, her face lined from tossing and turning all night on the saggy mattress on her antique bed. The thought of Richard and his thin, malevolent lips makes me queasy. Neither of us brings up the subject, which is something new for us. I'm surprised to find I also don't want to talk about the Editor either. Not now or maybe ever again, and certainly not with my mother. But she still wants me to stay. To talk about something, anything.

"I stopped off at the market and bought some things for dinner," she says. "The asparagus is in."

"I have plans," I remind her.

T HE next day, a Saturday, I'm sitting on Andrew's porch when Mum pulls up in her car and starts shouting from the driver's-side window. She's shouting in my direction. Enraged. The reason, it transpires, is that the dress I'm wearing is hers, not mine. She's correct. I took the dress from her closet the week before without asking. I have no excuse. I planned to give it back. I just liked it. "That's mine!" she screams. "Give it back! Take it off right now! You have *no right!*"

I stand up and walk halfway down the long garden path to the curb and ask her to please calm down; it's *embarrassing*. To calm her down, I promise to take the dress off and return it to her house later. Satisfied, she tosses her head, rolls up the window, and drives away in the rusted-out Mazda.

After she drives away, one of Andrew's roommates, who's been sitting hidden in his usual shady spot behind the barbecue, is quiet. He's thoughtful, laconic, a journalism student from the Maritimes. Eventually he looks up from the book he's reading. My mother wouldn't have seen him from the street. I'm painfully aware of this—that for her the scene was a private one.

"Do you think it's possible," Andrew's roommate says slowly, "that your mother is just a teeny-weeny bit jealous of you?"

I pretend to consider this seriously. The journalism student roommate rarely offers opinions, but when he does, they are generally worth listening to.

"Nah," I say. "She just really wants her dress back."

"Okey dokey." He goes back to reading his book. I mean to do the same, but instead I just sit there, staring at the empty street in silence.

WHEN I arrive for my shift at the Italian restaurant, The Editor is there. I'm not entirely surprised. His wife was in with a friend a few days before. At first I was terrified but we had a friendly exchange. She must have innocently mentioned the coincidence to him, that's how he knows where I work.

I arrange my face into a stiff smile and approach his table. It's a Friday, just before the six o'clock rush. Soon the pre-concert crowd will start drizzling in, groups of elderly women and couples who ask for half portions of pasta and quarter carafes of house wine on which they leave ten percent tips counted out in small change.

The Editor looks up from his legal pad.

"Leah," he says in an expectant way that confirms my suspicion it's an ambush. "I hope you don't mind my showing up like this."

His voice is a velvet purr. As always he is meticulously polite.

I pull a notepad and golf pencil from the pocket of my apron. "Good evening, sir, would you like to hear the specials? The fish of the day is grouper."

"I talked to Cecily. I asked her to ask you to call me. I didn't know how else to contact you."

"Of course, take your time. I'll get you some of our house focaccia to nibble on while you decide."

I turn and stride back to the kitchen, where I hide behind the bread station, pressing one cheek and then the other against the cool subway-tiled wall, waiting for the throbbing in my head to subside. When I reemerge, the Editor's table is empty. Under his empty wineglass is a twenty-dollar bill. Beneath that is a four-page letter written in longhand. I take it to the kitchen and read it quickly, then throw it in the scrap bin. I have no memory of what it said.

❖ ❖ ❖

THAT summer in Toronto, the summer of 1993, was a hot and wind-less season. Humidity insulated the alleys, insinuating itself into the crevices of the city. The Paul Bernardo murder trial dominated the news. The Scarborough Rapist who'd terrorized the suburbs in my high school years had been accused of the rape and murder of three teenaged girls. They were the same age as me when they were killed. I was fifteen and living at Beverley Street when the bodies of the second and third victims were found. Now, like everyone else, I knew their faces as well as my own. Bernardo's wife, Karla Homolka, was also charged; the first victim had been her younger sister. The cops made a mess of the inves-tigation, interviewing the handsome, charming Bernardo, who chuck-led at his own resemblance to the composite sketch and graciously provided a DNA sample. They let him go and for six months didn't bother to run a check. Later, figuring pretty Karla for the battered wife, the Crown struck a plea deal: protection from prosecution in exchange for her testimony. A few weeks later, videotapes emerged revealing she was complicit, an active and enthusiastic participant in the murders. In advance of the trial, their fairy-tale wedding photos were everywhere, bride and groom in an open-air horse-drawn carriage, waving and smiling, glistening faces emerging out of the voluminous froth of her gown. All through the spring and early summer the newsroom at the paper where my mother now worked was tense. The news editors were on tenterhooks, she said, debating how to cover the grisly details of the unfolding case.

After cashing out at the restaurant that summer, I'd walk the dozen blocks back to Andrew's place barefoot to air my blistered heels, weav-ing through the silent, sodium-lit streets of the Annex, picking leaves off the bushes as I went. One night just before the trial, my toes touched the pavement and I flinched. The sun had set hours before, but the side-walk was still hot, as if an electrical element had been laid underneath. I continued gingerly, and as I did, the neighborhood seemed to gather it-self around me and whisper. The feeling, the sound, reminded me of the singing of the northern lights—a celestial mutter interspersed by static.

I'd only heard it once, on a canoe trip in the North as a child, where it's possible to witness such things. The camp counselor explained it was the solar wind brushing up against the earth's hemisphere, creating a natural radio signal. The lights were green and blue and violet, babbling a gentle gibberish. A few of us slept out on the tennis court that night, tucked into our sleeping bags, absorbed by the magic of the sky. When we woke the next morning, our lips and eyelids were numbed with dew.

But this sound, the one from beneath the pavement of Toronto, was different. It rose and fell around me in urgent, thickening waves—an unintelligible bickering that rose almost to a point of conflict before dispersing into a scornful pixilated laughter. I felt humiliated by it somehow, as if I'd been tricked into eavesdropping on a private conversation I didn't want to hear. And then quite suddenly I was gripped by terrible fear, the worst I have ever felt. Worse than the night of the Peeper and, years later, the wailing alarms after Frankie's birth. It was the oily, unfathomable dread that can only be felt by a girl who is not yet a woman walking alone down a quiet city street at night.

I put on my shoes and ran. By the time I arrived, my feet were bleeding. Andrew's key was under the conch shell on the porch and he'd left me a present: a ripe black fig.

In bed the next morning, I told Andrew about the sound and how it had frightened me. I was hoping he'd make a joke about UFOs. Instead, he turned over on the floor mattress where we slept, propped his head in his hand, his face above mine, and waited for his glasses to un-fog. Then he said—I will never forget this—"I think it was them you heard."

"Who?"

"The lost girls."

THE following summer, Mum is sitting on the deck in Yarmouth Gardens when Basil, the librarian from *Maclean's*, cycles past. He stops and smiles. Mopping his brow, he explains breathlessly that he lives at the other end of our street. It takes a few weeks but eventually Mum musters up the courage to ask him for a second date. By the summer they're together. My mother is weightless and giddy. Together, we marvel that he is her first proper boyfriend since my father in high school. Basil is nothing like my father, of course, apart from the fact that he is tall and reliable and kind and good with dogs. A few months later, over dinner one night, Basil sinks to one knee and rolls a red rubber band onto my mother's finger. They set a date almost immediately. The wedding will be small and will take place in the chapel at Hart House, on the University of Toronto campus, where Basil is doing his master's in library sciences.

"Are you sure?" I ask my mother on the phone when she calls me at university to tell me the news.

"Don't be ridiculous," she says. "Of course I'm sure."

"But what's the big rush?" I'm thinking of our fridge motto, wondering if it's even still there.

"We're in love. That's the rush," Mum says.

I know I should be happy for my mother, but I'm apprehensive. I barely know Basil. I haven't had a chance to study him up close. What if he's a closet sociopath? I can't say this, so I steal her line.

"It's a long life," I say. "You get plenty of chances."

Mum laughs. "Not at my age you don't."

24

AFTER university, in the summer of 1998, Andrew and I rent a one-bedroom apartment on Dovercourt Road in Toronto. He publishes his first novel. I manage to sell a string of freelance pieces to magazines. It is all very exciting. And then, in an astonishing piece of good fortune, I land an internship at the *Globe and Mail*, the same paper where my mother now works. A couple of months in, Cathrin, the features editor, calls me into her office. She spins round in her chair and tells me I'm a hopeless speller, that I flunked my copyediting test. Then she adds that it doesn't matter because she's decided to hire me as a staff columnist.

At first Cecily and I don't even work in the same section. Any lingering awkwardness at our connection soon dissipates, because there is no shortage of distraction in the newsroom. There's a newspaper war on. Even upstairs in the "pansy patch"—as the news types derisively call the weekend sections—the work is exciting and relentless. My twenties pass in a blur of stories, meetings, travel, and relationship drama. Andrew breaks up with me in a way that is somehow heartbreaking, efficient and amicable. I relocate to London on a temporary posting. A year and a half later, when I return to Canada, it no longer seems strange that I work in the same office as my mother, who is now not only my best friend but my colleague. Since marrying Basil, she's gone part-time and become a copy editor in the features section. One day at lunch in the newsroom cafeteria Mum declares she's no longer ambitious. I am thirty-two and single at the time, living alone in a one-bedroom apartment in Little Italy. My mother is in her late fifties and has recently bought a pretty house in the country, on the banks of a small river.

"Were you ever really?" I ask.

She sniffs.

"Never trust ambitious people."

This was something my mother often told me. It was this oft-repeated scrap of advice that made me assume she wasn't ambitious herself. But as it turned out I was wrong.

A few weeks later, on a bright, cold midweek morning in April 2007, I am sitting at my desk in the newsroom when I get a call from my friend Liz, a producer at *The Gill Deacon Show*, a daytime chat show on CBC.

"Dude!" Liz says. Her voice is bright, recently caffeinated. "Just read your ma's piece in *Chatelaine*. *Yowza*. So listen, Gill is wondering if you both want to come on the show tomorrow to talk about it."

"What piece?"

The line goes silent. Liz is one of my best friends. I know her so well, I can actually hear her chewing her lip. I once rescued her from the women's toilets on the fourth floor of the CBC headquarters, just a few blocks from the *Globe* newsroom. She thought she was dying of a stroke but it turned out to be an anxiety attack.

"Seriously?" she says. "She really didn't tell you?"

"Tell me what?" I'm distracted, impatient, mentally rifling through a catalog of edgy, unsubstantiated social trend ideas I'm hoping to cast out at the ten o'clock features meeting. What Liz says next crushes my stomach like an olive entering a press.

"Leah, you need to stop whatever you're doing and go find a copy of this month's *Chatelaine*."

I amble casually through the Style section, past my mother's cubicle, where she sits editing a Saturday roundup of new kitchen gadgets. She's deep in the zone, fingers dancing across the keyboard, bifocals fixed on the screen, chin up, shoulders slumped—a posture that will exacerbate the pain in her scapula which radiates up her neck to the base of her skull. It's a pain everyone in the newsroom has, to some degree or other, and which my mother treats with two double Scotches a night. (I prefer cold white wine.) She does not look up as I pass. This is normal; we see each other so often we long ago dispensed with greetings at the office.

On the Style editor's empty desk, I find the latest copy of *Chatelaine*, then Canada's highest-circulation magazine (print readership 4.5 million). I thumb through the rhubarb pie recipes, the dress patterns, past the celebrity-fronted ads for perfume and anti-aging lotions, until I find it: my mother's byline under the headline GIVE ME MY LIFE BACK.

The four-page spread is illustrated with a still from the film *The Hours*. In the photo, Julianne Moore sits on a bed, dolled up like a blank-eyed 1950s housewife, an aesthetic homage to Sylvia Plath. "*The overwhelming sense of dread I felt while parenting my daughters was no passing affliction. For years, motherhood felt like an affliction.*" That's the pull quote.

The newsroom floor tilts beneath my feet; the fluorescent bulbs overhead streak like comets at the edges of my vision. I can't walk by her desk with the magazine in my hands, so I steady myself against the filing cabinet and begin to read. As I do, a strange thing happens. My mother's voice, which is never far from my mind, is right there, in my ear, as if *she* were right there, which of course she is. My eyes lift from the page and fall on the back of her head, about ten feet away, gray roots seeping along her highlighted hairline like the inevitable creep of dawn. A harmless, well-preserved fifty-something woman in a blue cashmere sweater I'd given her as a gift last Christmas.

What, I wonder, would my life have been like if I'd never embarked on this impossible adventure? Why does the love I feel for my children feel like a prison? How can I reconcile my desire to lay down my life for them with a simultaneous impulse to run for my life? This is the impossible ambivalence of motherhood.

I turn the page and my eyes fall upon a photo of the three of us. I remember the moment it was taken, by an obliging tourist, on a bridge over the Arno River in Florence, during Mum and Meg's 2002 trip to Italy. I'd been overseas with the paper and Dad had generously offered to pay Meg's way over. Meg had never been to Europe and our father thought it would be nice for us to take our first trip together, just the two of us. At the time his business was struggling and he couldn't really afford it, but he still insisted. He said he hoped it would be a chance for us to finally bond after all the lost years. At the last minute, on a whim, Mum decided to join.

In the photo, Mum and I stand abreast in identical black V-necks, looking like older and younger versions of the same person, our pale, fine hair illuminated by the flash, same set jawline and nervous, half-smiling squint. Meg stands adjacent, owning the foreground. My sister, I think, looks entirely herself: head slightly thrown back, wide, toothy grin, jean jacket misbuttoned in a way I once heard some cultures consider a sign of good fortune. One of her thick dark-blond curls licks my cheek like a Labrador's tongue.

I skim through the article to the end.

I have never been very good at this mothering thing which requires a degree of selflessness that simply has never been in me. The truth is that I am not the sort of person who should have had children.

I walk back to my desk, pick up my bag and coat, and walk home through the slush. On the way, I call Cathrin and leave a message saying I feel sick and will miss the ten o'clock meeting. Liz does not bother to call back to ask if I will go on *The Gill Deacon Show*. The next day I return to work, where Mum and I greet each other coolly. For days, possibly weeks or months, we barely speak. There must have been a confrontation but I can't recall it. What I remember is less emotion than a physical sensation. The dazed humiliation after the sucker punch.

25

On our last night in New York, my mother and I go to see Laura Linney in *My Name Is Lucy Barton*. This time Mum has chosen the play. It's a one-woman show adapted from the novel by Elizabeth Strout. Lucy is a woman from a bleak rural background who becomes a successful middle-aged writer, eventually divorcing her first husband and leaving her two daughters in order to write. She remarries happily, but her daughters never quite forgive her choices which they perceive as selfish and she defends as a matter of survival. In her books, Lucy ends up excavating the painful secrets, the shame of her childhood: poverty, neglect, and abuse. She makes a success of herself through the honesty of her writing, but she suffers. My mother has recently reread the novel and we discuss it as we're dressing to leave the hotel. Brilliant but grim, we agree. Not life-affirming like *Olive Kitteridge*, but still very good. I'm in the bathroom sweeping powder under my eyes when Mum stands in the door and reads to me her favorite line from the book, which comes near the end. It's a piece of advice Lucy's college mentor gives her.

"'You're a writer,'" my mother reads. "'Be ruthless.'"

The words settle like the steam in the tiny bathroom mirror. Leaning in beside me, my mother uses the side of her fist to clear a circle in the fog. She unsheathes a golden tube and applies her lipstick. It's matte, the color of dried blood. I watch as she pulls her mouth above her gums and revolves her chin, checking her teeth for stains. She smacks her lips once, then nods, satisfied.

A couple of hours later, when Linney delivers the line onstage, it is different. Her bare white feet are grounded apart under a thin hospital gown. Her face is pale and shiny, so open it's embarrassing to look at, like gazing into the splayed petals of a lily.

"Be ruthless. Be ruthless!"

Linney's voice is urgent, almost desperate. Honest as a tuning fork struck in the dark. This time I receive the line not as a dare but a promise. A precursor to something better. The fear that gives way to wonder. The possibility of joy. The actress lifts her head to the gallery and looks directly at my mother—I am sure of it—her chin tilts up, and she says the words one last time. Mum takes my hand and the lights fall. She squeezes and I squeeze back. We sit this way, silently conjoined, sweating into each other's palms as the applause rises to thunder and the audience stands and shouts and then sits down and stands again. We remain fixed to our seats until the houselights come on and the people around us blink and murmur, twisting round searching for their coats.

THE next morning my mother leaves early to catch the airport shuttle. She will fly to Toronto, then drive two hours north to her tiny, snow-dusted village. Before she goes, we embrace and discuss how she might return to London for Easter. If not then, we'll see each other in the summer when I come over with Rob and the boys.

I fall back to sleep, and when I awake, I see she's texted me from the airport. She says she forgot to tell me something. She's just finished the final volume of Knausgaard and it's all about the terrible things that happened to him after he wrote honestly about the people in his life. Then she sends another, final text, which she signs off with love:

I get the "be ruthless" thing but you will pay a price.

✦ ✦ ✦

I DON'T regret having children but in fairness to my mother, I didn't have me as a daughter. I do, however, find it exceedingly hard to contain. To me, motherhood often feels like a force that is simultaneously expanding inside me and swallowing me whole. When my children are with me, quite often I am anxious for them to go. This is how it feels, much of the time, at least to me—a constant state of longing for the next moment or step, the endless incremental nudging along. I want them to go to bed or to school or to come to the table, or just to be in a place, anyplace, that is not the place where I am. My office on a weekday or my bedroom at 4 a.m. And then, when they go, when they stumble away, in the direction of whatever it is I have urged them toward, a canyon yawns in my chest. I cannot think, in these moments, why it was I ever wanted my children to go. *Why have they left me alone?* The feeling—a mixture of ferocious protectiveness and abject self-pity—usually recedes within a minute or two, allowing me to get on with my work, "my life," as I call it. But other times my ribcage becomes a whirling centrifuge, one that threatens to pull me apart until the moment I can finally put my hands upon them again, pull them toward me, inhale the spice of their skin, tickle the playground dust from their hair until they run away shrieking, batting off my hands, glancing back and daring me to follow.

If I am good at any of it, it's the in-between moments. The sound of them playing in the next room while I read in bed. Noticing the twitch of their mouths as they mutter in a dream. Catching sight of one or both of them through a window, lost in the private world of a game. That pure unmediated play that growing up is a process of unlearning, then trying to replicate in various unsatisfactory ways. I love their indecipherable spy codes and pirate tests of courage. It's these bewildering, liminal moments in which I love my children best, by which I mean in the present tense, without wariness or uncertainty. It's a cheat, like the smug relief of scrolling through photos of the baby after it's finally asleep. The truth is I don't care. Because these are the shimmering moments in which I cannot fail my children.

My mother was right: commitment does suck the life right out of you. Raising kids, loving them, more than anything else, makes the passage of time impossible to ignore. Their relentless desires, the way they conflict with your own, the endless push and tug—this is the drip, drip, drip all of us are trying and failing to ignore.

What kills me are the bits of life that can't be saved. The stuff that slips through the sieve, too diffuse to be photographed, too unwieldy for the page. The dander of our skin, mixed up and swirling in the half-light of the empty house. A half-chewed apple, bruised and abandoned on the stairs. The headless triceratops who, for the past thirty-eight months, has guarded the back of the boot closet. The flesh of this morning's porridge pot giving way to Fairy soap in the sink. The way my husband drops a passing kiss on my head while I'm treating Batman's war wound with a collage of plasters. The broken robot dog croaking from the bottom of the toy bin. Frankie eating his raspberries, one by one, off the tip of each finger.

Some days I am able to absorb these things, even luxuriate in them, then at some point, perhaps after too little coffee or too much wine or an inexplicable argument with Rob—or just because it's ten past three on a December afternoon—I will think: *I am impossible to love.*

This is when I am most like my mother.

26

THE summer before the pandemic, I fly to Ottawa with my eldest son. The plan is for us to stay with my mother and Basil at the simple A-frame cottage they rent on a quiet lake in Quebec. It's just Solomon and me, because Rob is busy at work and Frankie's nursery runs through summer. My mother invited me as she always does and as usual I'd wavered. We'd had an argument over the phone over whether or not I should rent a car. I told her I couldn't justify the expense, which was true. Mum said if I thought she was going to spend her holiday chauffeuring me around cottage country, I had another thing coming.

But the flights are booked. Meg is due to give birth any day, so instead I arrange to stay with my old friend Hannah from high school, who lives nearby and has a daughter Solly's age. After I arrive at Hannah's house, Mum calls me again and begs me to stay with her. She sounds desperate on the phone, close to tears. It is so unlike her, I immediately agree to come. I don't want her to cry. I'm frightened of what might happen if she does. After marrying Basil, my mother declared she'd quit crying for good. She wasn't kidding. When my grandmother died of a cerebral contusion in her nineties, Mum arranged the entire funeral without shedding a single tear. The reception, I later realized, was held at the riding club, in the very clubhouse where the Horseman had raped her. My mother and I sat on the yellow vinyl sofa listening to the speeches, eating crustless egg sandwiches, drinking warm white wine. A funeral at a crime scene. Brilliantly perverse. A classic.

The point is my mother never cries. Not even at her own mother's funeral while sitting in the spot where she was violated as a child. If she does cry, I am certain something terrible will happen, so I agree to bring Solomon to stay at the cottage as planned. But the moment I see her I know it's a mistake. We meet in an outdoor outfitters shop in Ottawa where I'm buying Solly a list of things for his first time at summer camp. I find Mum browsing through a sale rack of snowshoes. "Oh!" she says, as if I am a distant work acquaintance and she is startled by the unexpected coincidence. She collects herself with a sigh and gazes past me into the middle distance. "Well," she murmurs. "Hello, then."

Solly—thank god for him—flies into his grandmother's arms, wetting her with kisses and chattering about the plane ride. I reach out to pat my mother's arm but she flinches then pivots away, refusing eye contact, as she will continue to do, with agonizing consistency, for all six of the days and nights I will spend with her.

The cottage is eerily still after the cacophony of London.

"Mummy, how can quiet be so loud?" Solomon asks warily.

On the path to the dock I can feel the snap of each twig underfoot. The humidity is settling on the lake, drawing around us like a suffocating shroud. My stepfather is on a new heart drug that makes him tired. He sits all day reading in a shady corner of the deck, ankle balanced on one knee, devouring a series of fantasy novels. In the evening he rouses himself to grill large portions of pre-marinated meat. He interacts evenly with Solly but barely acknowledges my presence. When I ask him a question, he stiffens. Basil is an introvert, my mother says. A quiet man with a large presence, like the roll of distant thunder. He has wide shoulders and a powerful neck. His white hair bristles above watery blue eyes. When he is aggrieved, his face involuntarily flushes scarlet. Once or twice in his drinking days I felt the full force of his temper. He's teetotal now, but I have no wish to see it again.

I think I can speak for both of us when I say my stepfather and I don't lie awake at night yearning for each other's company, but over the years we have learned to be tolerant and polite, at the best of times kind and even mildly affectionate. Our visits in recent years have been amicable and without incident. This arrangement bothers no one but my mother, for whom it's a point of lament. I tell her not to take it personally. Why should Basil be expected to adore his wife's elder daughter or vice versa? He has no children of his own and never wanted children. He's fonder of Meg, who sees them more often because she lives in Canada. "It's fine," I tell my mother. This is my position. But on this particular visit Basil's careful good humor seems more fragile. The atmosphere is wearing thin. By the third day, I feel as if I'm clinging to the edge of a cliff, breathing through a straw.

I know what the problem is. The book. The one I'm writing about my mother and me. The book that started as a collaborative investigation into the Horseman and has now come untethered from him and evolved into something else entirely. I continue to work on it at the cottage, writing furtively in snatched moments when Solly is swimming or sleeping or smashing up rocks in the woods. Once or twice I try to broach the subject with my mother, but she tells me to drop it. So I do.

But I don't.

My mother thinks the problem between me and Basil is that he somehow displaced me. I'm not speculating here; she's told me so explicitly on a number of occasions.

"I know how hard it was for you when I remarried" is how she has put it.

I don't feel envious of my stepfather. Not consciously. How can I be sure I don't secretly long to be my mother's live-in soul mate? Perhaps because it's a role I never wanted in the first place. An uxorious partner was what she wanted. Those were her terms, and as a child I accepted them. I did not wish to be her honorary sister, her colleague, her best friend or confidante, though at various times I have played all these roles. I certainly never wanted to be her rival. The only thing I have ever really wanted is to be recognized by her as what I am and always will be: her daughter. The other roles I played because they allowed me to bask in the glow of her attention. I did not choose them any more than she chose to be the Horseman's lover. Yes, I participated enthusiastically in our strange enmeshment, and it's true I was a precocious child. "A little actress," as my mother has said. But I was also frightened and desperately lonely at times, a confused little girl in a chaotic situation I did not understand or create. Is a child who inspires the affections of an adult guilty of seduction?

No.

A child is vulnerable by definition. Even if she pretends to be worldly, it is just that: a pretense. Play-acting. A child cannot consent to anything. This is especially true of a child in pursuit of an adult's love.

"Your goodness as a child was a manipulation." This is what my mother has said.

If there is one thing I want my mother to understand, it's this: *I was good.* If I was acting, it was a play I did not stage, a script I did not write. My innocence was not a trick. I will not wear her shame in exchange for the lie that I am special. Everyone is special. And all children are good. Even the bad ones.

I DID a lot of swimming that summer at the cottage in Quebec. Once, sometimes twice a day, just to escape the tension, I'd swim half a mile offshore and do a lazy breaststroke round the uninhabited pine-forested island. Often I found myself floating like a starfish, studying the contrails in the sky. It was on one of these occasions I understood my mother was right about one thing: I was the problem.

It was me—not her—who was looking for closure, and in all the wrong places. I'd believed that by solving the mystery of the Horseman I would expose the banality of his evil; render him harmless. But I'd been naive and deluded. The Horseman, I came to realize, was just a handy prop. A narrative concept I'd allowed to propel the plot of our relationship for far too long. He was the suitcase of cash in a heist movie that in the end, when finally popped open, proved empty.

There's something I haven't mentioned. Something I did not tell my mother that summer. Nor did I mention it in the long, difficult months of the pandemic that followed. It's something that doesn't matter. And its not mattering was what made it so interesting. Since I've made you curious, here it is. I did find out a few things about the Horseman that summer. I dug them up the old-fashioned way, by combing land registries, employment records, police files, old classified ads, and birth, death, and wedding announcements. I managed to enlist the help of a private detective who owed me a favor.

What emerged was a vague outline of a man who matched his name and description, a small-town bounder with a spotty career in animal husbandry and a history of petty crime, reckless philandering, and drunk driving infractions. If he ever got caught for being a predatory serial hebephile, it didn't make the papers. Remember, the Horseman had other victims. He has a family. Many of his descendants are still alive. I will not name him. I could pretend I'm being noble and respectful but the truth is I don't want his name in my book.

The Horseman was born, he lived, he did bad things. For the most part, he escaped punishment. He died. I'm leaving out a few things but trust me when I say they don't matter. So, that's the gist.

I didn't promise you purgation.

What I understood that day in the lake was that it wasn't the Horseman that compelled me. The story I needed to untangle, if it was possible, was how my mother's story flowed into and formed my own. I decided I would write a book about what it was like to grow up as the daughter of a victim who refused to be silent or still. A woman who made me and loved me in all the right and wrong ways and whose love I return with the same relentless imperfection.

Stories are like children, and children are like barn fires. You can make one. It's usually easy. You can do it on purpose or by accident. Go ahead, toss a match in the hay. After that the thing will live and breathe. It will go where it wants. You cannot pretend to own it any more than you can control it. But here's the catch: you can, and will, be blamed for the outcome. This is especially true if you are the mother. I'm not saying it's fair. I'm saying that's how it is. You need to prepare.

All suffering is not equal—yet somehow we are all victims and perpetrators both—heroes of our own self-serving redemption narratives.

Whatever luck or misfortune has paved the way for your wickedness and goodness, here you are in the muck, rubbing along with the rest of us. We must prepare and be accountable.

So tell your story. Give the whole world a full and forensic accounting of your pain. But also prepare to be accountable. Force yourself to face the blaze. The one you created with nothing more than a shrug and a flick of your wrist. Let yourself be dazzled by it. Let yourself be warmed. Listen to the roar of the story you didn't write and don't want to hear. The story you will be blamed for, however unjustly. Later you can sift through the ashes and find wisdom. It's in there.

You'll see. We must love each other relentlessly, imperfectly. This is the struggle. There's nothing else.

FLOATING on my back in the lake in Quebec in the summer of 2019, I was forced to admit that when it came to my mother, I was equally guilty of self-serving delusion. Not only did I want her to acknowledge my feelings, I wanted her to actually feel them herself. Like the piano student victim in *Downstate*, I wanted to condemn and be comforted by the adult who'd confused me and broken my heart. I wanted to be both the hero of my story—our story—and also its victim.

It was not a tenable position.

ON my last night at the cottage the crackle in the atmosphere seems to dissipate. It's early evening and Solly is in bed, worn out from swimming. Basil is grilling steak. Mum and I are down at the dock, sipping twin gin and tonics, eating vinegar chips from separate bowls. The ice cubes are half-melted. Soon the sun will dip below the trees and we will shiver, but for now everything is fine.

"I've been seeing a new therapist," she says. Her tone is breezy, bemused. She's itching to tell me something.

"You mentioned," I say. "How's it going?"

"She's very good, actually. Insightful. Especially about you. About us."

"Tell me," I say. And she does.

+ + +

Solomon goes off to camp and I escape for two nights, deeper into the woods—a last-minute reunion with Joni and Hannah. It's the first time we've been together, just the three of us, since the year of Scott's pool party. Almost thirty years have passed.

Hannah is now a senior bureaucrat in Ottawa like my sister. Her husband runs a successful canoe-tripping company and they have two preteen children, a boy and a girl. Joni is a licensed reiki energy healer married to a Swedish actuary. They have two cats named Frank and Earnest and live in Santa Fe, which she hates because it's dry, and full of rich hippies whose auras she manipulates for a living. While Hannah and I have remained close—I was her maid of honor and vice versa—my contact with Joni has been less frequent. She and Hannah have not seen each other since my wedding. In the car we are giddy, fizzing with energy, girlfriends on the lam. We turn up the stereo and sing along to Billy Joel: *Only the good die young.*

Hannah drives us to a secret spot—a lake on a hundred acres, deep in the forest north of the Gatineaus. A kind of private campsite, loaned to us for the weekend. There's a fully kitted outdoor kitchen with a propane stove and a roof tank that catches and warms rainwater for showers. Two small bunkhouses for sleeping, a wood-fired sauna, a dock, and a composting outhouse. The lake is small—a large pond, really—but it's clear and warm and deep. By the time we arrive, it's evening: the cicadas have gone to bed and the bullfrogs are belching. We run from the mosquitoes, cover ourselves with repellent, make warm margaritas with half-melted ice. We carry our drinks down to the dock, strip off our sweaty sundresses, and dive in naked, floating on our backs, staring up at the rising gibbous moon. Joni has made a body scrub out of coffee grinds and rose water and olive oil. We slather it over ourselves, massaging the grinds into our legs and faces and feet. Joni stands naked on the edge of the dock staring out at the water, every inch of her skin glistening and flecked with espresso. She draws her hands into prayer and surprises us by bellowing out a chant, "Oṃ Maṇi Padme Hūṃ." She repeats it three times, deep low tones that reverberate up from her belly and across the lake. Hannah asks what it means and Joni explains very seriously it's an ancient Buddhist compassion mantra that translates to "don't be an asshole." We all join hands and jump back in the water.

Hannah, the responsible, organized grown-up, has brought a prepre-pared homemade dinner: salads and dips and grilled meat. For dessert we eat squares of dark, raw cannabis chocolate Joni purchased on the Internet. I open the bottles: champagne, then white, then red wine. We drink and we dance—Billy Joel, Beyoncé, the Band. When we are tired of dancing, we build a fire and sit around it, huddling under blankets, telling stories of lovers we might have married, books and screenplays we forgot to write, friends who have drifted away, changed gender, gotten rich or addicted, or died. We talk of faraway countries we've been to and long to revisit, share stories of miscarriages, weddings, religious experiences at yoga retreats, inheritances, mortgages, aborted babies, and love affairs. We talk of the people we used to be and know and ask each other, "What happened to her?"

Hannah asks idly if I've spoken to Scott much. Beside me, I feel Joni shift on her stump.

"I saw him last summer," I say. He dropped by for a visit when I was in Cobourg, I say, where my father and MJ still live. He was in town from Vancouver, where he's a successful music producer. I'd flown over with the boys and stayed the entire summer on a friend's farm. Scott was staying at a friend's cottage in the area, so he came for lunch and brought his younger sister, whom I remembered vaguely from school. They stayed for a couple of hours. What can I say about Scott?

"He was the same as always. Maybe a bit less obsessed with work."

"I never hear from him anymore," Hannah says, staring into the fire. Scott was close to Hannah in high school, closer than he was to me, or certainly Joni, who left arts school after the second year and transferred to a private girls' school downtown. Hannah, who was the first to get married, was the one Scott always swore he'd propose to. I can't re-member if he was invited to her wedding, but he wasn't there. Hannah laughs and repeats his strange refrain:

"'You gotta marry a Hannah.' Remember that?"

Hannah and I laugh. Joni is silent.

"But what did he mean?" I say. "Was it a joke or a threat, or neither?"

Hannah shrugs. "I saw that old photo he posted on Facebook. The one of the two of you."

"The one at graduation?"

"No, no, the one from the pool party," she corrects. "You're sitting on the diving board and your hair is wet."

"Right."

"That's just fucking weird," Joni says. She's almost never on Facebook.

"Jeff had lots of pool parties," I say. "I'm not sure it was *that* night."

But it was that night. I know, because I remember what I was wearing and what he was wearing and what Joni was wearing too. I don't know what time it was taken except that it was light enough that it must have been before anything happened.

I look terrible in the photo: sullen, slope-shouldered, as if I'm willing my body to absorb itself. Scott sits erect, shoulders square to the camera, his chest still firm and tight, right arm clamped around my shoulder. He looks fantastic. Probably that's why he posted it.

"You weren't in the picture," I say to Joni, and reach for her hand under the blanket. She squeezes my fingers, then slowly withdraws her hand.

"I don't talk to him either," Joni says, then touches her face, which is how I know she's crying. Hannah hands her one of the cloth napkins she packed in the cooler with our picnic dinner.

"Joni, I'm so sorry about what happened." It's all I can think of to say.

I search for Hannah's eyes, but she gazes evenly into the fire.

Joni presses her chin deeper into the camp blanket and sighs, then blows her nose into the napkin. "Yeah, well."

"It was messed up."

"I'm sorry too," she says. "For the way I shut you out after. I just didn't know how to handle any of it."

"I still—I mean—me neither." I am fumbling. "Obviously, what happened, it wasn't right. It wasn't the plan."

I'm suddenly aware that we are using the passive tense, and that feels like a cop-out. I turn to look at Joni, but she ignores my gaze and stares deeper into the fire. Her nostrils flare. Her neck is tight, almost quivering.

"But it didn't happen to *you*, Leah, it happened to *me*."

Joni's tone is gentle but defiant. A shiv glinting from the breast pocket of a velvet coat. I understand she is laying claim to the narrative. She is saying to me: This story? The one about the pool party? You cannot have it. It's mine.

Be ruthless, but you will pay a price.

When I write my story, I understand that Joni will perceive it as a violation, a burglary of her truth. And we both know I will write it. I have told her I am writing a book and that is how it starts. This is the inevitability that chills the air around the campfire. The knowledge that what I want—what I will do—cancels out what she does not.

If I could go back to the campfire this is what I would say to Joni: We were wasted. We were children, we were reckless and confused. We hurt and got hurt. All of us. This is not the same as saying the story is simple. It's not.

All I have now are these fragments: The underwater tea party, the mermaid game, taking off our bathing suits on the count of three. The bleary trinity on the edge of the pool. Me holding your hand, Scott trying and failing. It isn't much and it doesn't make the story mine but it matters.

There is no ledger, no debt to be settled. There never was. That was a lie.

"It happened to all of us," I say carefully.

"Leah—" Joni begins, then stops when I raise a finger.

"Hear me out."

For the first time, I tell Joni and Hannah what happened later that night, with me and Scott in the bedroom. It's the first time I've told anyone since I told my mother at the kitchen table. It's not that I considered it a huge secret. If it was ever shameful, it's certainly not now. The truth is, until quite recently I've thought of it glancingly if at all. Then I started to think about it a lot. It lingered. For a long time it seemed the least interesting thing about that night in the context of everything else that happened, both before and especially after—the gossip at school, the breakup with Joni, my mother's story. The importance it held, and continues to hold, is in the vivid clarity of the memory: the shock and the sadness I felt afterward. It troubles me, but do I consider it a trauma? Not really. Perhaps I'm self-blaming, or deluded, but what bothers me most is the blatant disregard I showed for myself, not just that night but on other nights and days in other rooms with other men. All the figurative rapes that I prepared myself for by blow-drying my hair and filing my nails just so. For a long time I hated myself for that. And then I hated the world and I hated myself for hating the world and then, around age forty, after Frankie's birth, I began to feel as if the world hated me. I was older, unbeautiful. It was the unvarnished truth, as predictable and astonishing as the dawn. But what startled me more than anything was that all the hating, the self-hating in particular, had not actually prepared me for any of it. So I waited for the inevitable shame to descend. The real kind of shame—as literal, hard-won, and well-deserved as the creases on my throat and the droop of my pelvic floor. I waited and waited but it never arrived. I understood then I was free. That was the hardest part.

After I finish telling the story, everyone is silent. Joni is the first to speak.

"I had no idea. I'm so sorry that happened to you."

"It's not a huge deal," I say. "It was weird."

Hannah coughs. The wind has changed direction. She blinks through a scrim of woodsmoke then shifts to the next stump over. For some reason I think of the poem on her fridge, the one her mother didn't write:

As far as possible, without surrender, be on good terms with all persons.

"I'm not mad at Scott," I say. "Maybe I should be, but I'm not. Maybe I should blame him but I don't. The whole situation was so fucked-up."

Joni shakes her head. "No. That's not how it works."

But he was just a kid, I think. *Fourteen.* Like us he was a child. He was vulnerable by definition, incapable of consent.

If there's anything I learned from that night, or indeed from any of the many painful, messy moral complications in which I've found myself over the years—including with my mother—it's this: I wish we'd been kinder to each other. I wish we'd been gentler, more careful with ourselves. I regret the disdain we showed for our unbroken hearts and smooth young bodies. The way we treated our innocence as a babyish toy to be hidden and disposed of. I wish we'd cherished our own innocence not for the value it held in the world—about which we were ludicrously naive—but for the simple fact it was ours.

I want to say all these things to Joni, but instead I say nothing. Under the blanket, I squeeze her hand while she cries.

27

Weeks pass, then months. A cataclysmic event occurs—the pandemic—in which everything and nothing happens. The whole world grinds to a halt but London sails on impervious. My older son comes home from school one day and tells me about a new game he has learned in which one child lies on the ground pretending to be dead while the rest kneel round chanting, "Light as a feather, stiff as a board, light as a feather, stiff as a board," before levitating the body with their fingers.

I narrow my eyes. "Who taught you that?"

"We learned it in history," he says. "Did you know 'Ring a Ring o' Roses' is about the bubonic plague?"

During this bewildering time, my mother and I do not speak. In the post she sends me a card with David Milne's *Lilies* on the front. Her handwriting is large and erratic. When I touch the script, her rage blisters my fingertips. I carry the card upstairs into the corner of the bedroom my husband now uses as an office and read it aloud to him.

I am deeply sorry for what happened. I abandoned you, my children, in order to fulfil my own interests. It was wrong and I deeply regret the pain it caused you, the pain it caused all of us. I want you to know that in spite of my selfishness and carelessness I have never stopped loving you.

"That's nice, isn't it?" Rob says.

I explain that it's like one of those Maoist propaganda poems that contains a message of resistance. He laughs.

"So your mother is the rebel poet and you're the totalitarian state?"

"My point is that it's disingenuous."

He looks at me wearily. "Maybe you should give her the benefit of the doubt," he says. "She's your mother."

"I'm acutely aware of that."

I place the card in a box with the stolen strawberry obsidian from the hipster hotel. It sits on top of a stack of old photographs: the photo of my mother and the professor and my father on the boat. The photo of my mother cuddling me as a toddler and my sister as a baby. The one of her in the sitting room at Vogrie with Richard just out of frame. In another she stands in the kitchen of the flat on Beverley Street looking startled in a green-gold gown on New Year's Eve. There is a photograph of me as a baby, smiling in a white bonnet on the grass. My mother leans over me tenderly, a burning cigarette smoldering in her hand.

Months pass and she sends me another unsolicited note. This one says:

I feel betrayed. I feel violated. I feel exploited. And I feel very angry. This project of yours will cause untold damage to me, to our relationship, and by extension I would think, to you. It is also creating divisions in our family that may never heal. I know everything pales in the light of Covid-19, but there it is.

Ah, I think. *Now we're getting somewhere.*

Weeks pass, then months. My mother sends me a link to a two-page personal essay she has published in a Canadian literary magazine. Her latest—and possibly final—literary ambush. This time she does not bury the lede.

"In June 1964, a few weeks before my thirteenth birthday I was raped by a man old enough to be my father." After that, she tells her life story, or the story she understands as her life. It's one I have heard many times before, a story she has published other versions of in other places, but this time she does not exclude anything. She gives all the details of her passive rape at the age of twelve at the hands of the Horseman. The ensuing clandestine affair. She records dates, places, details. She names the club and the Horseman and mentions his wife and children, two of whom are older than her and likely still living in Canada. I wonder if she hopes they will read it. She explains my grandfather's part in the story, how her shame at disappointing him led to her early marriage to my father, to young motherhood—and ultimately to her subsequent divorce after her father's death. These decisions, my mother explains, resulted in years of emotional chaos, a tortured love affair with a "dark prince" (Richard), and eventually, once her elder daughter had left home, a contented second marriage to the "good prince" (Basil). The happy ending to the twisted fairy tale of her life is marred by a thorn: her elder daughter's upcoming book, a "tell-all" appropriation of her story.

Here is the final paragraph:

I have not led a blameless life. I own every mistake I have made— every one. I feel my daughter's pain as if it is my own . . . but I will say this as vigorously and directly as I can: This story, this one, is mine.

Over dinner, I tell Rob it's odd my mother thinks I'm out to steal her story. Of all the stories she gave to me, the one about the Horseman is the one I accepted least willingly. I was just a kid when I first heard it and because of that I did not recoil, which is different from saying I enjoyed it. For years, I did my best to shake it off but the Horseman was always lurking under the surface of our conversations, waiting for my mother to bring him up. She raised the subject often with me, perhaps because she thought I was used to it, the person least likely to flinch at the mention of his unmentionable name. Like my mother I am not afraid of the dark. She has every right to tell her story, but my mother is wrong to think I have designs on it. It was never mine to steal.

I never wanted it in the first place.

28

T HE year of the pandemic lumbers on. Summer, fall, and Christmas come and go. Each day is like watching an ice cube melt, pool into water, then gradually be sopped by the sun. My children and husband loom so large in my field of vision, I feel as if we have absorbed each other. I am so grateful to have them. They are all I've ever wanted and for anything that is not them. Mostly I am desperate to escape.

One gloomy January afternoon Frankie walks into my office for the seventh or eighth time in that day and that minute and demands "another peanut butter toast not toasted," which means cut the way he likes in two triangles joined at the center like bat wings. I smile at him and touch his curls. Then without a word I get up from my desk, walk through the garden into the house and out the front door. In the bedroom window I can see Rob Zooming on the encrypted desktop he recently had couriered from the office. His face looks bluish in the screen light and he is nodding in agreement with an unseen colleague. I get in the car and drive around North London aimlessly, blasting one of Solly's hip-hop playlists. Eventually I park on an unremarkable street in Cricklewood I have never been down before. A long, curved row of pebbledash suburban terraces. Beside me is a cylindrical London post box. Its red paint is glossed with dripping rain. The letter slot, I notice, is protected by the brim of its jaunty cap. For most of an hour

I sit in silence contemplating the genius of the post box's design. Before driving home I look around the car and think, *Maybe this wouldn't be such a bad place to live?*

Early in the new year, another email arrives from my mother. She says she's not sure why it's taken her so long to get to this point. She's ready to listen. She says she now realizes her trauma became my trauma. "I know I've apologized all over hell's half acre for being an inadequate parent, but those apologies, I see now, were a form of narcissism on my part. They were not for you, they were for me. I was trying to make myself feel better."

I wait a day or so, then respond with a brief chatty note filled with news about the boys and work, but I know this is not what my mother wants. She wants the old thing, the intensity. *Enmeshment.* She wants me to tell her everything, but for the first time in my life, I won't. Our correspondence peters out. She calls and calls, and when I pick up, I say, "Hi, Mum!" and put her on FaceTime with the boys.

After that, she sends me a series of single-line emails. No body text, just a subject heading.

I miss you Leah.
I will always love you Leah.
Leah, I love you so much.

Then finally she sends a link to a recent story from the *Atlantic*: "The Psychology of Silent Treatment as Abuse."

I begin to feel that my mother is using our one-way correspondence in order to have an agonized conversation with herself. For me to say anything at this point would be rude, an intrusion on a private conversation.

A present arrives in the post. It's a large hardback book. The collected poems of Mary Oliver, entitled *Devotions.*

I call my mother to thank her. I tell her I love Mary Oliver.

"Well," she sniffs. "I know you better than you think."

"What's going on with you?" I ask.

Mum tells me she has a new puppy, a terrier cross named Lulu. She tells me about her seventieth-birthday plans, a family party at my aunt and uncle's fishing lodge. She does not bother to invite me; we both know I will not be coming back to Canada anytime soon. She says she's sorry about the essay she published about me stealing her story.

"I just wanted to get it off my chest. You know—get out ahead of the story."

She says she doesn't care about my book anymore. People are more important than words on the page. She doesn't care who's right or what's true. In relationships, she says, truth is relative, not empirical. Voices can't be appropriated. It's all nonsense; she knows this now. It doesn't matter; none of it matters. The only thing that matters is us.

"And besides—" she begins, but I cut her off.

"Writers write?"

We laugh, then lapse into silence. We are, I think, equally astonished that we have both lived long enough to be capable of experiencing a moment in which we are simply responsive to each other. For the first time in years, possibly ever, our mutual focus is not on what each of us is or is not getting from the other. We are just here, together, on the phone. An ocean apart, but rubbing along all the same.

"Little Leah," she says. "Are you still there?"

"Yes, Mum."

"I'm your mother, you know. I'll always be your mother."

"Really?" I joke. "Are you sure, absolutely sure?"

"As a matter of fact, I am."

I cradle the phone to my ear and stare out the window of my writing shed, past the goldfinches on the feeder, over the back fence, across the four-track railway, to the church steeple. Behind it, the sun is orange and sinking fast.

There's a warm front spreading across the Atlantic. The days are getting longer in London. Spring is rolling over into summer, and soon my mother will be seventy. Frankie is tapping lightly at the window of my shed, asking for an ice lolly. A pink one. The watermelon not the strawberry kind. I tell my mother I love her—that I'll always love her—but now I have to go.

Acknowledgments

I am very grateful to my father, Jim McLaren, without whose quiet support and unwavering trust this book would not exist.

Enormous thanks also to my agent, Felicity Blunt, for her encouragement, wisdom, and steadfast loyalty in the many times one or both of us needed to prioritize babies over books.

Thank you to my dream team of editors: Sarah Stein at Harper US, Jocasta Hamilton at John Murray UK, Pamela Murray and Anne Collins at PRH Canada. I could not have hoped for a more experienced and talented collection of editorial brains, eyes, ears, and hearts.

Thanks also to Alexandra Machinist at ICM, Rosie Pierce at Curtis Brown UK, Hayley Salmon, Abigail Scruby, Linda Friedner, Dori Ross, Mary Jane McLaren, and Tara Quish for patience, kindness, and support along the way.

Many old friends helped me to parse and compare memories of childhood and adolescence: thanks to Joanna Baker, Max Mandel, Marni Schuster, and Shawna Rich. Others generously read early drafts and provided invaluable feedback: Robert Yates, Jill Offman, Andrew Pyper, Daniel Richler, Bea Longmore, Cathrin Bradbury, Harriet Sachs, Clayton Ruby, and Daisy Aitkins.

I'm deeply grateful to the Writers' Trust of Canada and the Leacock Foundation for providing much-needed financial support in a crunch. Thank you to Richard Salmon and Frances Jones Davies of the Golden

Grove Trust in Carmarthenshire, Wales, for giving me a quiet place to write. To the Bawds of Euphony, thank you for the poetry and sanity in lockdown.

Finally and most important, I am lucky to be the number one groupie, back-up dancer, and official sandwich-maker for North West London's most underrated punk band, Rob and the Yates boys. Thank you, Jack, Solomon, and Frank. Yo fam! (Did I say it right?) I love you more than you love me stamped-it-no-erasies-cross-my-heart-and-hope-to-die-stick-a-needle-in-my-eye. Thank you for tolerating my many inexcusable absences, literal and figurative, and for remembering to feed His Ruthlessness, The Honorable Ratter of the Exchequer, Vice Regent Tabby-in-Chief, Lord Cromwell, Governor of Wakeman Road, Baron of Kensal Green so he doesn't kill us in our sleep.

About the Author

LEAH MCLAREN is an award-winning journalist, screenwriter, and novelist. Her two novels, *The Continuity Girl* and *A Better Man*, have been published in half a dozen countries and translated into several languages. She has also written for film and television.

She began her career as a columnist for the *Globe and Mail*, where she spent a decade on staff and was posted to the London bureau. For many years she was Europe correspondent for *Maclean's* magazine. Her work is regularly published in the *Guardian*, the *Observer Magazine*, the *Spectator*, the *Sunday Times Magazine*, the *Walrus*, *Chatelaine*, and *Toronto Life*, among others. In 2013, she won a gold National Magazine Award in the long-features category.

She was born in rural Ontario, and grew up in Cobourg and Toronto, Ontario. Today she lives in London, England, with her husband and two sons.